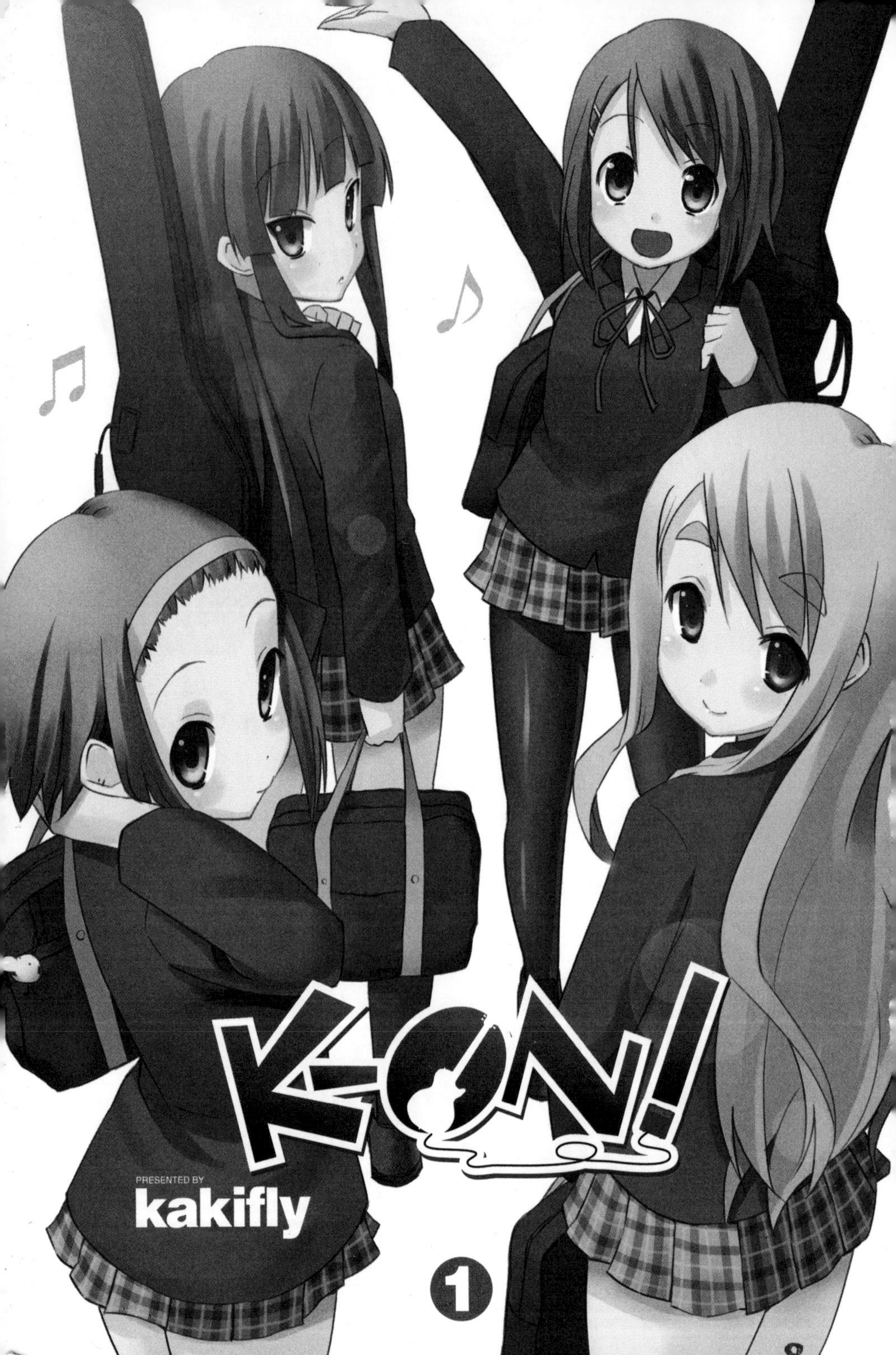
K-ON!
PRESENTED BY
kakifly
1

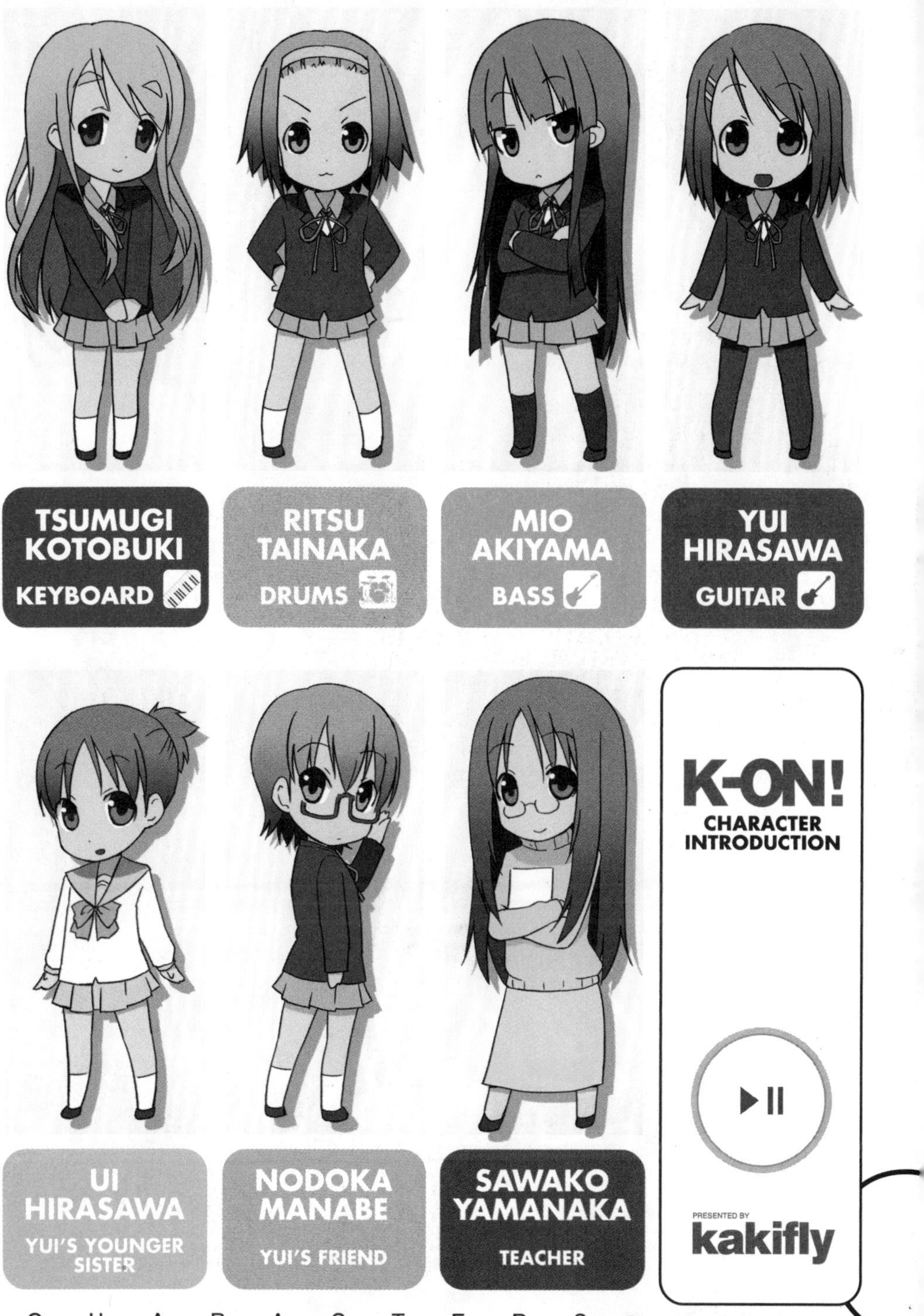
TSUMUGI KOTOBUKI
KEYBOARD
RITSU TAINAKA
DRUMS
MIO AKIYAMA
BASS
YUI HIRASAWA
GUITAR
UI HIRASAWA
YUI'S YOUNGER SISTER
NODOKA MANABE
YUI'S FRIEND
SAWAKO YAMANAKA
TEACHER
K-ON!
CHARACTER INTRODUCTION
PRESENTED BY
kakifly
C H A R A C T E R S

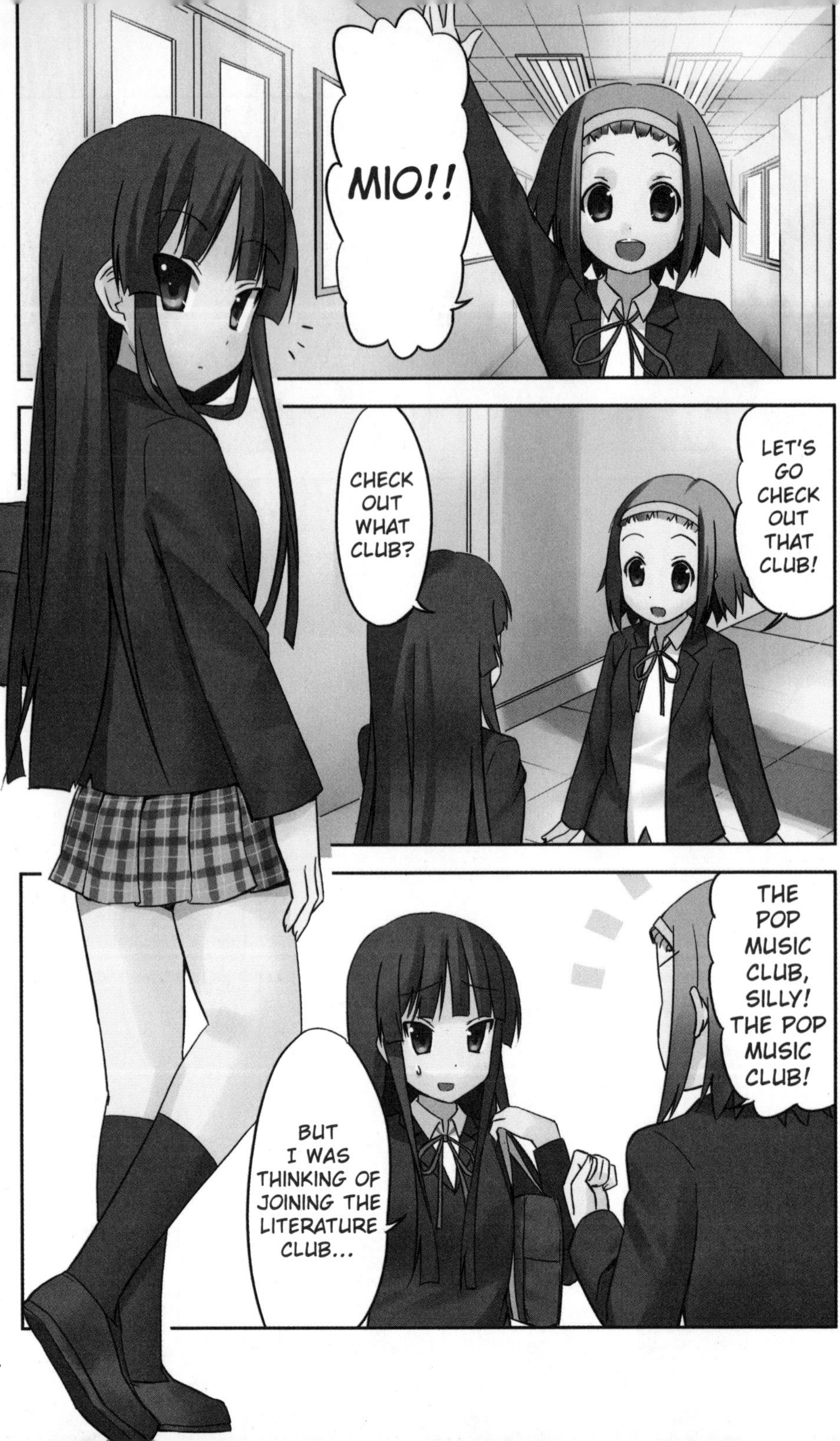
MIO!!
LET'S GO CHECK OUT THAT CLUB!
CHECK OUT WHAT CLUB?
THE POP MUSIC CLUB, SILLY! THE POP MUSIC CLUB!
BUT I WAS THINKING OF JOINING THE LITERATURE CLUB...

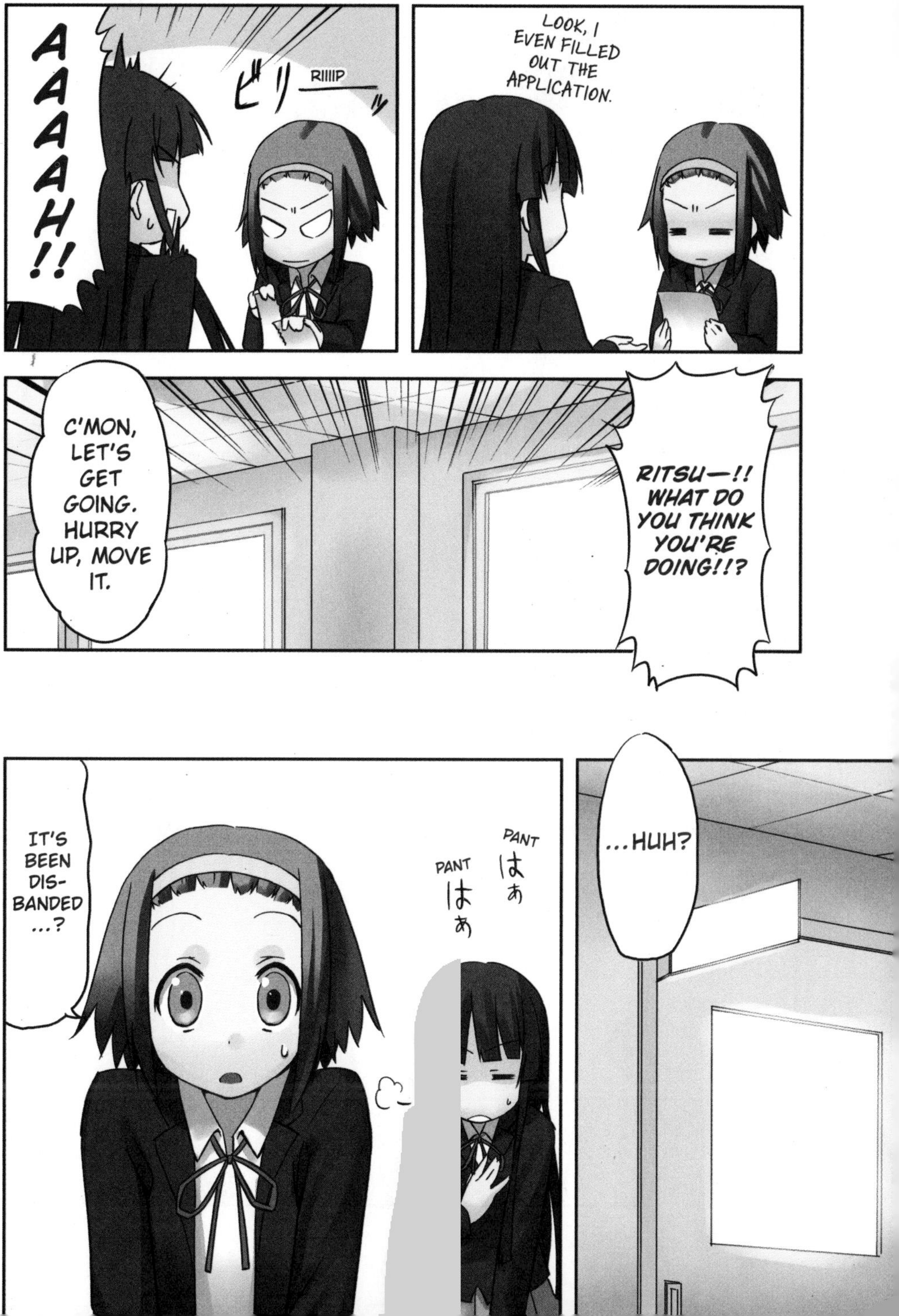
LOOK, I EVEN FILLED OUT THE APPLICATION.
ビリー ッ
RIIIIP
AAAAAH!!
RITSU—!! WHAT DO YOU THINK YOU'RE DOING!!?
C'MON, LET'S GET GOING. HURRY UP, MOVE IT.
...HUH?
PANT はぁ
PANT はぁ
IT'S BEEN DIS-BANDED...?

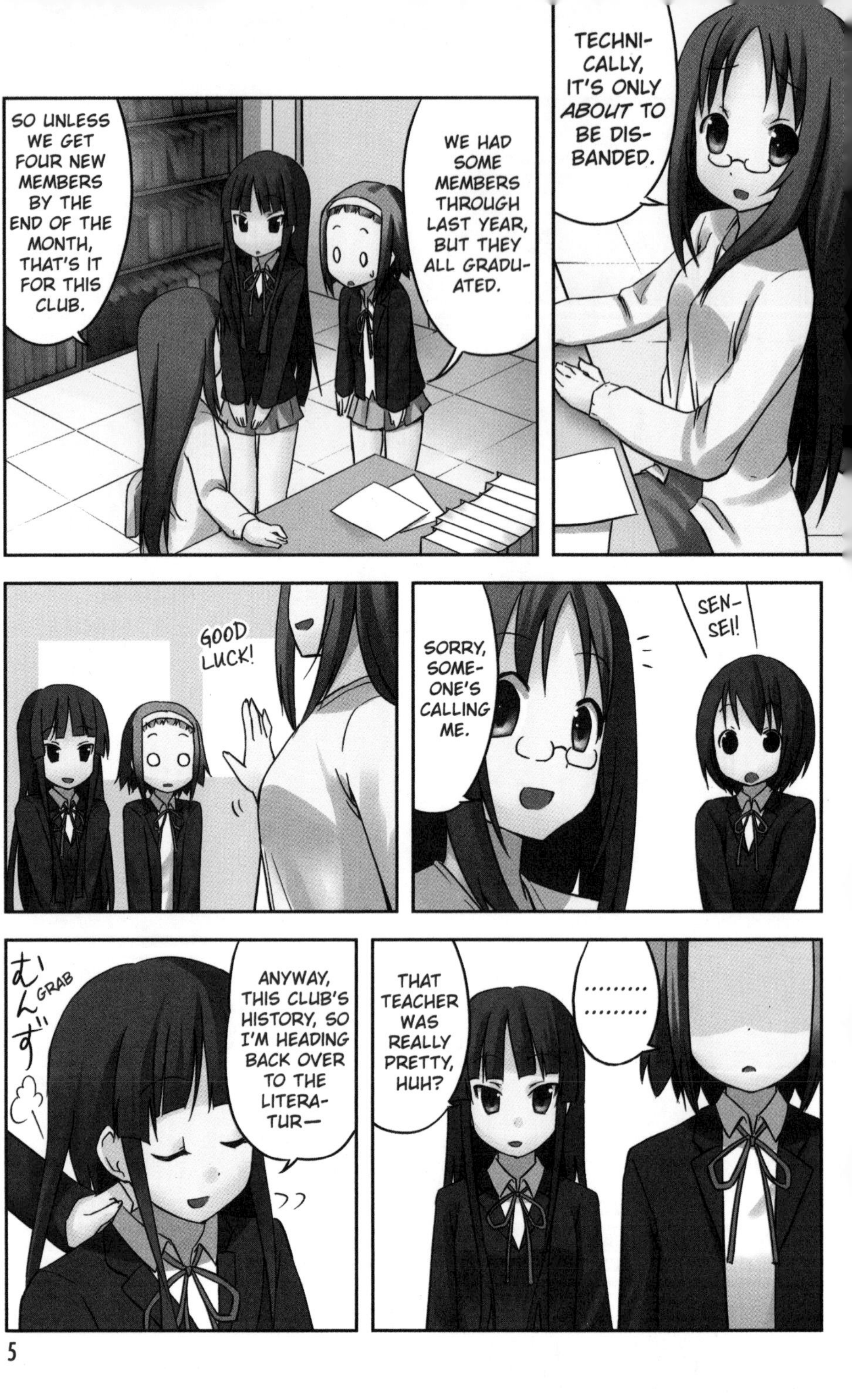
TECHNICALLY, IT'S ONLY *ABOUT* TO BE DISBANDED.
WE HAD SOME MEMBERS THROUGH LAST YEAR, BUT THEY ALL GRADUATED.
SO UNLESS WE GET FOUR NEW MEMBERS BY THE END OF THE MONTH, THAT'S IT FOR THIS CLUB.
SENSEI!
SORRY, SOMEONE'S CALLING ME.
GOOD LUCK!
....
....
THAT TEACHER WAS REALLY PRETTY, HUH?
ANYWAY, THIS CLUB'S HISTORY, SO I'M HEADING BACK OVER TO THE LITERATUR—
むんず GRAB

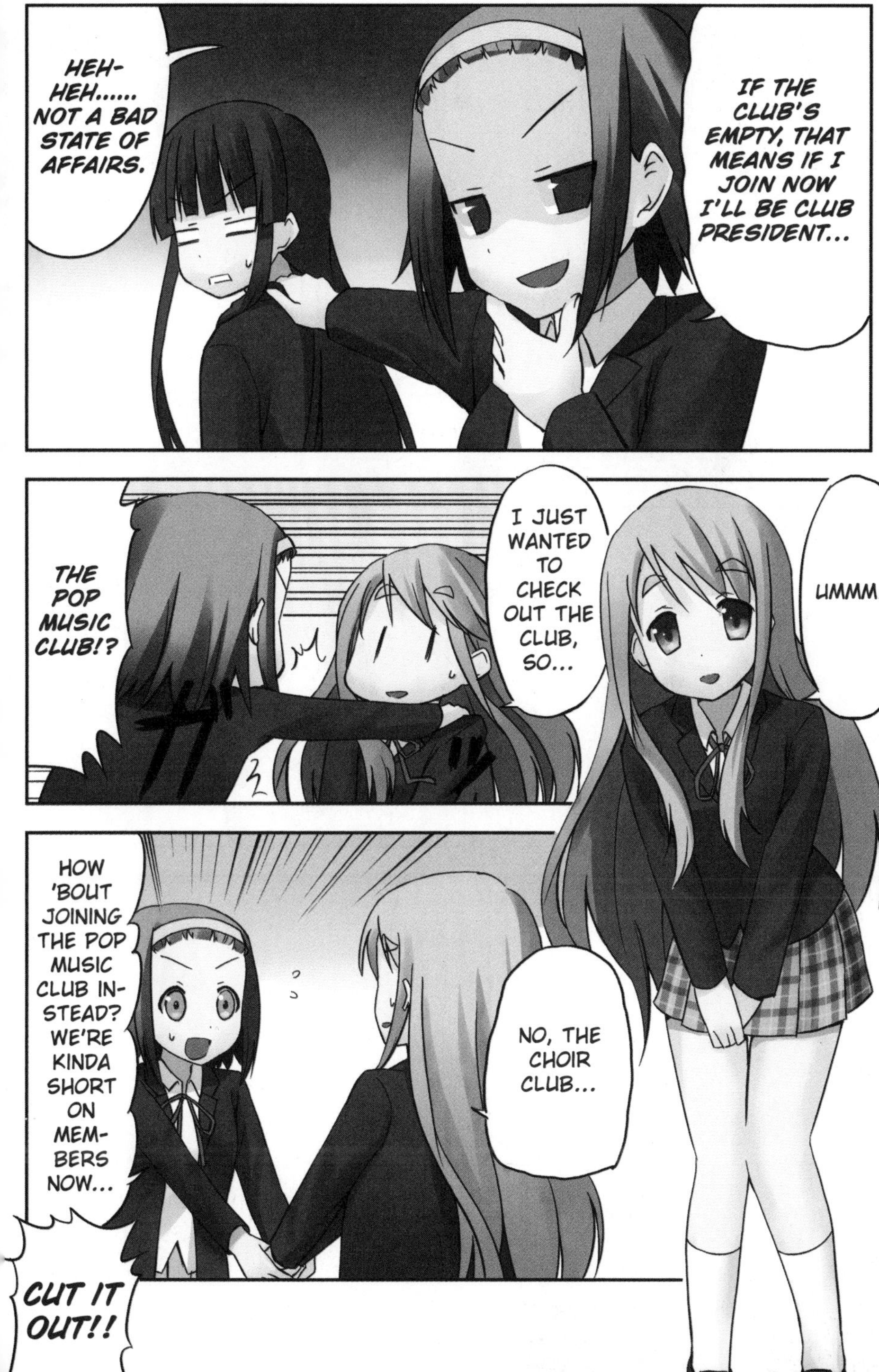
IF THE CLUB'S EMPTY, THAT MEANS IF I JOIN NOW I'LL BE CLUB PRESIDENT...
HEH-HEH...... NOT A BAD STATE OF AFFAIRS.
UMMM...
I JUST WANTED TO CHECK OUT THE CLUB, SO...
THE POP MUSIC CLUB!?
NO, THE CHOIR CLUB...
HOW 'BOUT JOINING THE POP MUSIC CLUB INSTEAD? WE'RE KINDA SHORT ON MEMBERS NOW...
CUT IT OUT!!

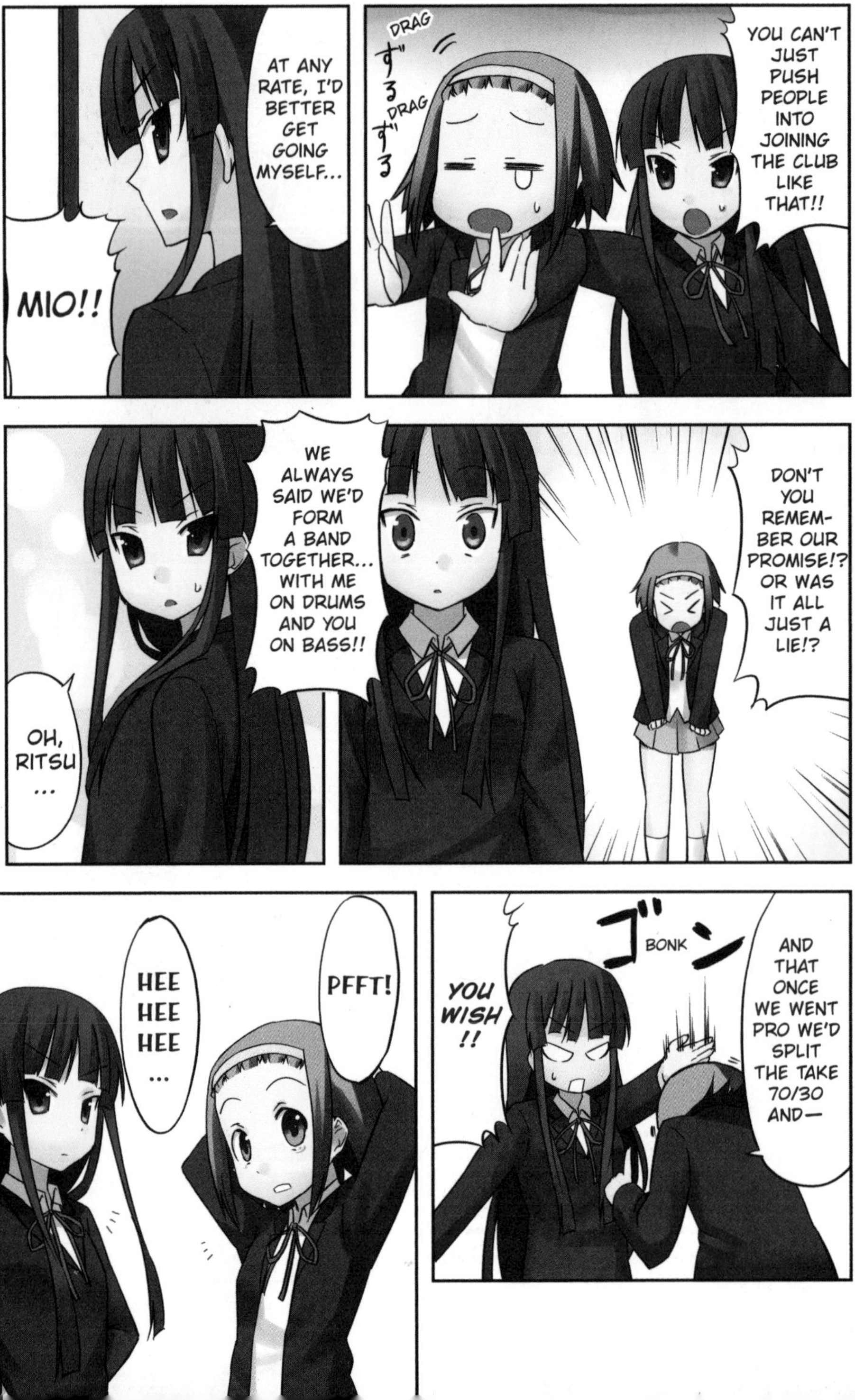
YOU CAN'T JUST PUSH PEOPLE INTO JOINING THE CLUB LIKE THAT!!
ずる DRAG ずる DRAG
AT ANY RATE, I'D BETTER GET GOING MYSELF...
MIO!!
DON'T YOU REMEMBER OUR PROMISE!? OR WAS IT ALL JUST A LIE!?
WE ALWAYS SAID WE'D FORM A BAND TOGETHER... WITH ME ON DRUMS AND YOU ON BASS!!
OH, RITSU...
AND THAT ONCE WE WENT PRO WE'D SPLIT THE TAKE 70/30 AND—
ゴン BONK
YOU WISH!!
PFFT!
HEE HEE HEE...

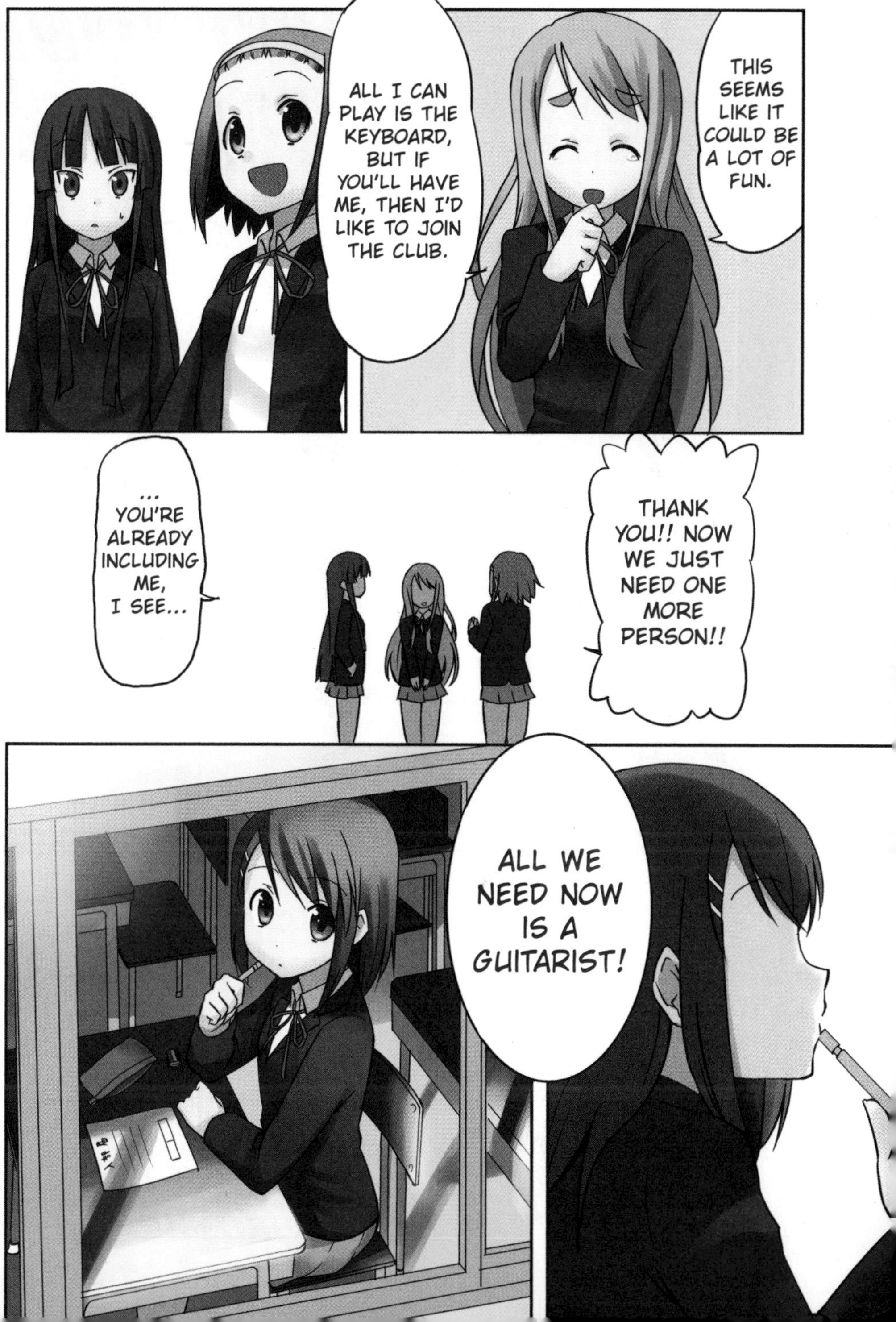
THIS SEEMS LIKE IT COULD BE A LOT OF FUN.
ALL I CAN PLAY IS THE KEYBOARD, BUT IF YOU'LL HAVE ME, THEN I'D LIKE TO JOIN THE CLUB.
THANK YOU!! NOW WE JUST NEED ONE MORE PERSON!!
... YOU'RE ALREADY INCLUDING ME, I SEE...
ALL WE NEED NOW IS A GUITARIST!

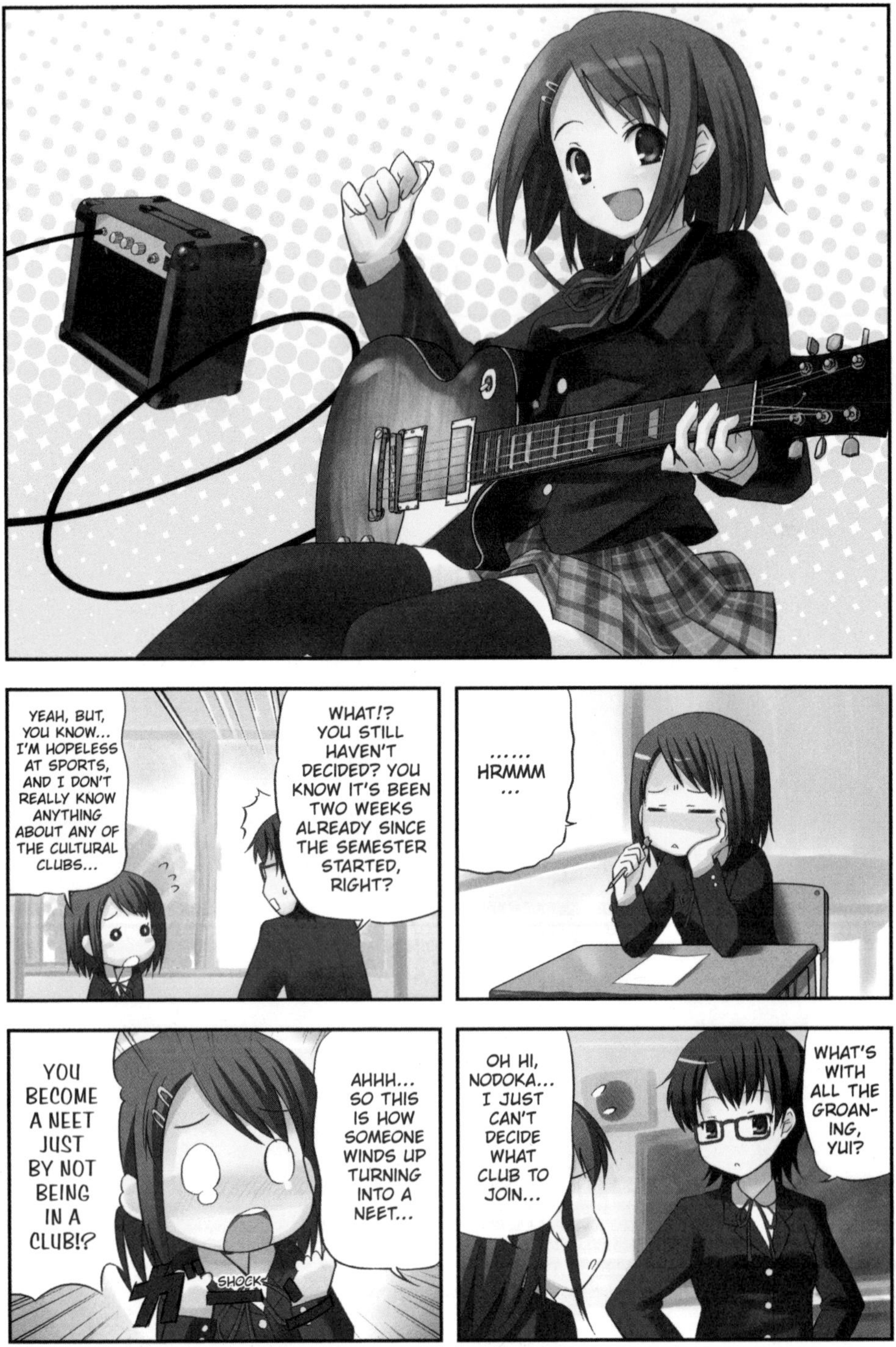
……
HRMMM
…
WHAT!? YOU STILL HAVEN'T DECIDED? YOU KNOW IT'S BEEN TWO WEEKS ALREADY SINCE THE SEMESTER STARTED, RIGHT?
YEAH, BUT, YOU KNOW… I'M HOPELESS AT SPORTS, AND I DON'T REALLY KNOW ANYTHING ABOUT ANY OF THE CULTURAL CLUBS…
WHAT'S WITH ALL THE GROAN-ING, YUI?
OH HI, NODOKA… I JUST CAN'T DECIDE WHAT CLUB TO JOIN…
AHHH… SO THIS IS HOW SOMEONE WINDS UP TURNING INTO A NEET…
YOU BECOME A NEET JUST BY NOT BEING IN A CLUB!?
SHOCK

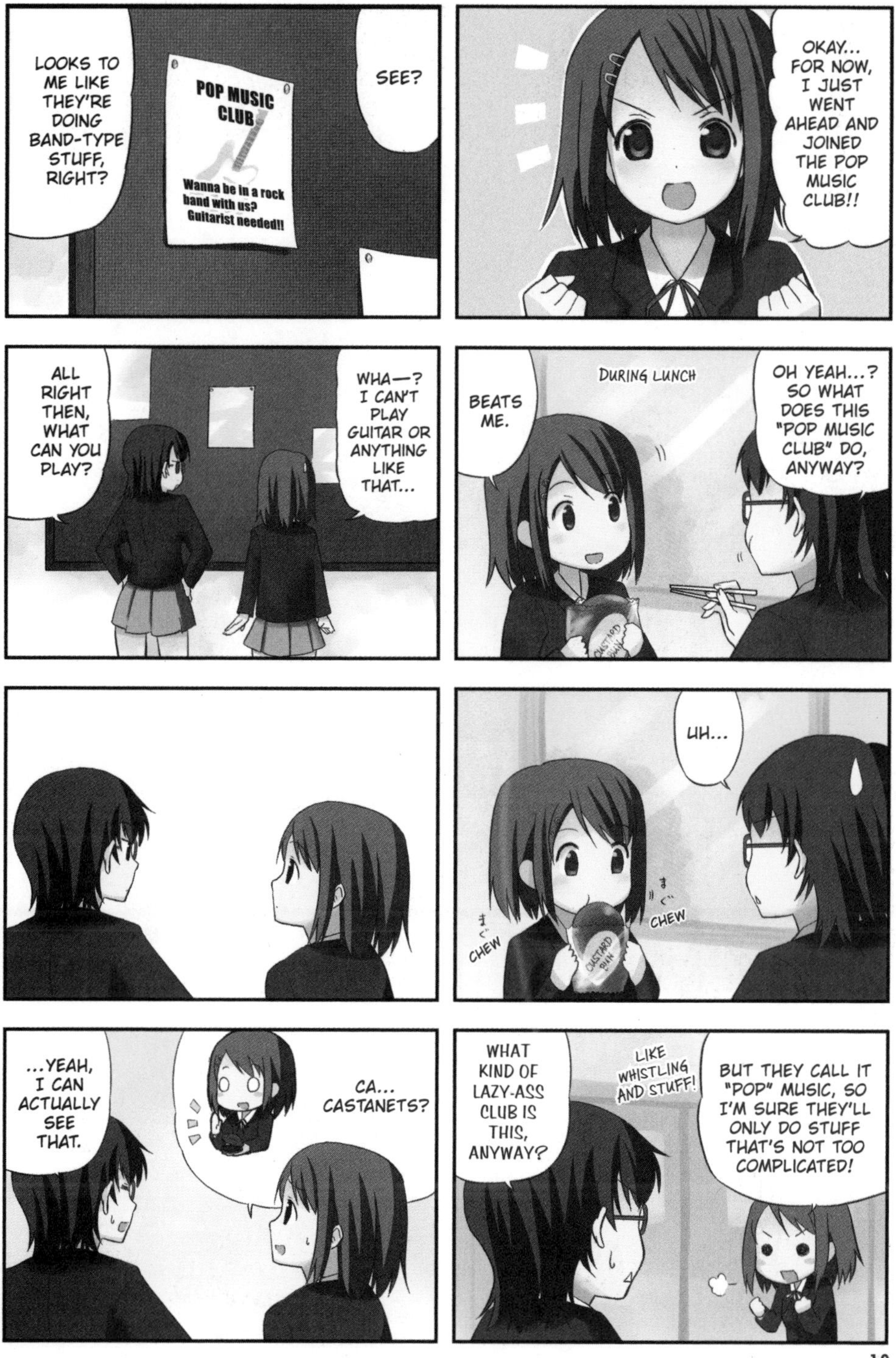
OKAY... FOR NOW, I JUST WENT AHEAD AND JOINED THE POP MUSIC CLUB!!
DURING LUNCH
OH YEAH...? SO WHAT DOES THIS "POP MUSIC CLUB" DO, ANYWAY?
BEATS ME.
CUSTARD BUN
UH...
まぐ CHEW
まぐ CHEW
CUSTARD BUN
BUT THEY CALL IT "POP" MUSIC, SO I'M SURE THEY'LL ONLY DO STUFF THAT'S NOT TOO COMPLICATED!
LIKE WHISTLING AND STUFF!
WHAT KIND OF LAZY-ASS CLUB IS THIS, ANYWAY?
SEE?
LOOKS TO ME LIKE THEY'RE DOING BAND-TYPE STUFF, RIGHT?
POP MUSIC CLUB
Wanna be in a rock band with us? Guitarist needed!!
WHA—? I CAN'T PLAY GUITAR OR ANYTHING LIKE THAT...
ALL RIGHT THEN, WHAT CAN YOU PLAY?
CA... CASTANETS?
...YEAH, I CAN ACTUALLY SEE THAT.

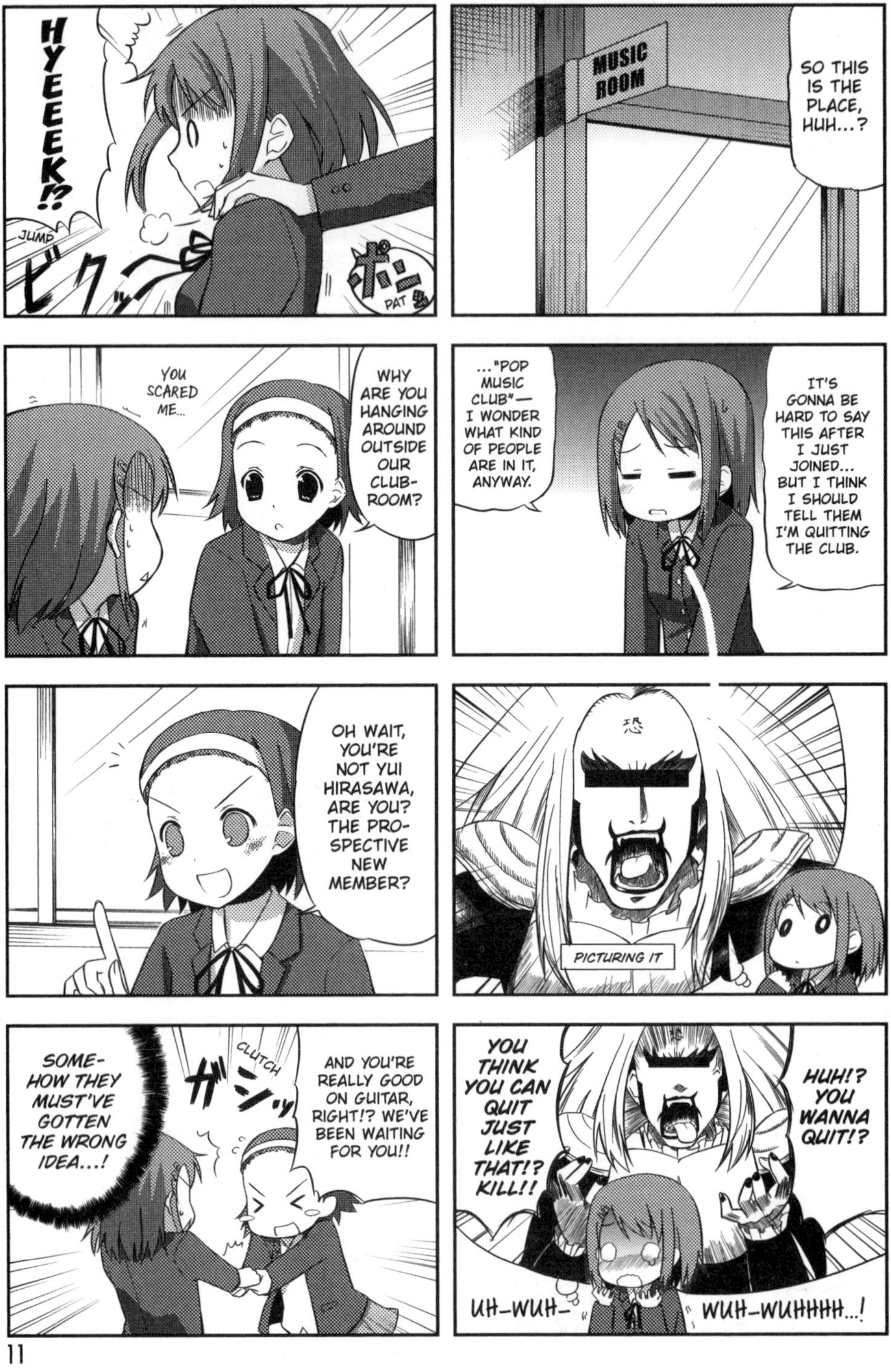
MUSIC ROOM
SO THIS IS THE PLACE, HUH...?
IT'S GONNA BE HARD TO SAY THIS AFTER I JUST JOINED... BUT I THINK I SHOULD TELL THEM I'M QUITTING THE CLUB.
..."POP MUSIC CLUB"— I WONDER WHAT KIND OF PEOPLE ARE IN IT, ANYWAY.
恐
PICTURING IT
HUH!? YOU WANNA QUIT!?
YOU THINK YOU CAN QUIT JUST LIKE THAT!? KILL!!
UH-WUH-
WUH-WUHHHH...!
ポン
PAT
HYEEEK!?
ビクッ
JUMP
WHY ARE YOU HANGING AROUND OUTSIDE OUR CLUB-ROOM?
YOU SCARED ME...
OH WAIT, YOU'RE NOT YUI HIRASAWA, ARE YOU? THE PRO-SPECTIVE NEW MEMBER?
AND YOU'RE REALLY GOOD ON GUITAR, RIGHT!? WE'VE BEEN WAITING FOR YOU!!
ガシッ
CLUTCH
SOME-HOW THEY MUST'VE GOTTEN THE WRONG IDEA...!

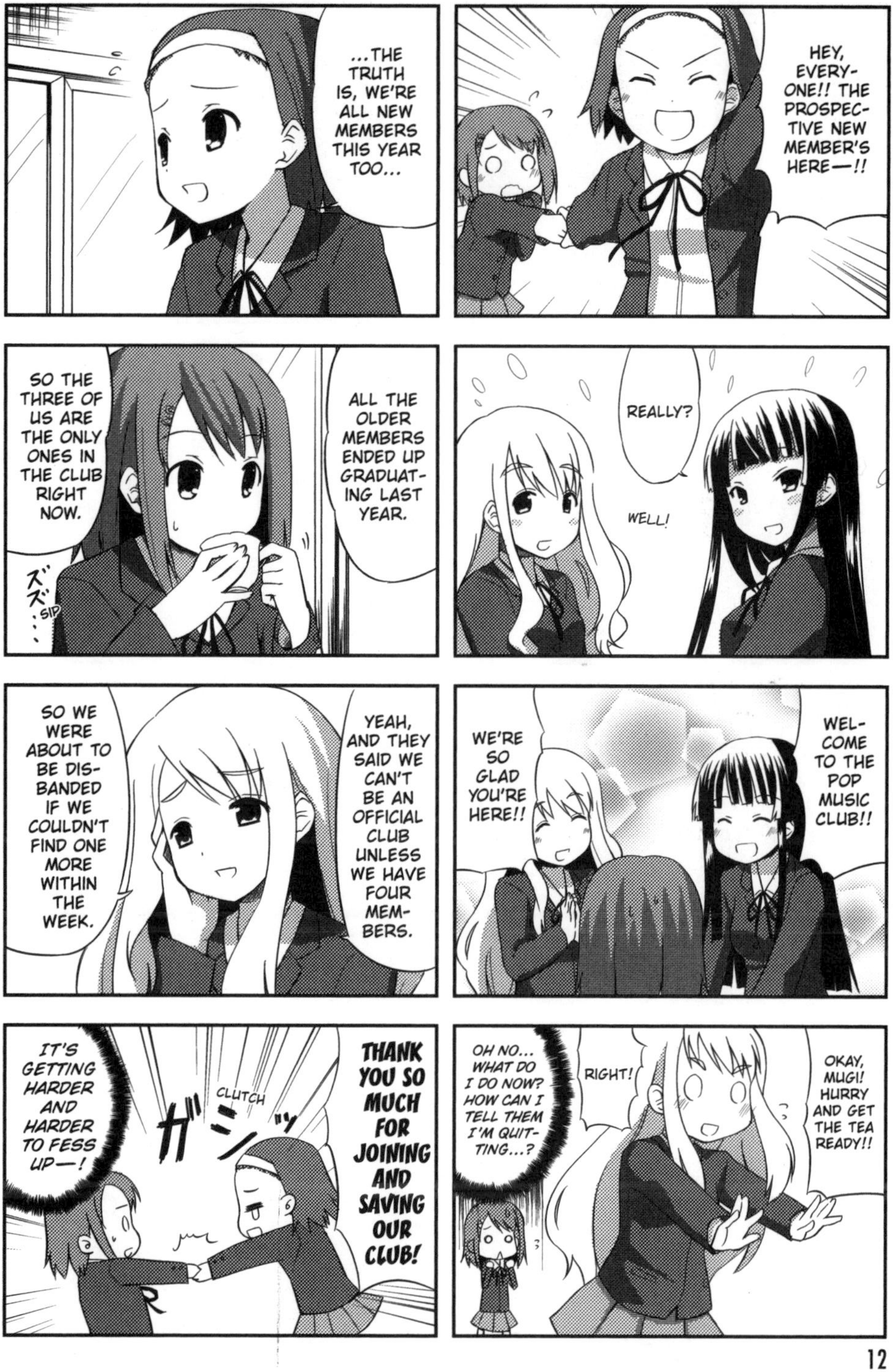
HEY, EVERYONE!! THE PROSPECTIVE NEW MEMBER'S HERE—!!
REALLY?
WELL!
WELCOME TO THE POP MUSIC CLUB!!
WE'RE SO GLAD YOU'RE HERE!!
OKAY, MUGI! HURRY AND GET THE TEA READY!!
RIGHT!
OH NO... WHAT DO I DO NOW? HOW CAN I TELL THEM I'M QUITTING...?
...THE TRUTH IS, WE'RE ALL NEW MEMBERS THIS YEAR TOO...
ALL THE OLDER MEMBERS ENDED UP GRADUATING LAST YEAR.
SO THE THREE OF US ARE THE ONLY ONES IN THE CLUB RIGHT NOW.
ズズ…
SIP
YEAH, AND THEY SAID WE CAN'T BE AN OFFICIAL CLUB UNLESS WE HAVE FOUR MEMBERS.
SO WE WERE ABOUT TO BE DISBANDED IF WE COULDN'T FIND ONE MORE WITHIN THE WEEK.
THANK YOU SO MUCH FOR JOINING AND SAVING OUR CLUB!
ガシッ
CLUTCH
IT'S GETTING HARDER AND HARDER TO FESS UP—!

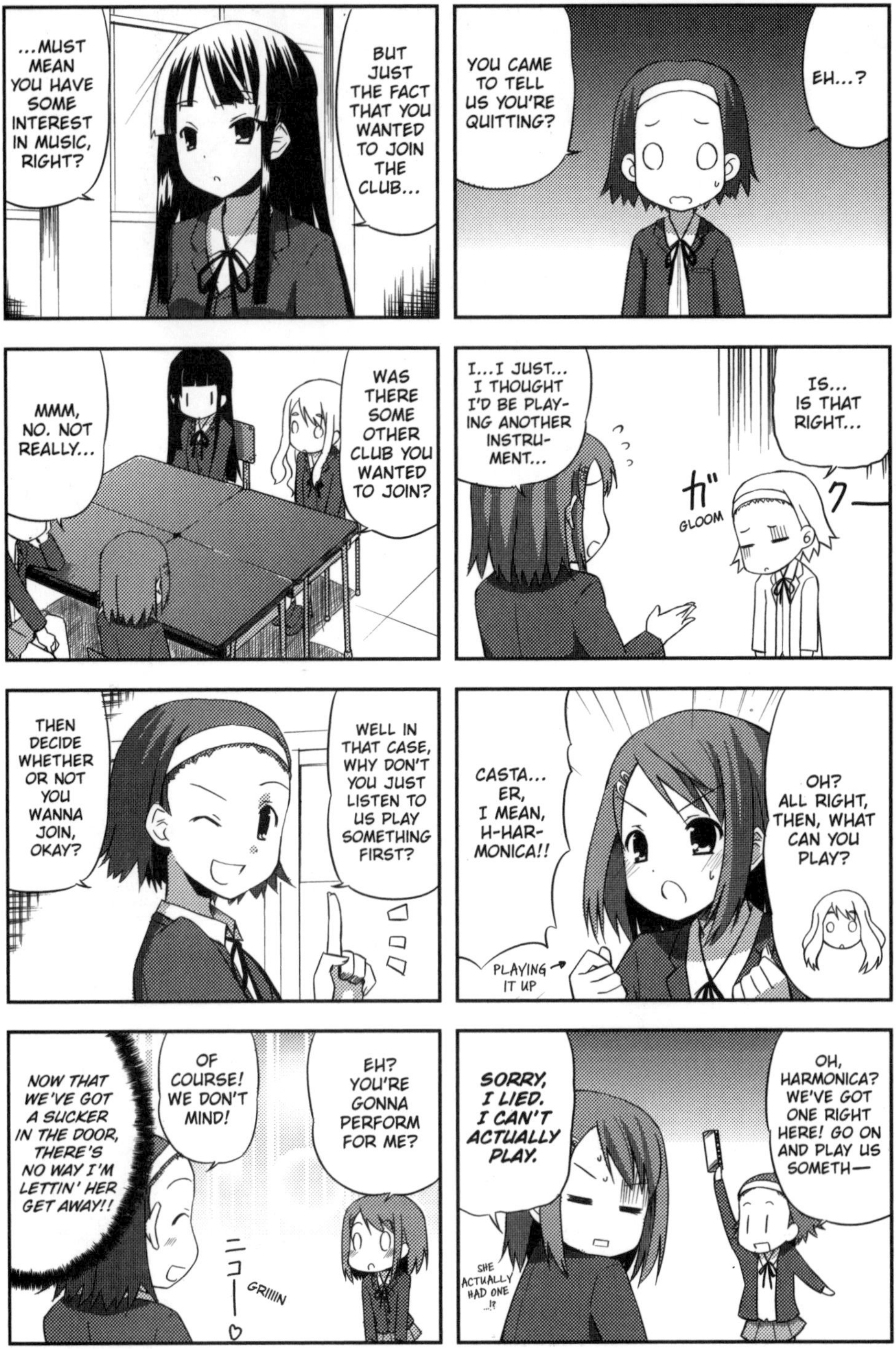
EH...?
YOU CAME TO TELL US YOU'RE QUITTING?
IS... IS THAT RIGHT...
ガクー
GLOOM
I...I JUST... I THOUGHT I'D BE PLAYING ANOTHER INSTRUMENT...
OH? ALL RIGHT, THEN, WHAT CAN YOU PLAY?
CASTA... ER, I MEAN, H-HARMONICA!!
PLAYING IT UP
OH, HARMONICA? WE'VE GOT ONE RIGHT HERE! GO ON AND PLAY US SOMETH—
SORRY, I LIED. I CAN'T ACTUALLY PLAY.
SHE ACTUALLY HAD ONE ...!?
BUT JUST THE FACT THAT YOU WANTED TO JOIN THE CLUB...
...MUST MEAN YOU HAVE SOME INTEREST IN MUSIC, RIGHT?
WAS THERE SOME OTHER CLUB YOU WANTED TO JOIN?
MMM, NO. NOT REALLY...
WELL IN THAT CASE, WHY DON'T YOU JUST LISTEN TO US PLAY SOMETHING FIRST?
THEN DECIDE WHETHER OR NOT YOU WANNA JOIN, OKAY?
EH? YOU'RE GONNA PERFORM FOR ME?
OF COURSE! WE DON'T MIND!
NOW THAT WE'VE GOT A SUCKER IN THE DOOR, THERE'S NO WAY I'M LETTIN' HER GET AWAY!!
ニコー
GRIIIN

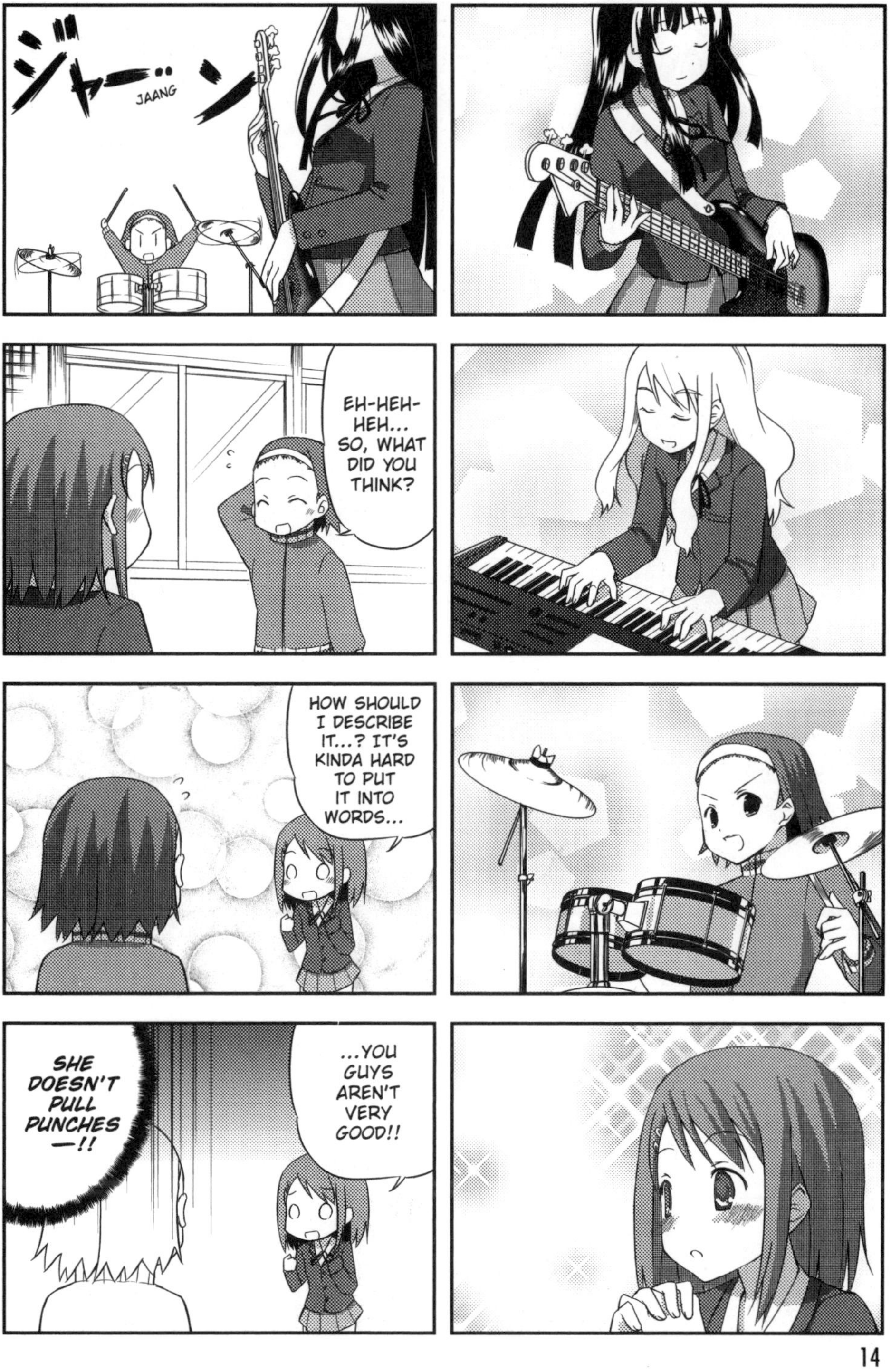
ジャーン
JAANG
EH-HEH-HEH... SO, WHAT DID YOU THINK?
HOW SHOULD I DESCRIBE IT...? IT'S KINDA HARD TO PUT IT INTO WORDS...
...YOU GUYS AREN'T VERY GOOD!!
SHE DOESN'T PULL PUNCHES—!!

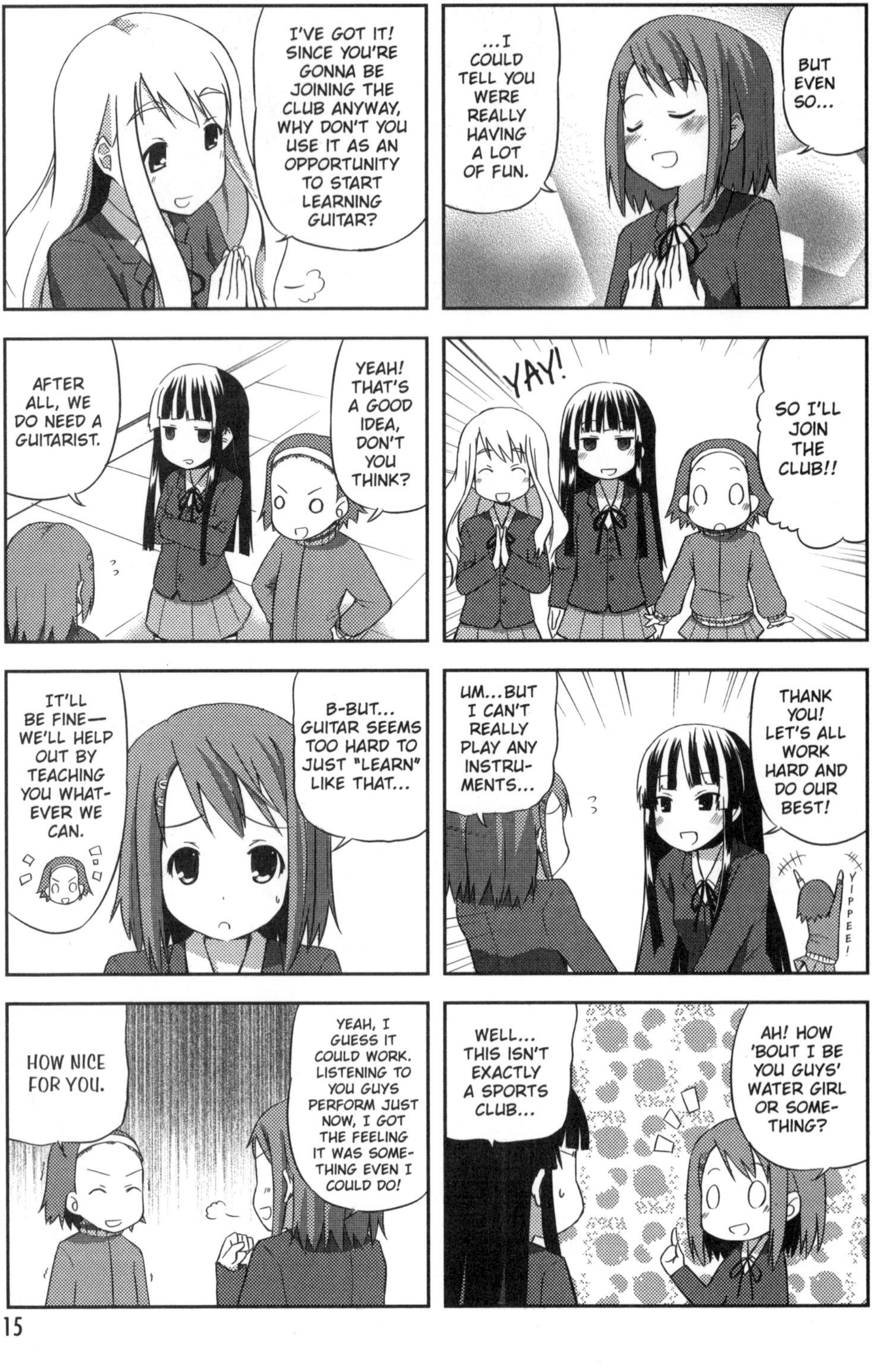
BUT EVEN SO...
...I COULD TELL YOU WERE REALLY HAVING A LOT OF FUN.
SO I'LL JOIN THE CLUB!!
YAY!
THANK YOU! LET'S ALL WORK HARD AND DO OUR BEST!
YIPPEE!
UM...BUT I CAN'T REALLY PLAY ANY INSTRU-MENTS...
AH! HOW 'BOUT I BE YOU GUYS' WATER GIRL OR SOME-THING?
WELL... THIS ISN'T EXACTLY A SPORTS CLUB...
I'VE GOT IT! SINCE YOU'RE GONNA BE JOINING THE CLUB ANYWAY, WHY DON'T YOU USE IT AS AN OPPORTUNITY TO START LEARNING GUITAR?
YEAH! THAT'S A GOOD IDEA, DON'T YOU THINK?
AFTER ALL, WE DO NEED A GUITARIST.
B-BUT... GUITAR SEEMS TOO HARD TO JUST "LEARN" LIKE THAT...
IT'LL BE FINE—WE'LL HELP OUT BY TEACHING YOU WHAT-EVER WE CAN.
YEAH, I GUESS IT COULD WORK. LISTENING TO YOU GUYS PERFORM JUST NOW, I GOT THE FEELING IT WAS SOME-THING EVEN I COULD DO!
HOW NICE FOR YOU.

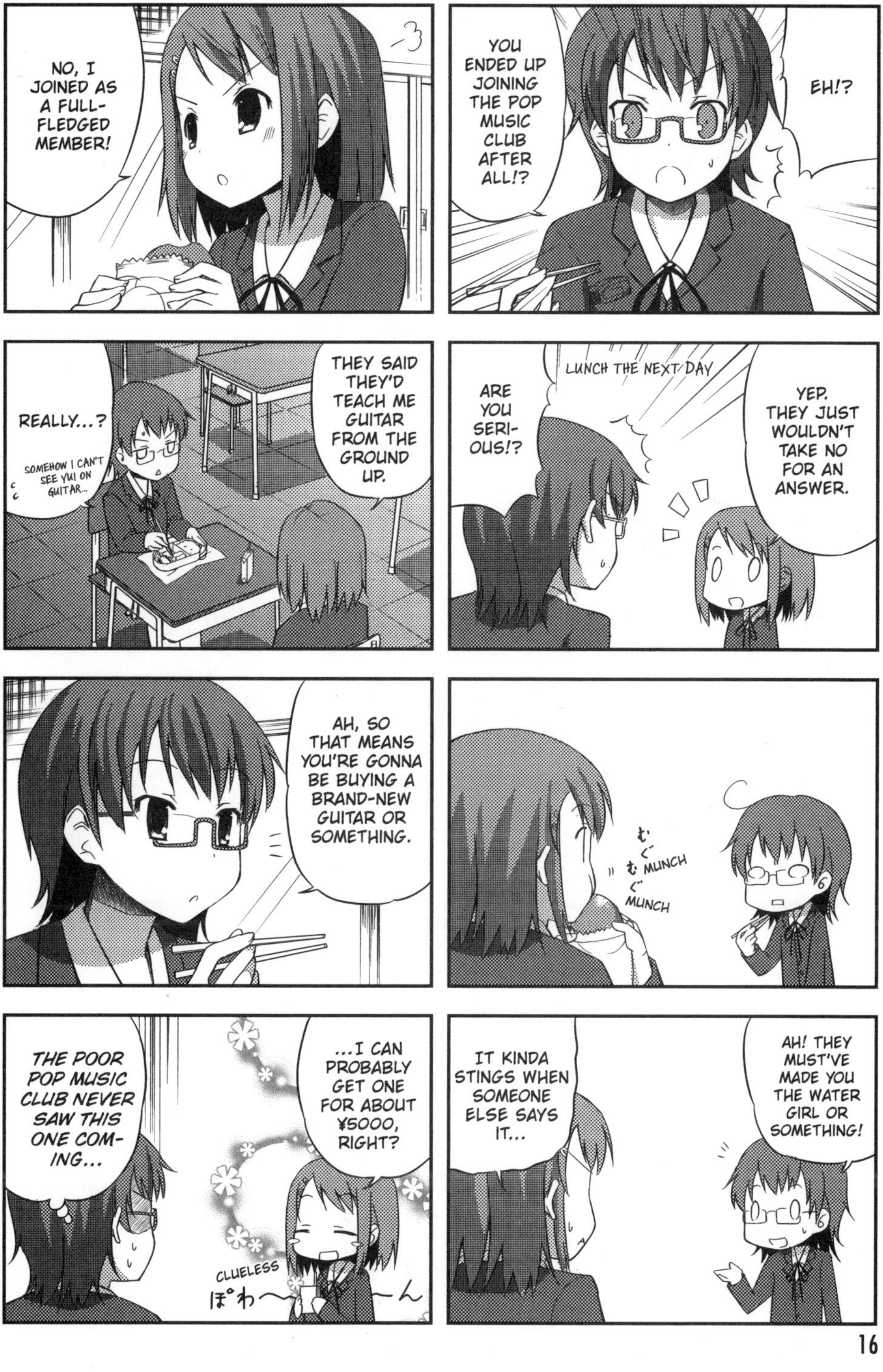
YOU ENDED UP JOINING THE POP MUSIC CLUB AFTER ALL!?
EH!?
LUNCH THE NEXT DAY
ARE YOU SERI-OUS!?
YEP. THEY JUST WOULDN'T TAKE NO FOR AN ANSWER.
MUNCH MUNCH
AH! THEY MUST'VE MADE YOU THE WATER GIRL OR SOMETHING!
IT KINDA STINGS WHEN SOMEONE ELSE SAYS IT...
NO, I JOINED AS A FULL-FLEDGED MEMBER!
THEY SAID THEY'D TEACH ME GUITAR FROM THE GROUND UP.
REALLY...?
SOMEHOW I CAN'T SEE YUI ON GUITAR...
AH, SO THAT MEANS YOU'RE GONNA BE BUYING A BRAND-NEW GUITAR OR SOMETHING.
...I CAN PROBABLY GET ONE FOR ABOUT ¥5000, RIGHT?
THE POOR POP MUSIC CLUB NEVER SAW THIS ONE COMING...
CLUELESS

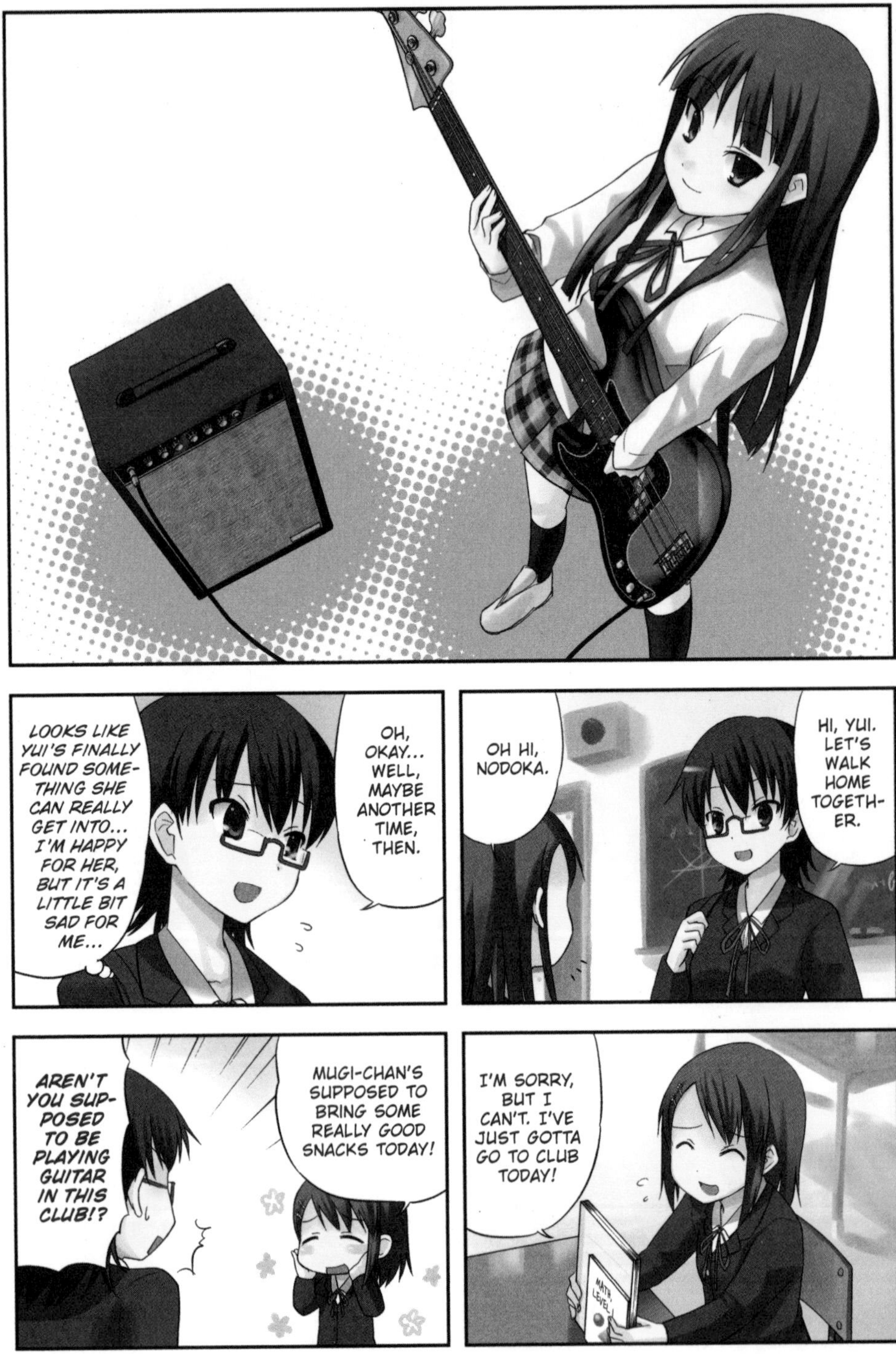
HI, YUI. LET'S WALK HOME TOGETHER.
OH HI, NODOKA.
OH, OKAY... WELL, MAYBE ANOTHER TIME, THEN.
LOOKS LIKE YUI'S FINALLY FOUND SOMETHING SHE CAN REALLY GET INTO... I'M HAPPY FOR HER, BUT IT'S A LITTLE BIT SAD FOR ME...
I'M SORRY, BUT I CAN'T. I'VE JUST GOTTA GO TO CLUB TODAY!
MUGI-CHAN'S SUPPOSED TO BRING SOME REALLY GOOD SNACKS TODAY!
AREN'T YOU SUPPOSED TO BE PLAYING GUITAR IN THIS CLUB!?

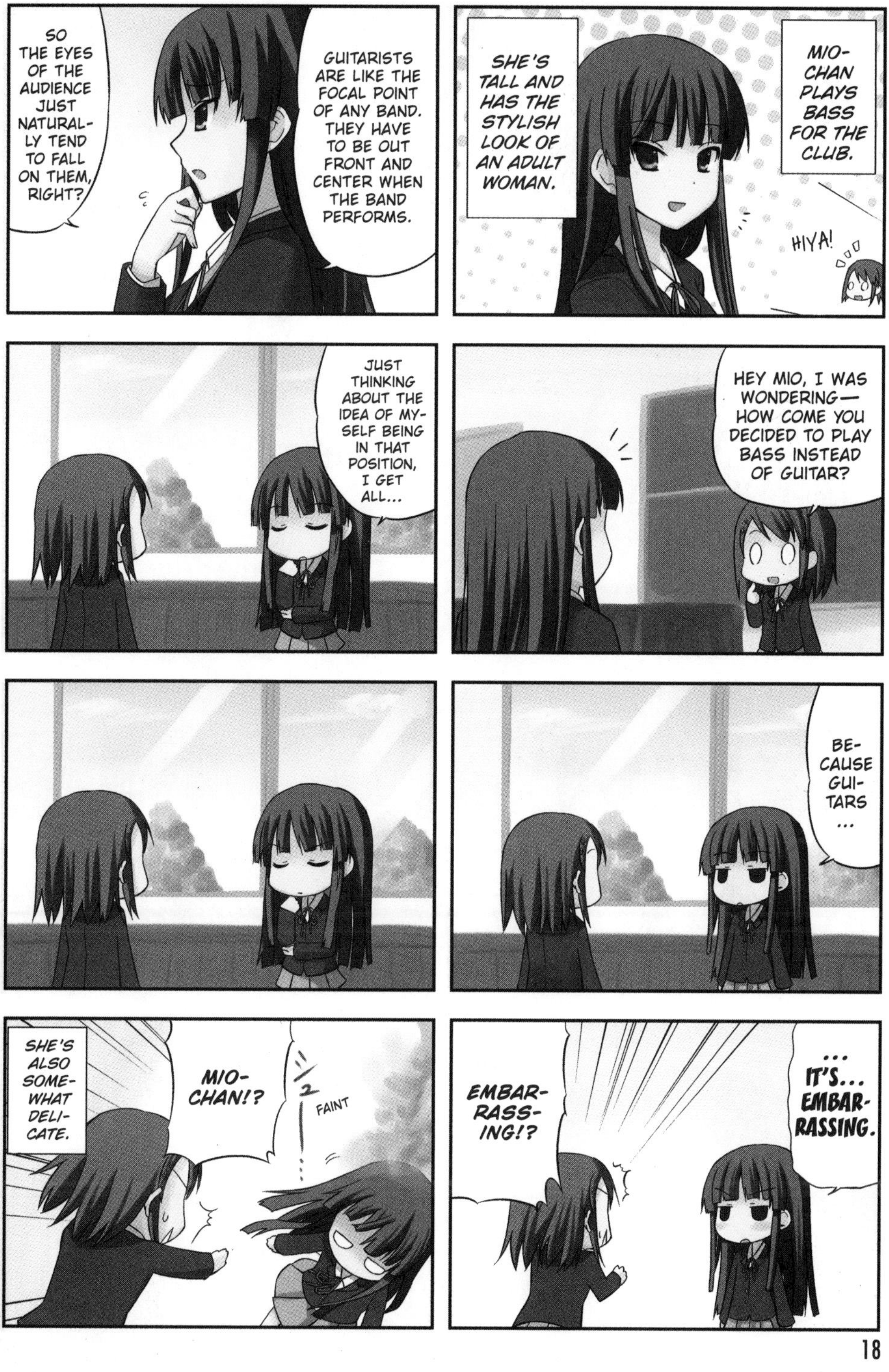
MIO-CHAN PLAYS BASS FOR THE CLUB.
SHE'S TALL AND HAS THE STYLISH LOOK OF AN ADULT WOMAN.
HIYA!
GUITARISTS ARE LIKE THE FOCAL POINT OF ANY BAND. THEY HAVE TO BE OUT FRONT AND CENTER WHEN THE BAND PERFORMS.
SO THE EYES OF THE AUDIENCE JUST NATURALLY TEND TO FALL ON THEM, RIGHT?
HEY MIO, I WAS WONDERING— HOW COME YOU DECIDED TO PLAY BASS INSTEAD OF GUITAR?
JUST THINKING ABOUT THE IDEA OF MYSELF BEING IN THAT POSITION, I GET ALL...
BECAUSE GUITARS...
...IT'S... EMBARRASSING.
EMBARRASSING!?
SHE'S ALSO SOMEWHAT DELICATE.
MIO-CHAN!?
FAINT

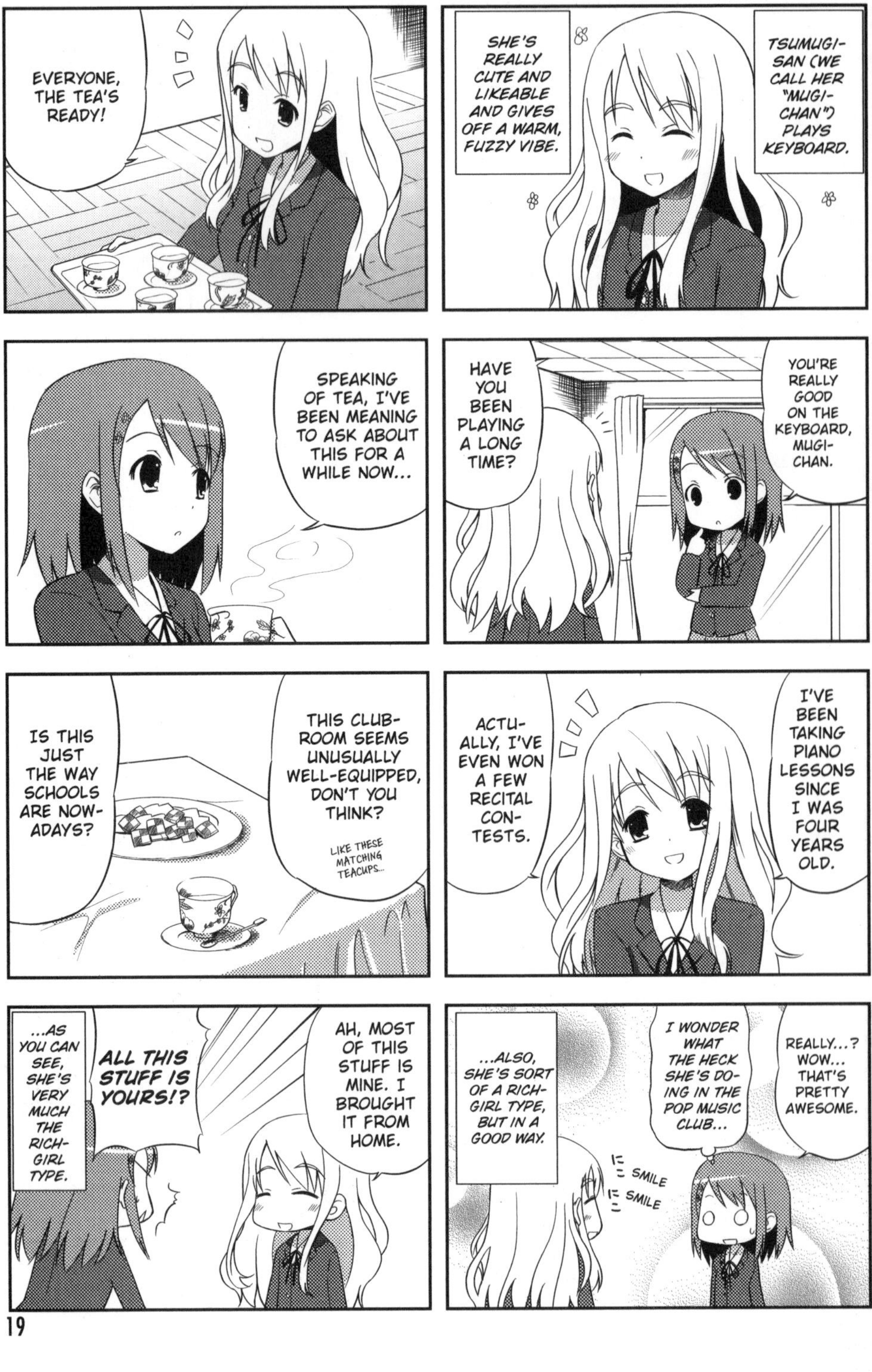
TSUMUGI-SAN (WE CALL HER "MUGI-CHAN") PLAYS KEYBOARD.
SHE'S REALLY CUTE AND LIKEABLE AND GIVES OFF A WARM, FUZZY VIBE.
YOU'RE REALLY GOOD ON THE KEYBOARD, MUGI-CHAN.
HAVE YOU BEEN PLAYING A LONG TIME?
I'VE BEEN TAKING PIANO LESSONS SINCE I WAS FOUR YEARS OLD.
ACTUALLY, I'VE EVEN WON A FEW RECITAL CONTESTS.
REALLY...? WOW... THAT'S PRETTY AWESOME.
I WONDER WHAT THE HECK SHE'S DOING IN THE POP MUSIC CLUB...
SMILE
SMILE
...ALSO, SHE'S SORT OF A RICH-GIRL TYPE, BUT IN A GOOD WAY.
EVERYONE, THE TEA'S READY!
SPEAKING OF TEA, I'VE BEEN MEANING TO ASK ABOUT THIS FOR A WHILE NOW...
THIS CLUBROOM SEEMS UNUSUALLY WELL-EQUIPPED, DON'T YOU THINK?
LIKE THESE MATCHING TEACUPS...
IS THIS JUST THE WAY SCHOOLS ARE NOWADAYS?
AH, MOST OF THIS STUFF IS MINE. I BROUGHT IT FROM HOME.
ALL THIS STUFF IS YOURS!?
...AS YOU CAN SEE, SHE'S VERY MUCH THE RICH-GIRL TYPE.

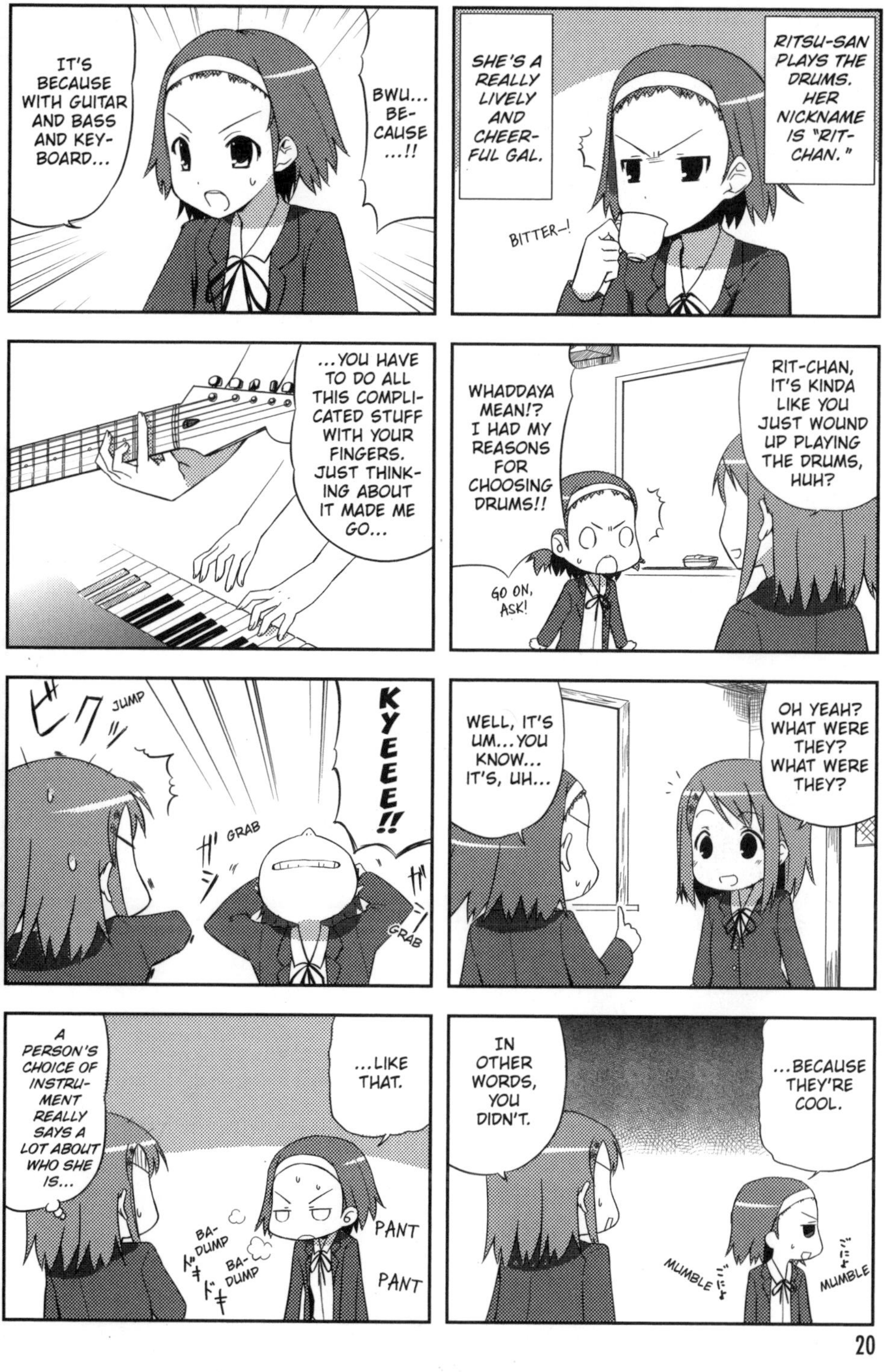
RITSU-SAN PLAYS THE DRUMS. HER NICKNAME IS "RIT-CHAN."
SHE'S A REALLY LIVELY AND CHEERFUL GAL.
BITTER—!
RIT-CHAN, IT'S KINDA LIKE YOU JUST WOUND UP PLAYING THE DRUMS, HUH?
WHADDAYA MEAN!? I HAD MY REASONS FOR CHOOSING DRUMS!!
GO ON, ASK!
OH YEAH? WHAT WERE THEY? WHAT WERE THEY?
WELL, IT'S UM... YOU KNOW... IT'S, UH...
...BECAUSE THEY'RE COOL.
IN OTHER WORDS, YOU DIDN'T.
MUMBLE
MUMBLE
BWU... BE-CAUSE ...!!
IT'S BECAUSE WITH GUITAR AND BASS AND KEY-BOARD...
...YOU HAVE TO DO ALL THIS COMPLICATED STUFF WITH YOUR FINGERS. JUST THINKING ABOUT IT MADE ME GO...
KYEEEE!!
JUMP
GRAB
GRAB
...LIKE THAT.
A PERSON'S CHOICE OF INSTRUMENT REALLY SAYS A LOT ABOUT WHO SHE IS...
PANT
PANT
BA-DUMP
BA-DUMP

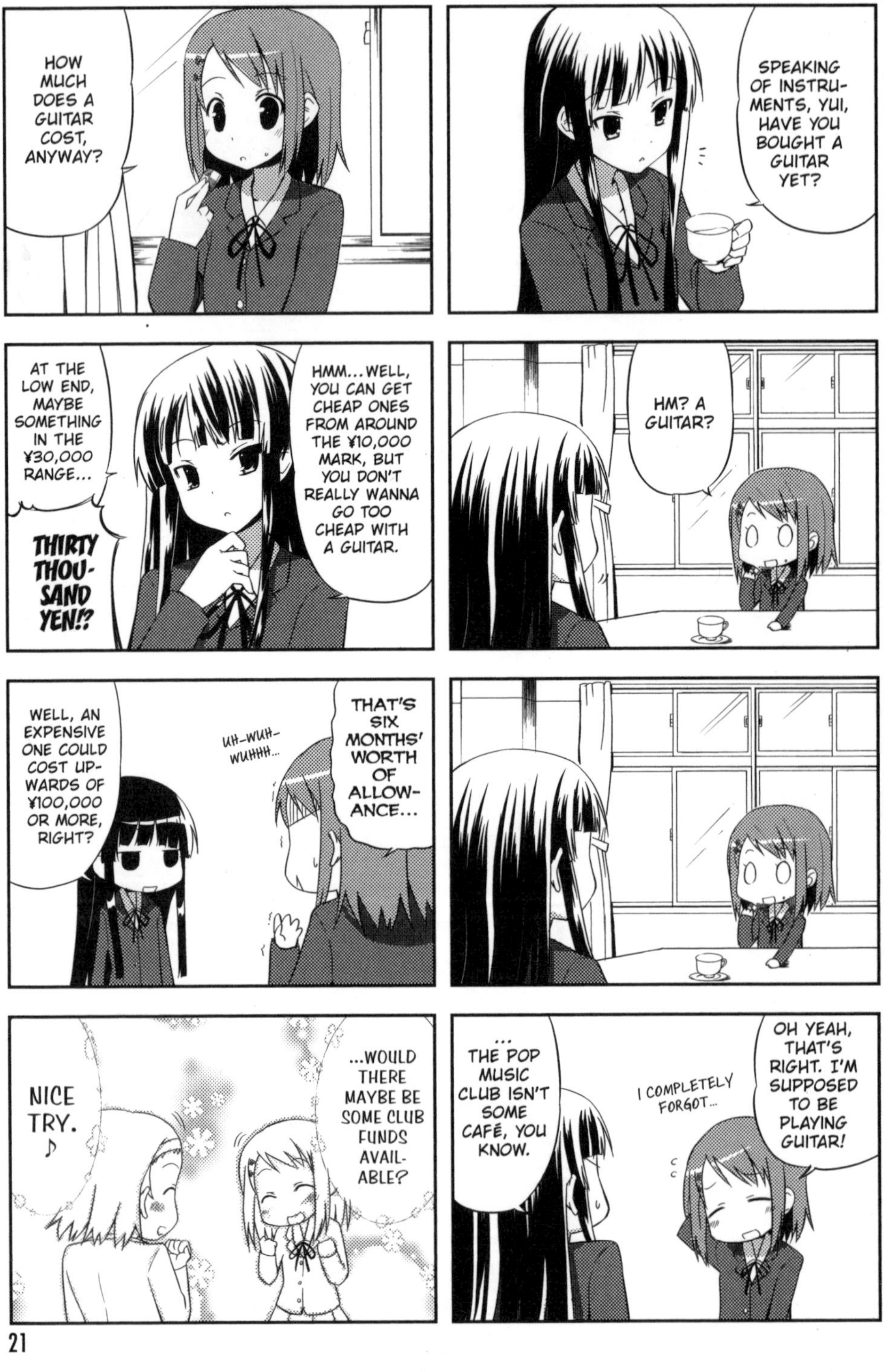
SPEAKING OF INSTRUMENTS, YUI, HAVE YOU BOUGHT A GUITAR YET?
HM? A GUITAR?
OH YEAH, THAT'S RIGHT. I'M SUPPOSED TO BE PLAYING GUITAR!
I COMPLETELY FORGOT...
... THE POP MUSIC CLUB ISN'T SOME CAFÉ, YOU KNOW.
HOW MUCH DOES A GUITAR COST, ANYWAY?
HMM...WELL, YOU CAN GET CHEAP ONES FROM AROUND THE ¥10,000 MARK, BUT YOU DON'T REALLY WANNA GO TOO CHEAP WITH A GUITAR.
AT THE LOW END, MAYBE SOMETHING IN THE ¥30,000 RANGE...
THIRTY THOUSAND YEN!?
THAT'S SIX MONTHS' WORTH OF ALLOWANCE...
UH-WUH-WUHHH...
WELL, AN EXPENSIVE ONE COULD COST UPWARDS OF ¥100,000 OR MORE, RIGHT?
...WOULD THERE MAYBE BE SOME CLUB FUNDS AVAILABLE?
NICE TRY. ♪

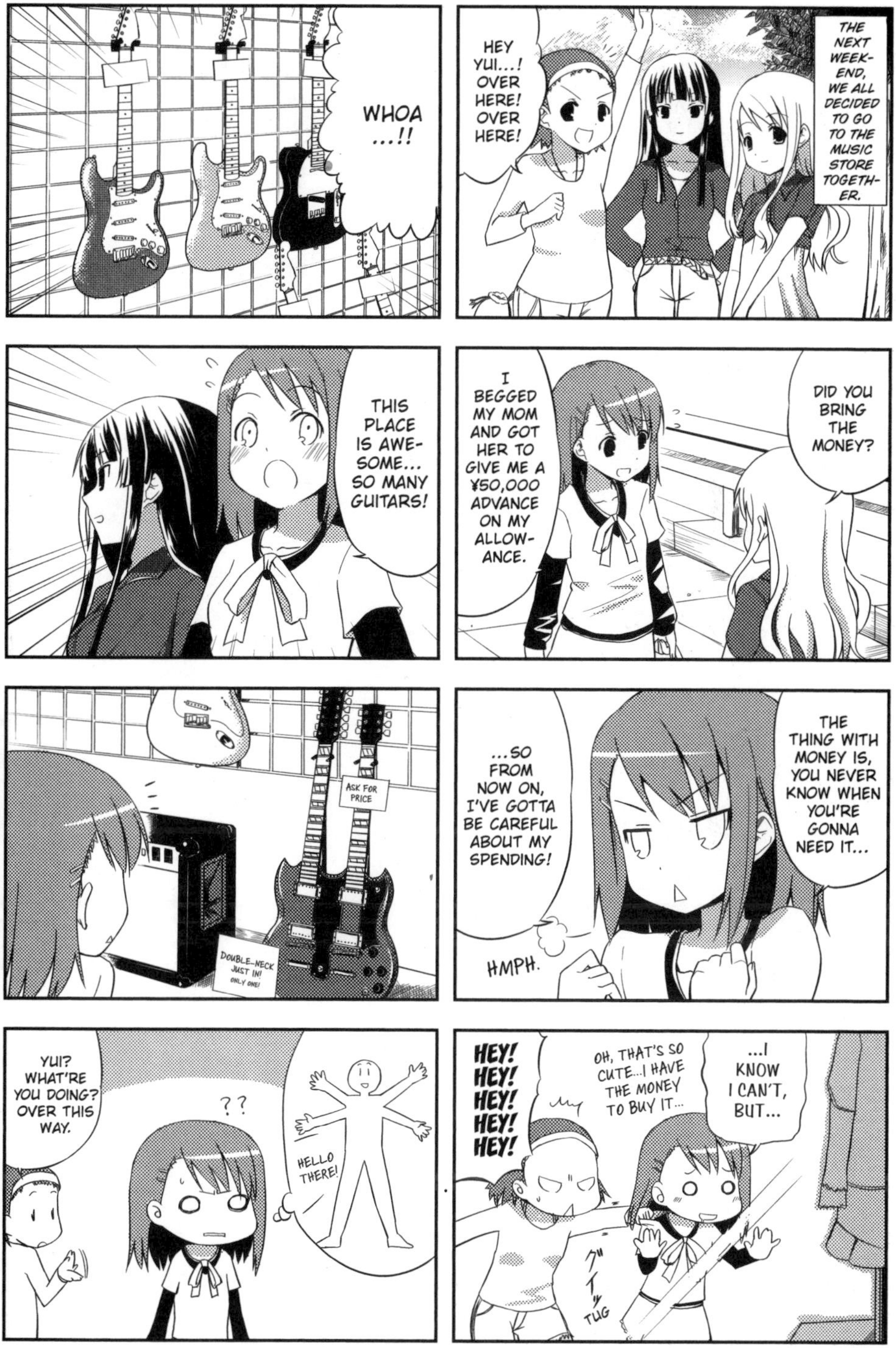
THE NEXT WEEKEND, WE ALL DECIDED TO GO TO THE MUSIC STORE TOGETHER.
HEY YUI...! OVER HERE! OVER HERE!
WHOA ...!!
DID YOU BRING THE MONEY?
I BEGGED MY MOM AND GOT HER TO GIVE ME A ¥50,000 ADVANCE ON MY ALLOWANCE.
THIS PLACE IS AWESOME... SO MANY GUITARS!
THE THING WITH MONEY IS, YOU NEVER KNOW WHEN YOU'RE GONNA NEED IT...
...SO FROM NOW ON, I'VE GOTTA BE CAREFUL ABOUT MY SPENDING!
HMPH.
ASK FOR PRICE
DOUBLE-NECK JUST IN! ONLY ONE!
...I KNOW I CAN'T, BUT...
OH, THAT'S SO CUTE...I HAVE THE MONEY TO BUY IT...
HEY! HEY! HEY! HEY! HEY!
TUG
HELLO THERE!
??
YUI? WHAT'RE YOU DOING? OVER THIS WAY.

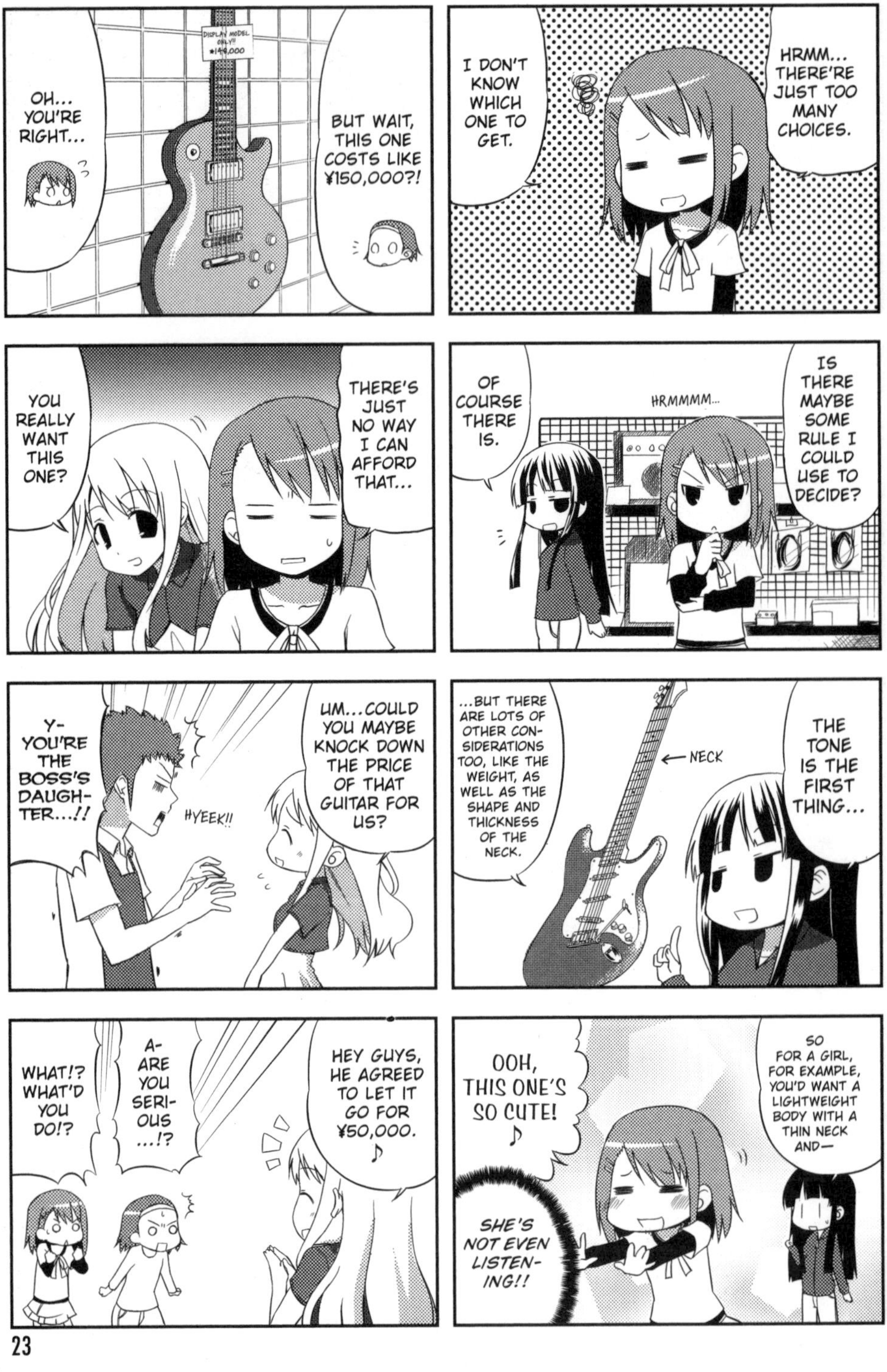
HRMM... THERE'RE JUST TOO MANY CHOICES.
I DON'T KNOW WHICH ONE TO GET.
IS THERE MAYBE SOME RULE I COULD USE TO DECIDE?
HRMMMM...
OF COURSE THERE IS.
THE TONE IS THE FIRST THING...
...BUT THERE ARE LOTS OF OTHER CON-SIDERATIONS TOO, LIKE THE WEIGHT, AS WELL AS THE SHAPE AND THICKNESS OF THE NECK.
NECK
SO FOR A GIRL, FOR EXAMPLE, YOU'D WANT A LIGHTWEIGHT BODY WITH A THIN NECK AND—
OOH, THIS ONE'S SO CUTE! ♪
SHE'S NOT EVEN LISTEN-ING!!
BUT WAIT, THIS ONE COSTS LIKE ¥150,000?!
OH... YOU'RE RIGHT...
THERE'S JUST NO WAY I CAN AFFORD THAT...
YOU REALLY WANT THIS ONE?
UM...COULD YOU MAYBE KNOCK DOWN THE PRICE OF THAT GUITAR FOR US?
HYEEK!!
Y-YOU'RE THE BOSS'S DAUGHTER...!!
HEY GUYS, HE AGREED TO LET IT GO FOR ¥50,000. ♪
A-ARE YOU SERI-OUS...!?
WHAT!? WHAT'D YOU DO!?

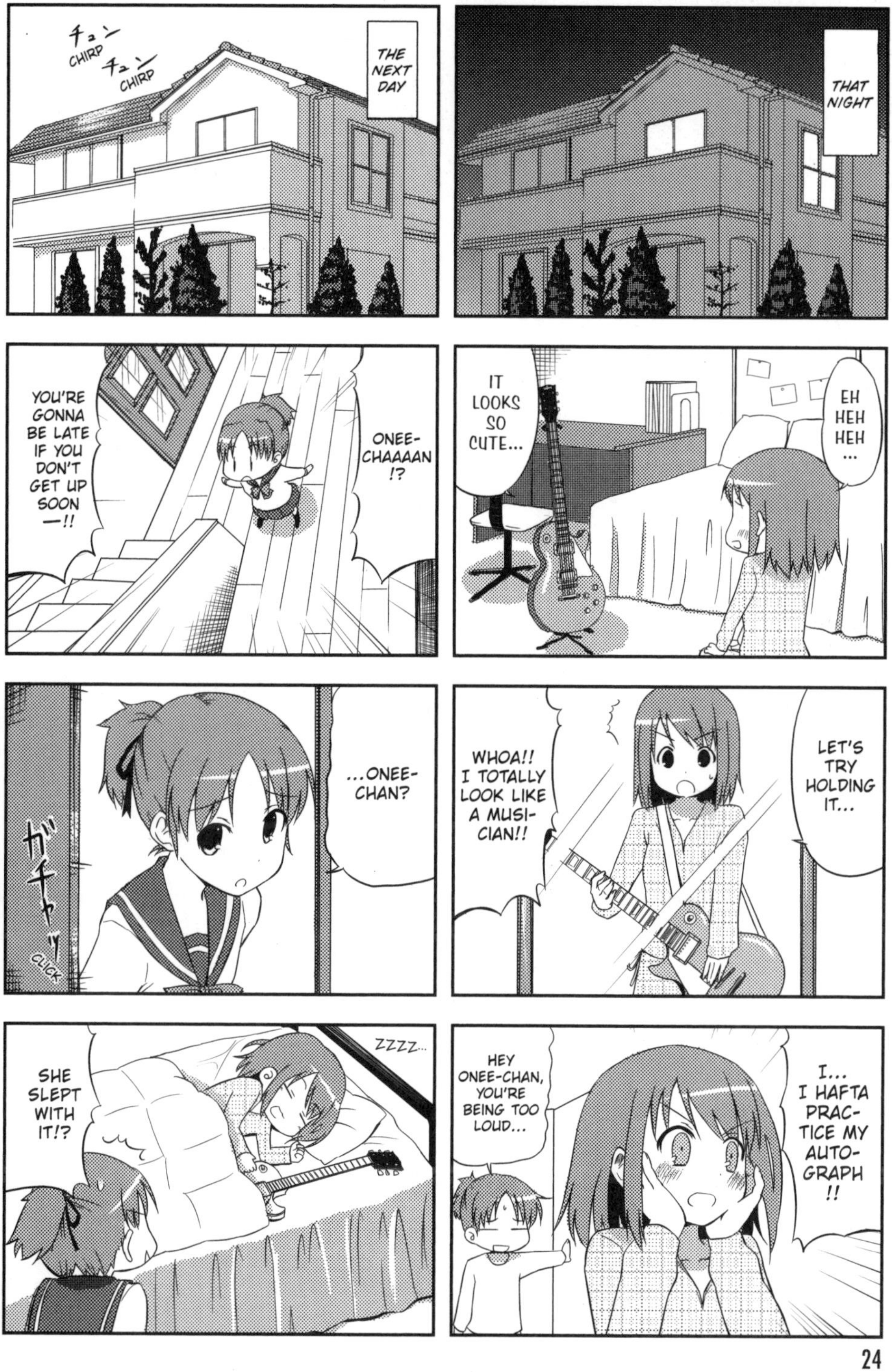
THAT NIGHT
EH HEH HEH...
IT LOOKS SO CUTE...
LET'S TRY HOLDING IT...
WHOA!! I TOTALLY LOOK LIKE A MUSICIAN!!
I... I HAFTA PRACTICE MY AUTOGRAPH!!
HEY ONEE-CHAN, YOU'RE BEING TOO LOUD...
THE NEXT DAY
チュン CHIRP チュン CHIRP
ONEE-CHAAAAN!?
YOU'RE GONNA BE LATE IF YOU DON'T GET UP SOON—!!
...ONEE-CHAN?
ガチャ CLICK
ZZZZ...
SHE SLEPT WITH IT!?

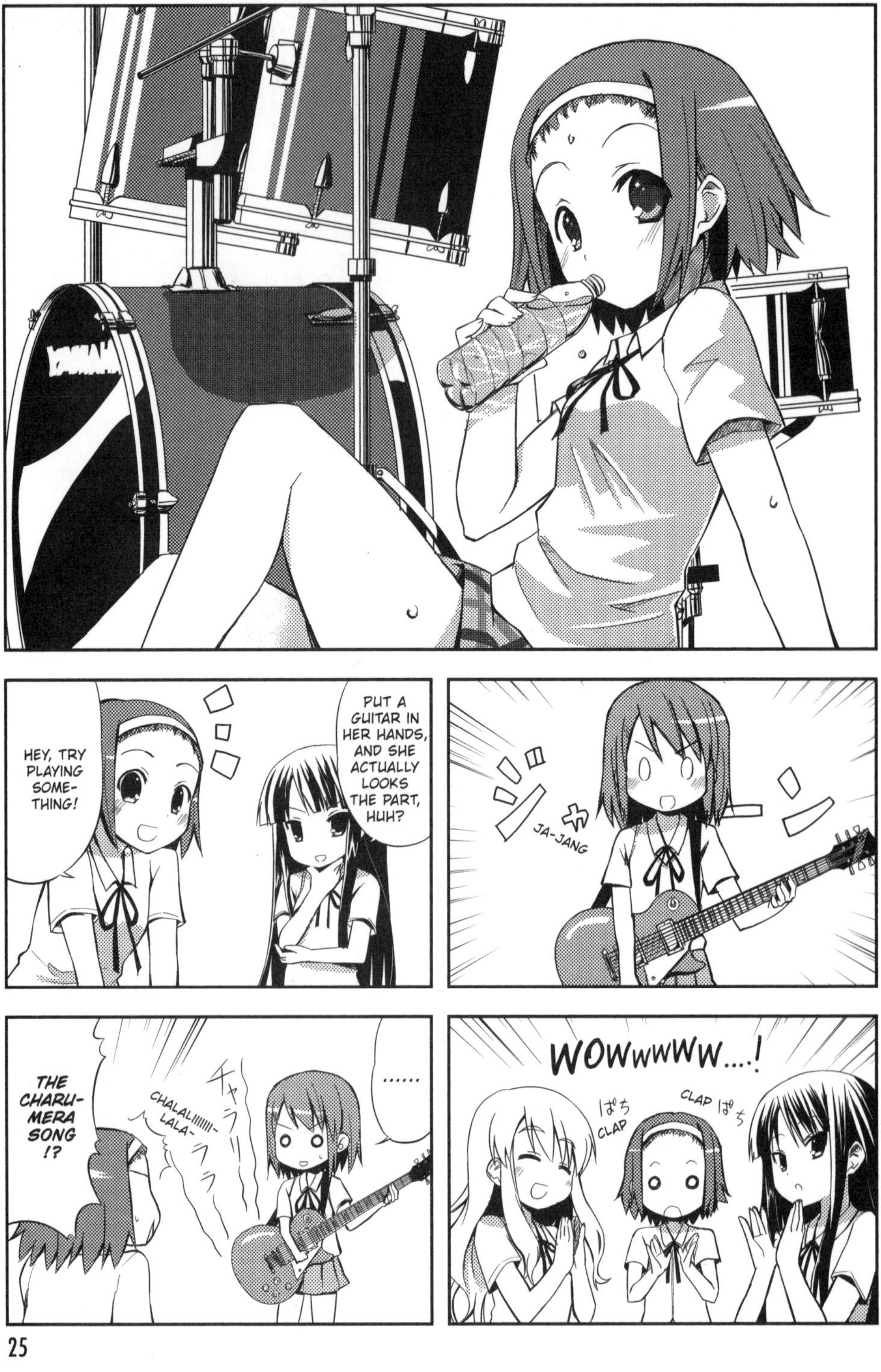
HEY, TRY PLAYING SOME-THING!
PUT A GUITAR IN HER HANDS, AND SHE ACTUALLY LOOKS THE PART, HUH?
ジャーン
JA-JANG
チャラーララ
CHALALIIIIII-LALA-
......
THE CHARUMERA SONG !?
WOWwwWW....!
ぱち CLAP
CLAP ぱち

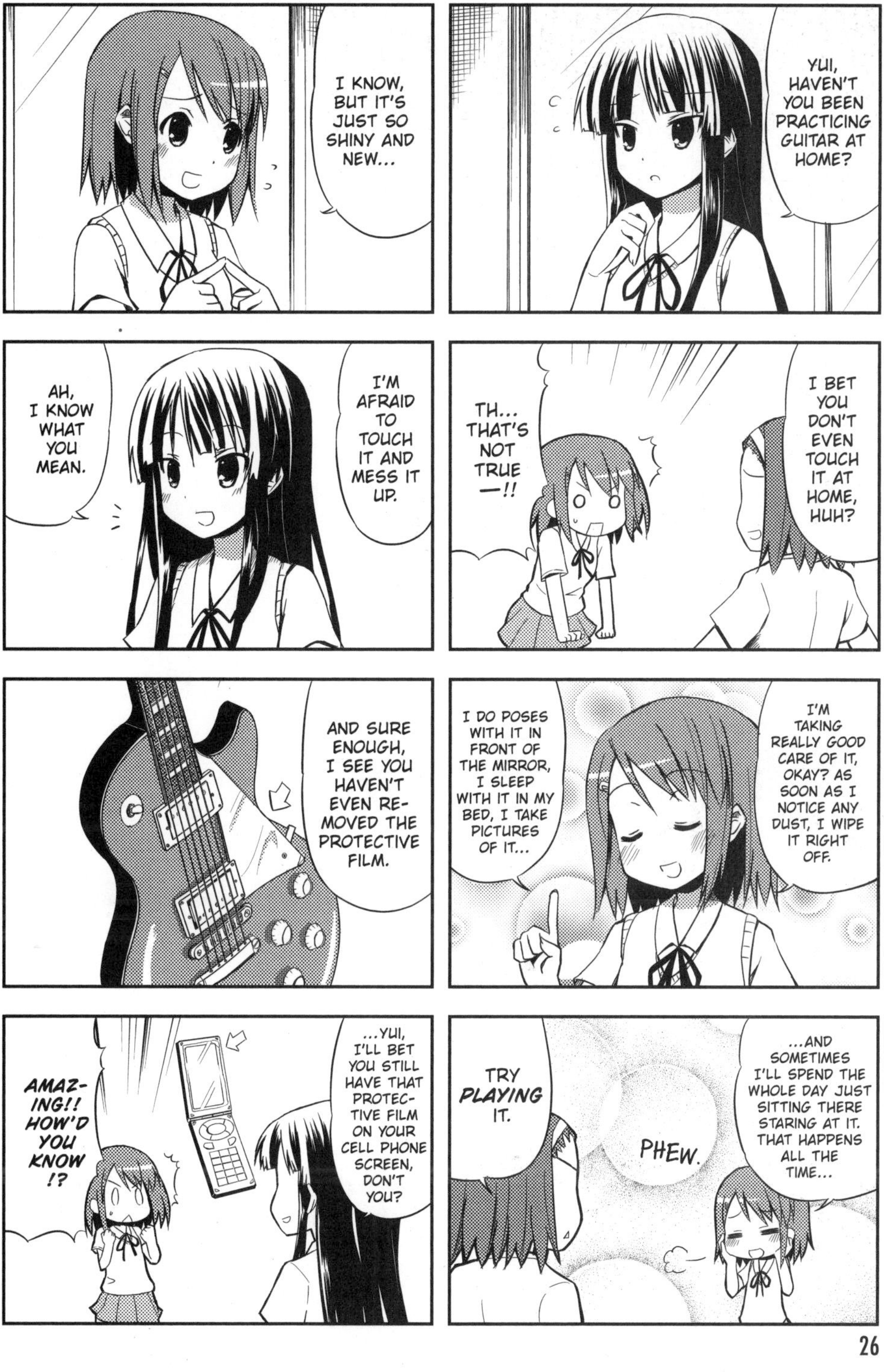
YUI, HAVEN'T YOU BEEN PRACTICING GUITAR AT HOME?
I BET YOU DON'T EVEN TOUCH IT AT HOME, HUH?
TH... THAT'S NOT TRUE—!!
I'M TAKING REALLY GOOD CARE OF IT, OKAY? AS SOON AS I NOTICE ANY DUST, I WIPE IT RIGHT OFF.
I DO POSES WITH IT IN FRONT OF THE MIRROR, I SLEEP WITH IT IN MY BED, I TAKE PICTURES OF IT...
...AND SOMETIMES I'LL SPEND THE WHOLE DAY JUST SITTING THERE STARING AT IT. THAT HAPPENS ALL THE TIME...
PHEW.
TRY *PLAYING* IT.
I KNOW, BUT IT'S JUST SO SHINY AND NEW...
I'M AFRAID TO TOUCH IT AND MESS IT UP.
AH, I KNOW WHAT YOU MEAN.
AND SURE ENOUGH, I SEE YOU HAVEN'T EVEN RE-MOVED THE PROTECTIVE FILM.
...YUI, I'LL BET YOU STILL HAVE THAT PROTEC-TIVE FILM ON YOUR CELL PHONE SCREEN, DON'T YOU?
AMAZ-ING!! HOW'D YOU KNOW!?

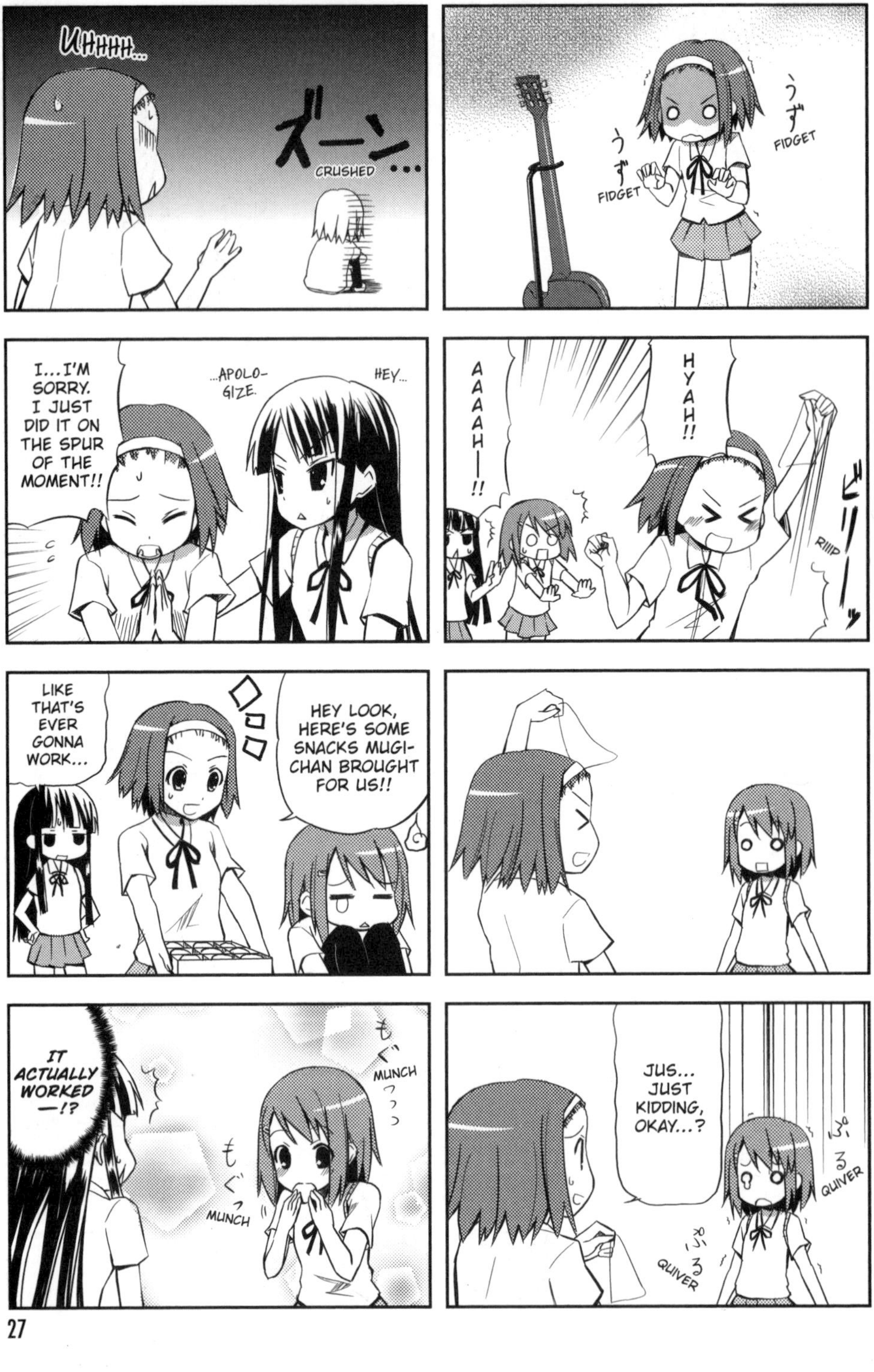

うず
FIDGET
うず
FIDGET
UHHHH...
ズーン
CRUSHED...
HYAH!!
ビリーーッ
RIIIP
AAAAH—!!
HEY...
...APOLOGIZE.
I...I'M SORRY. I JUST DID IT ON THE SPUR OF THE MOMENT!!
HEY LOOK, HERE'S SOME SNACKS MUGI-CHAN BROUGHT FOR US!!
LIKE THAT'S EVER GONNA WORK...
ぷる
QUIVER
JUS... JUST KIDDING, OKAY...?
ぷる
QUIVER
もぐっっっ
MUNCH
もぐっ
MUNCH
IT ACTUALLY WORKED—!?

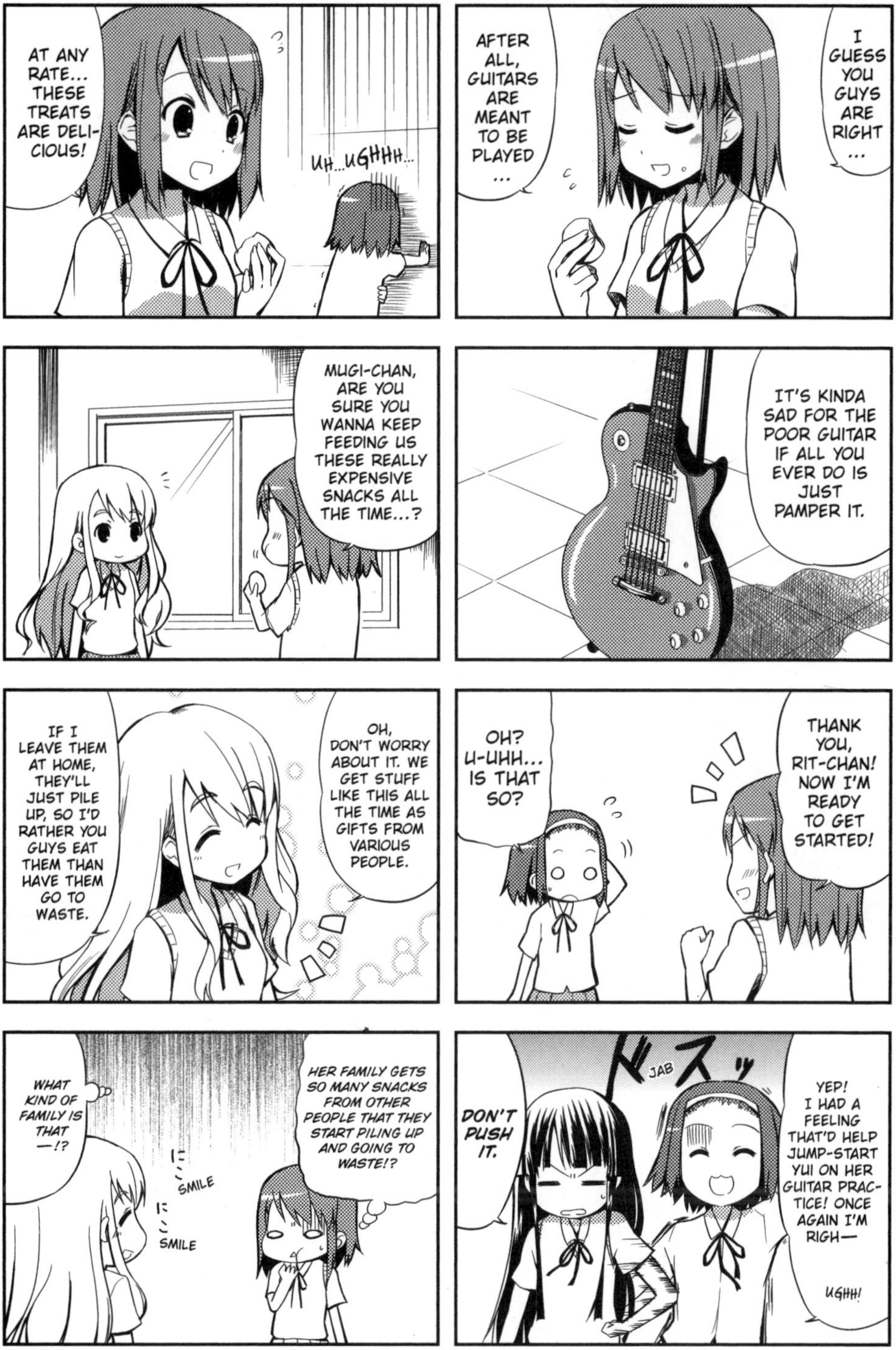
I GUESS YOU GUYS ARE RIGHT...
AFTER ALL, GUITARS ARE MEANT TO BE PLAYED...
AT ANY RATE... THESE TREATS ARE DELI-CIOUS!
UH...UGHHH...
IT'S KINDA SAD FOR THE POOR GUITAR IF ALL YOU EVER DO IS JUST PAMPER IT.
MUGI-CHAN, ARE YOU SURE YOU WANNA KEEP FEEDING US THESE REALLY EXPENSIVE SNACKS ALL THE TIME...?
THANK YOU, RIT-CHAN! NOW I'M READY TO GET STARTED!
OH? U-UHH... IS THAT SO?
OH, DON'T WORRY ABOUT IT. WE GET STUFF LIKE THIS ALL THE TIME AS GIFTS FROM VARIOUS PEOPLE.
IF I LEAVE THEM AT HOME, THEY'LL JUST PILE UP, SO I'D RATHER YOU GUYS EAT THEM THAN HAVE THEM GO TO WASTE.
YEP! I HAD A FEELING THAT'D HELP JUMP-START YUI ON HER GUITAR PRAC-TICE! ONCE AGAIN I'M RIGH—
ドスッ
JAB
DON'T PUSH IT.
UGHH!
HER FAMILY GETS SO MANY SNACKS FROM OTHER PEOPLE THAT THEY START PILING UP AND GOING TO WASTE!?
WHAT KIND OF FAMILY IS THAT—!?
SMILE
SMILE

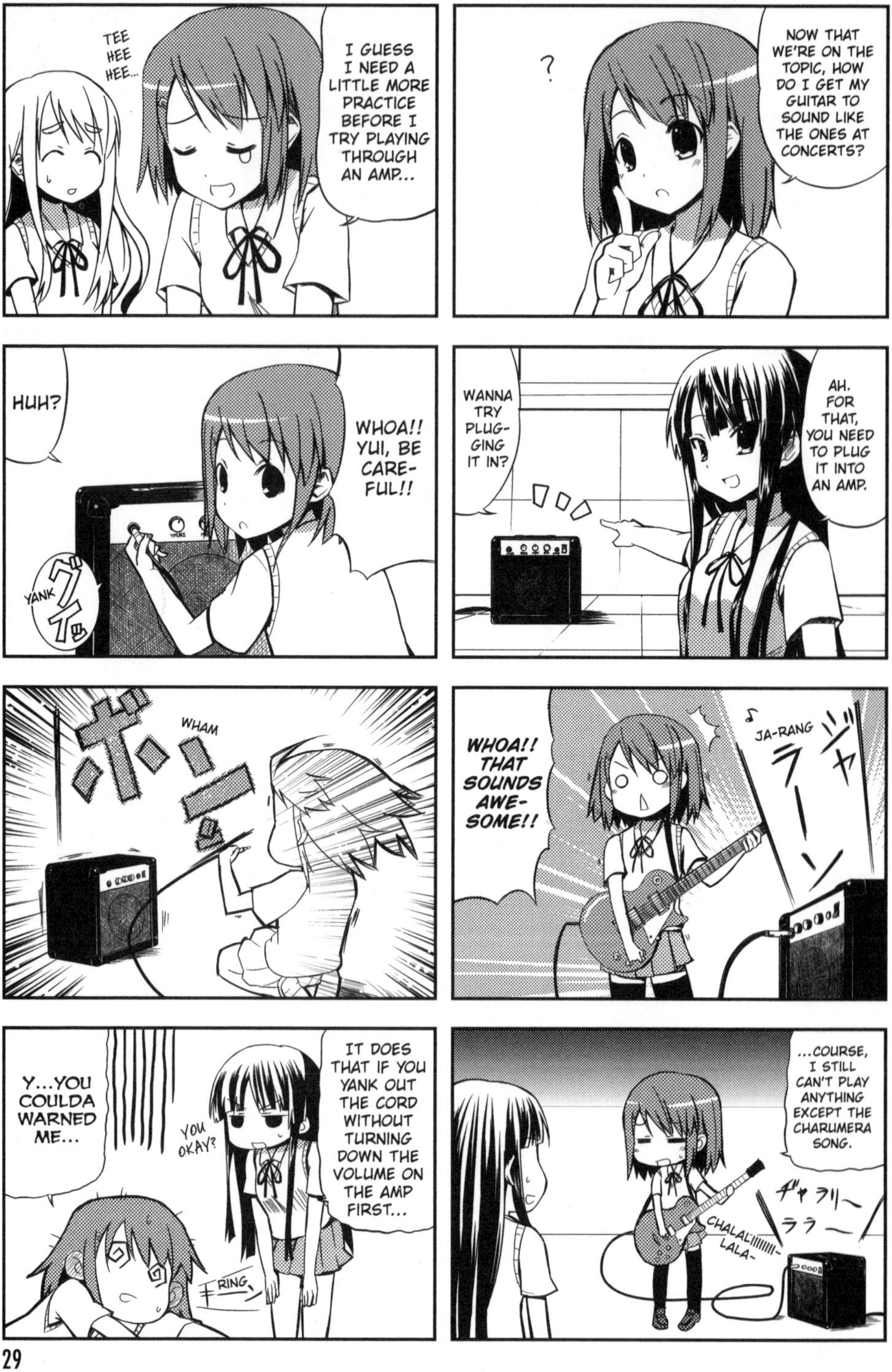
NOW THAT WE'RE ON THE TOPIC, HOW DO I GET MY GUITAR TO SOUND LIKE THE ONES AT CONCERTS?
?
AH. FOR THAT, YOU NEED TO PLUG IT INTO AN AMP.
WANNA TRY PLUG-GING IT IN?
JA-RANG
WHOA!! THAT SOUNDS AWE-SOME!!
...COURSE, I STILL CAN'T PLAY ANYTHING EXCEPT THE CHARUMERA SONG.
CHALAL'IIIIIII~ LALA~
I GUESS I NEED A LITTLE MORE PRACTICE BEFORE I TRY PLAYING THROUGH AN AMP...
TEE HEE HEE...
WHOA!! YUI, BE CARE-FUL!!
HUH?
YANK
WHAM
IT DOES THAT IF YOU YANK OUT THE CORD WITHOUT TURNING DOWN THE VOLUME ON THE AMP FIRST...
YOU OKAY?
Y...YOU COULDA WARNED ME...
RING

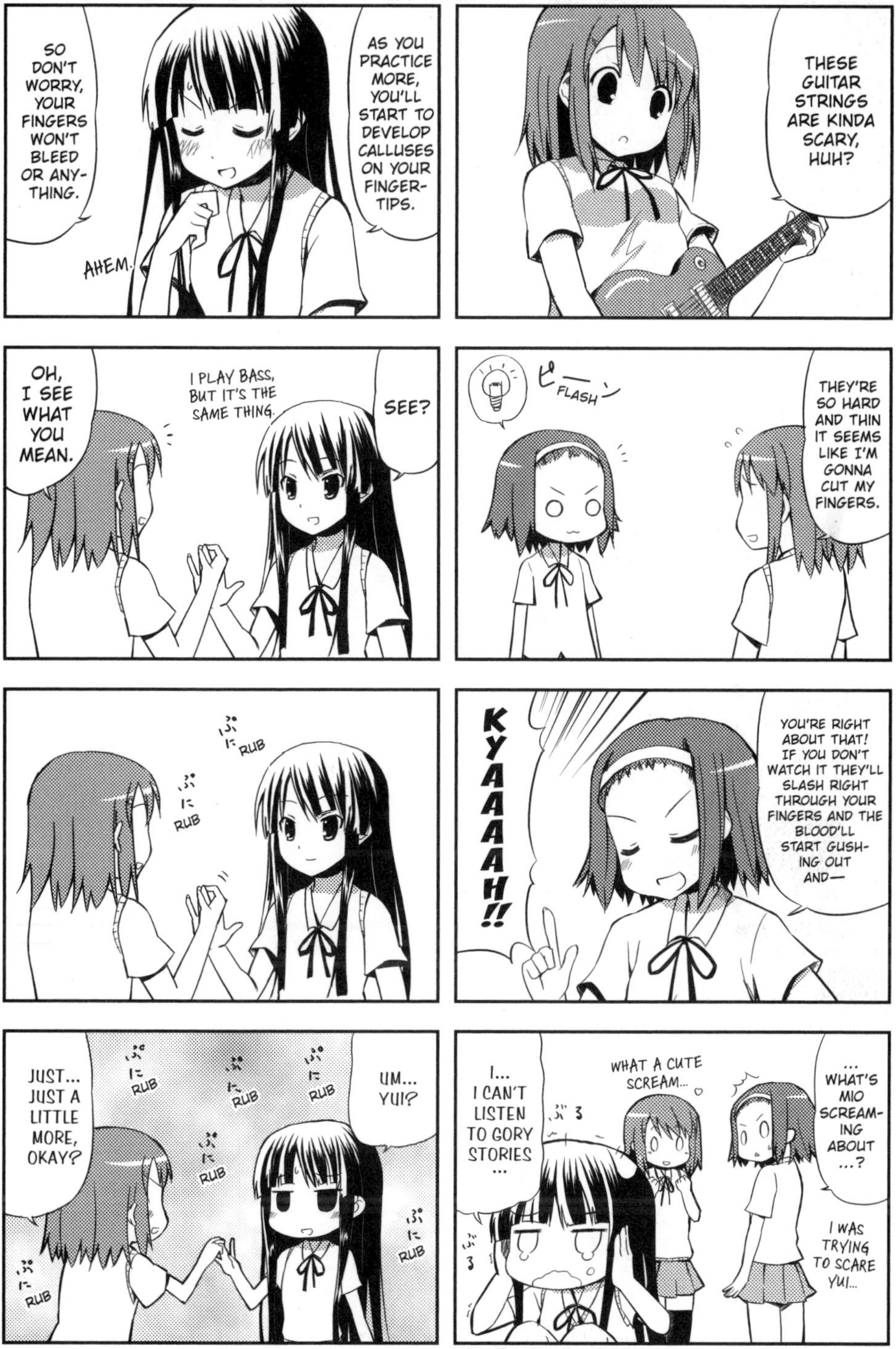
THESE GUITAR STRINGS ARE KINDA SCARY, HUH?
THEY'RE SO HARD AND THIN IT SEEMS LIKE I'M GONNA CUT MY FINGERS.
ピーン FLASH
YOU'RE RIGHT ABOUT THAT! IF YOU DON'T WATCH IT THEY'LL SLASH RIGHT THROUGH YOUR FINGERS AND THE BLOOD'LL START GUSHING OUT AND—
KYAAAAAH!!
...WHAT'S MIO SCREAMING ABOUT...?
I WAS TRYING TO SCARE YUI...
WHAT A CUTE SCREAM...
I... I CAN'T LISTEN TO GORY STORIES...
ぷる ぷる
AS YOU PRACTICE MORE, YOU'LL START TO DEVELOP CALLUSES ON YOUR FINGERTIPS.
SO DON'T WORRY, YOUR FINGERS WON'T BLEED OR ANYTHING.
AHEM.
SEE?
I PLAY BASS, BUT IT'S THE SAME THING.
OH, I SEE WHAT YOU MEAN.
ぷに RUB
ぷに RUB
UM... YUI?
JUST... JUST A LITTLE MORE, OKAY?
ぷに RUB
ぷに RUB
ぷに RUB
ぷに RUB
ぷに RUB
ぷに RUB

SFX: TREMBLE TREMBLE

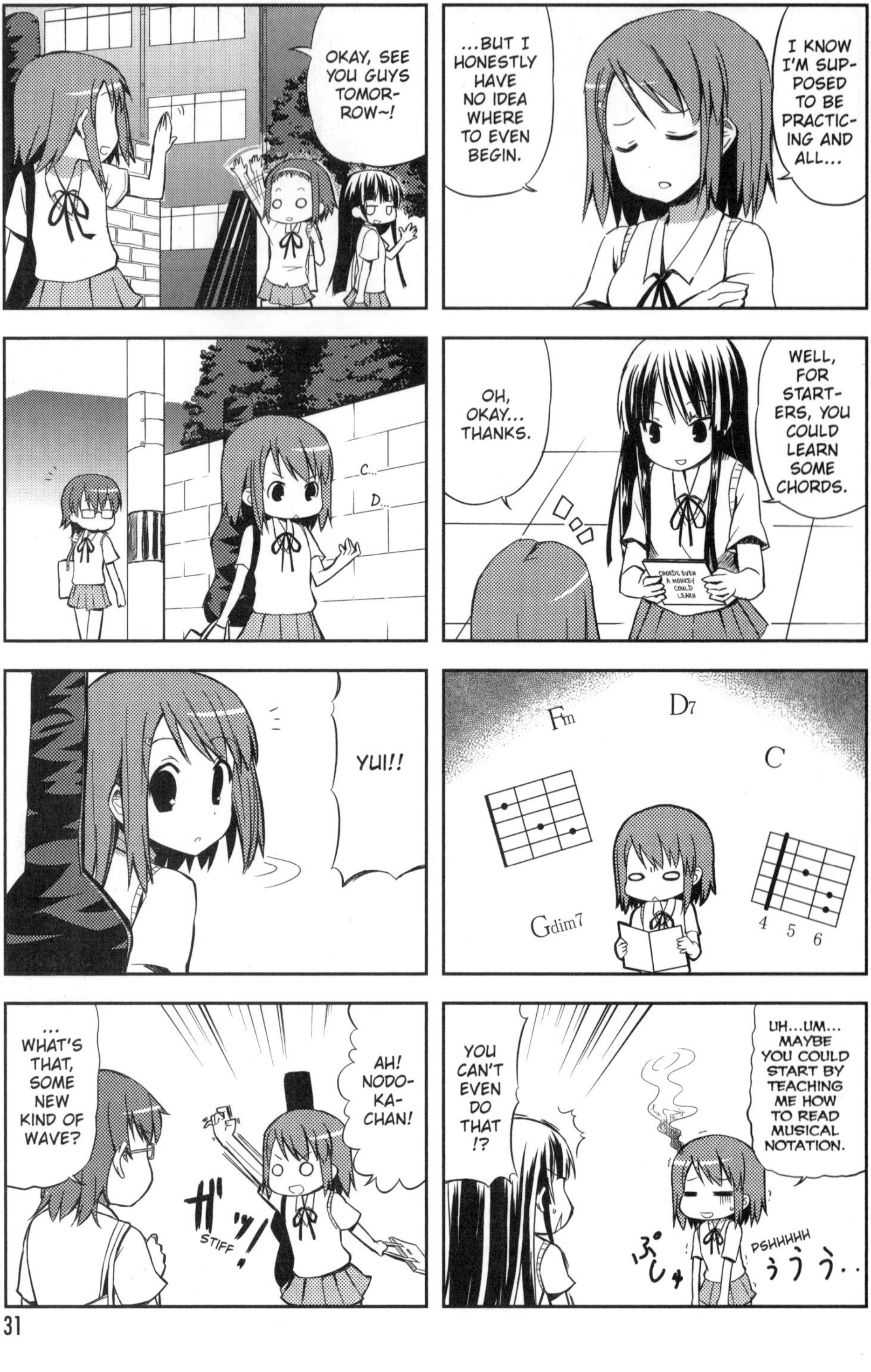
I KNOW I'M SUP-POSED TO BE PRACTIC-ING AND ALL...
...BUT I HONESTLY HAVE NO IDEA WHERE TO EVEN BEGIN.
WELL, FOR START-ERS, YOU COULD LEARN SOME CHORDS.
CHORDS EVEN A MONKEY COULD LEARN
OH, OKAY... THANKS.
D7
Fm
C
Gdim7
4 5 6
UH...UM... MAYBE YOU COULD START BY TEACHING ME HOW TO READ MUSICAL NOTATION.
PSHHHHH
YOU CAN'T EVEN DO THAT!?
OKAY, SEE YOU GUYS TOMOR-ROW~!
C...
D...
YUI!!
AH! NODO-KA-CHAN!
STIFF
...WHAT'S THAT, SOME NEW KIND OF WAVE?

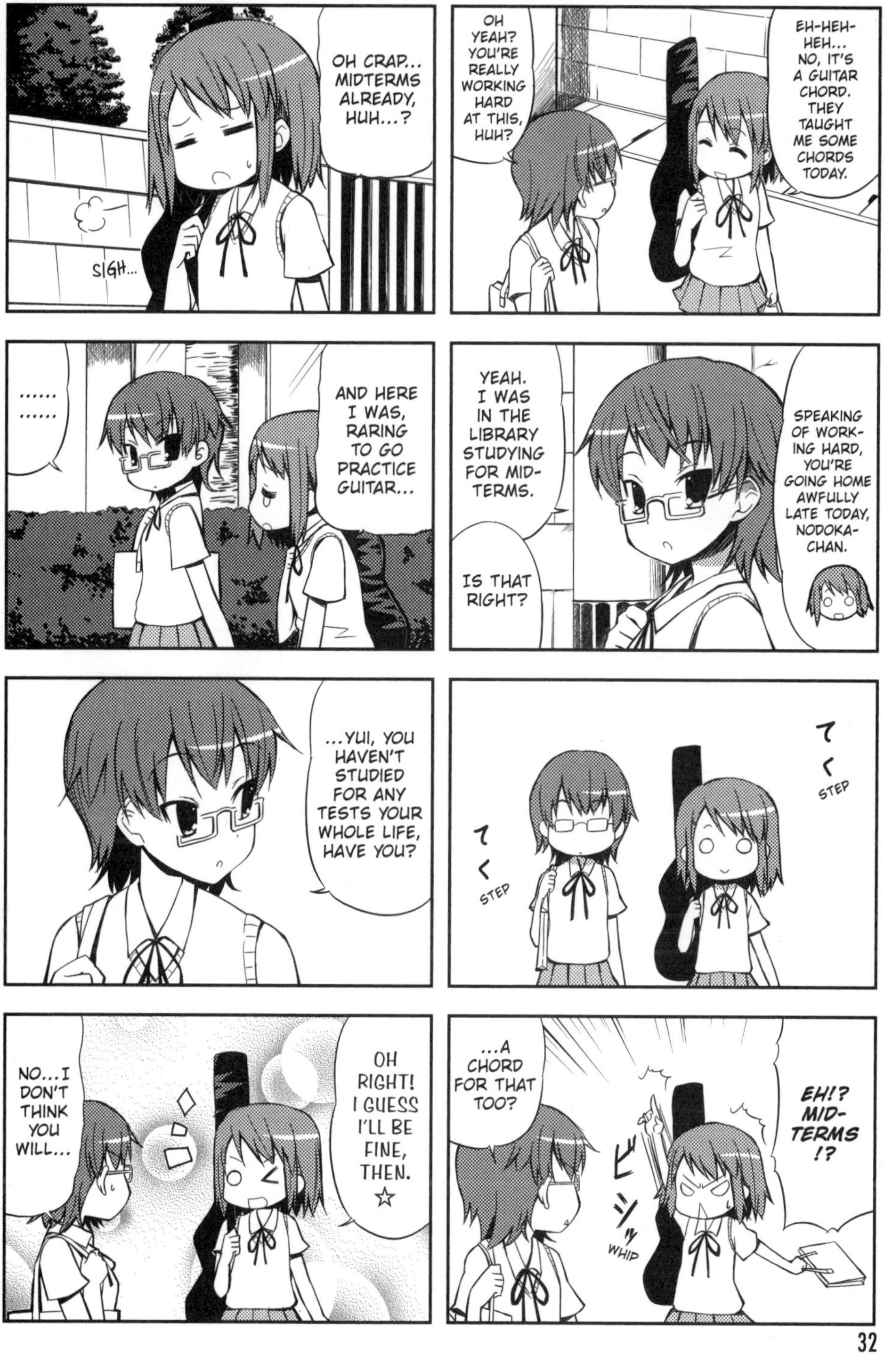
OH YEAH? YOU'RE REALLY WORKING HARD AT THIS, HUH?
EH-HEH-HEH... NO, IT'S A GUITAR CHORD. THEY TAUGHT ME SOME CHORDS TODAY.
SPEAKING OF WORKING HARD, YOU'RE GOING HOME AWFULLY LATE TODAY, NODOKA-CHAN.
YEAH. I WAS IN THE LIBRARY STUDYING FOR MID-TERMS.
IS THAT RIGHT?
てく
STEP
てく
STEP
EH!? MID-TERMS!?
...A CHORD FOR THAT TOO?
WHIP
OH CRAP... MIDTERMS ALREADY, HUH...?
SIGH...
AND HERE I WAS, RARING TO GO PRACTICE GUITAR...
......
......
...YUI, YOU HAVEN'T STUDIED FOR ANY TESTS YOUR WHOLE LIFE, HAVE YOU?
OH RIGHT! I GUESS I'LL BE FINE, THEN. ☆
NO...I DON'T THINK YOU WILL...

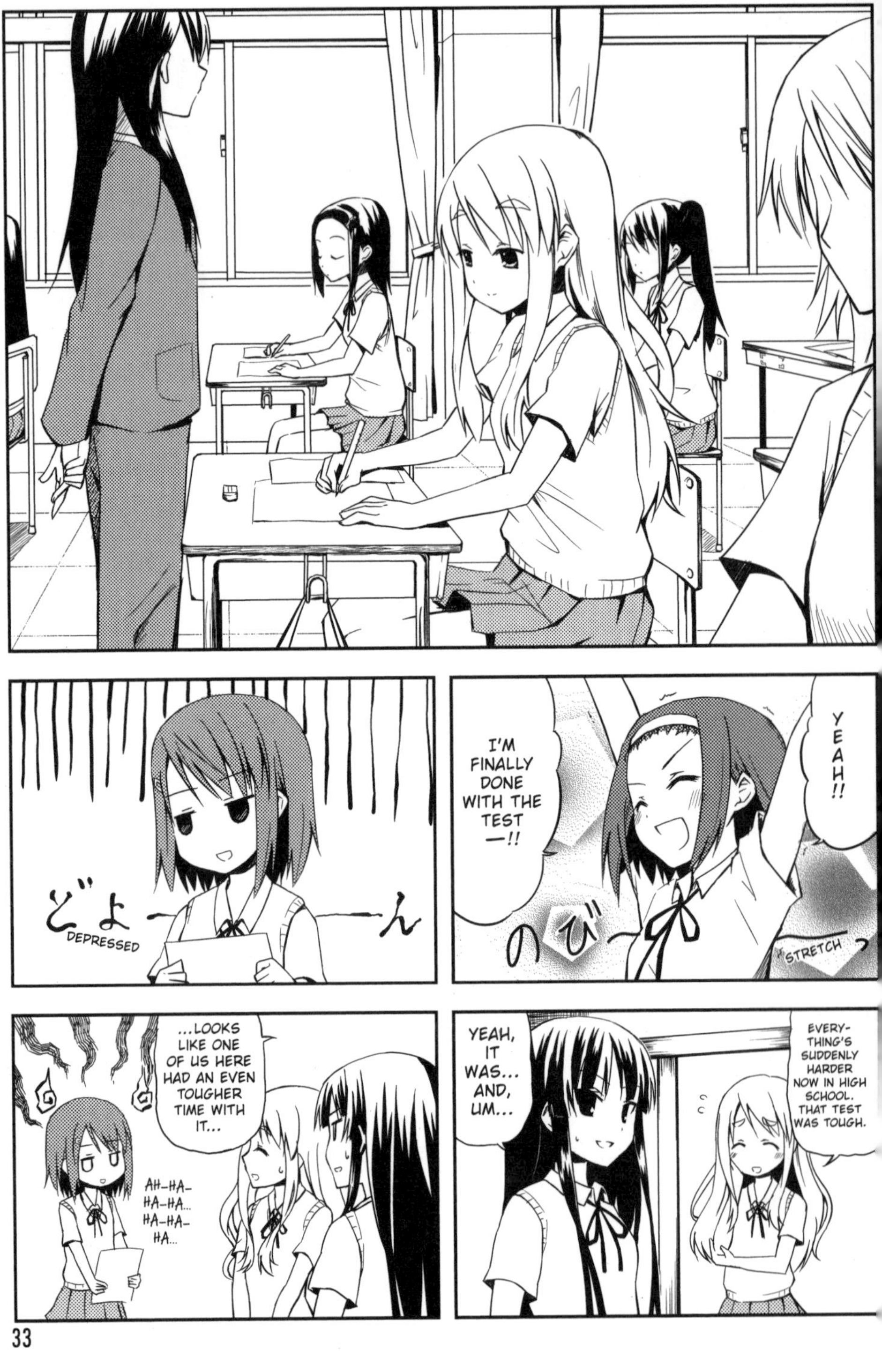
I'M FINALLY DONE WITH THE TEST—!!
YEAH!!
のび～
STRETCH
どよ～～ん
DEPRESSED
EVERYTHING'S SUDDENLY HARDER NOW IN HIGH SCHOOL. THAT TEST WAS TOUGH.
YEAH, IT WAS... AND, UM...
...LOOKS LIKE ONE OF US HERE HAD AN EVEN TOUGHER TIME WITH IT...
AH-HA-HA-HA... HA-HA-HA...

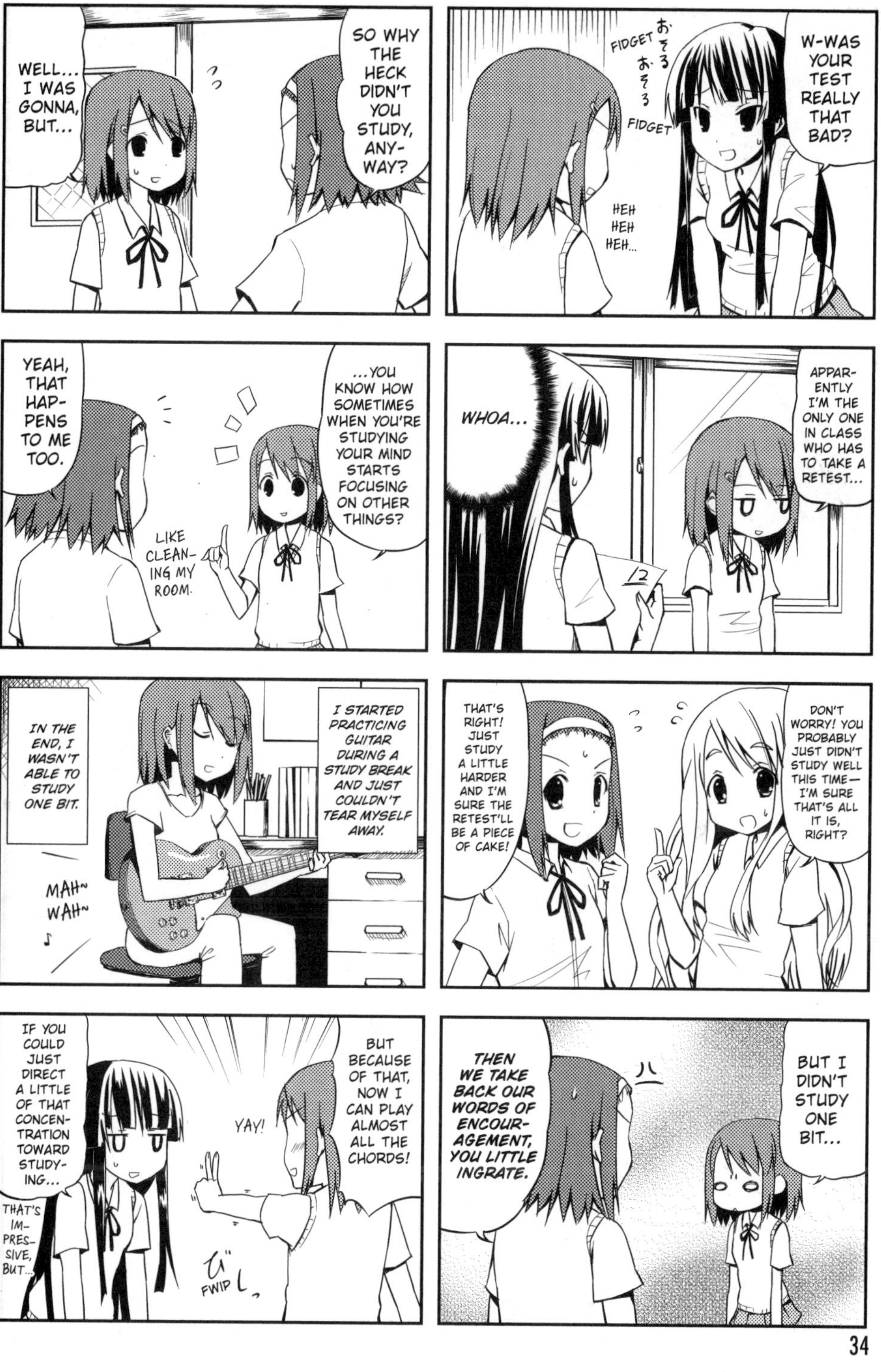
W-WAS YOUR TEST REALLY THAT BAD?
FIDGET おそる おそる FIDGET
HEH HEH HEH...
APPARENTLY I'M THE ONLY ONE IN CLASS WHO HAS TO TAKE A RETEST...
WHOA...
12
DON'T WORRY! YOU PROBABLY JUST DIDN'T STUDY WELL THIS TIME—I'M SURE THAT'S ALL IT IS, RIGHT?
THAT'S RIGHT! JUST STUDY A LITTLE HARDER AND I'M SURE THE RETEST'LL BE A PIECE OF CAKE!
BUT I DIDN'T STUDY ONE BIT...
THEN WE TAKE BACK OUR WORDS OF ENCOURAGEMENT, YOU LITTLE INGRATE.
SO WHY THE HECK DIDN'T YOU STUDY, ANYWAY?
WELL... I WAS GONNA, BUT...
...YOU KNOW HOW SOMETIMES WHEN YOU'RE STUDYING YOUR MIND STARTS FOCUSING ON OTHER THINGS?
LIKE CLEANING MY ROOM.
YEAH, THAT HAPPENS TO ME TOO.
I STARTED PRACTICING GUITAR DURING A STUDY BREAK AND JUST COULDN'T TEAR MYSELF AWAY.
IN THE END, I WASN'T ABLE TO STUDY ONE BIT.
MAH~ WAH~ ♪
BUT BECAUSE OF THAT, NOW I CAN PLAY ALMOST ALL THE CHORDS!
YAY!
ぴしっ FWIP
IF YOU COULD JUST DIRECT A LITTLE OF THAT CONCENTRATION TOWARD STUDYING...
THAT'S IMPRESSIVE, BUT...

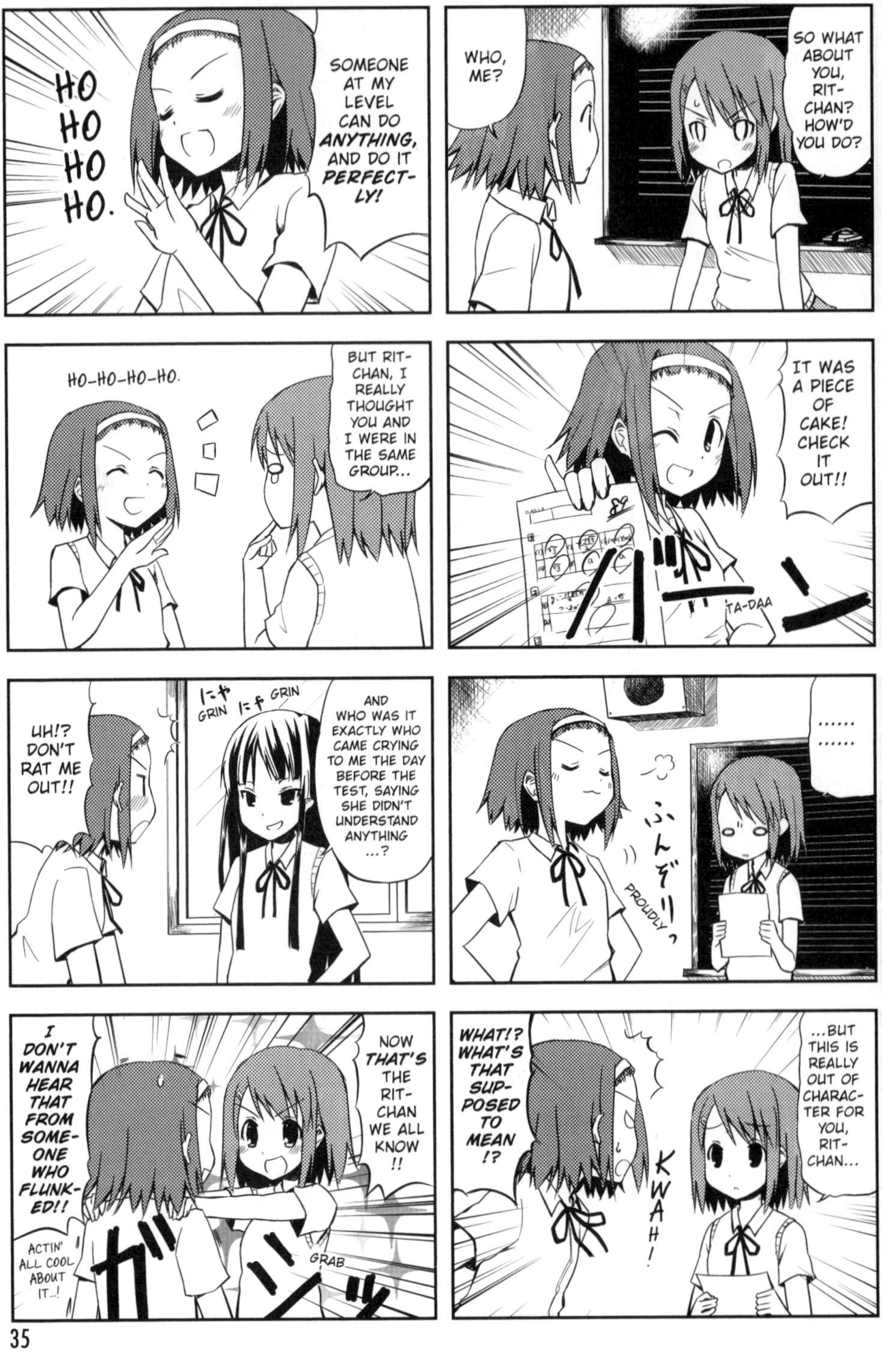
SO WHAT ABOUT YOU, RIT-CHAN? HOW'D YOU DO?
WHO, ME?
IT WAS A PIECE OF CAKE! CHECK IT OUT!!
TA-DAA
......
......
ふんぞりっ
PROUDLY
...BUT THIS IS REALLY OUT OF CHARACTER FOR YOU, RIT-CHAN...
WHAT!? WHAT'S THAT SUPPOSED TO MEAN!?
KWAH!
SOMEONE AT MY LEVEL CAN DO ANYTHING, AND DO IT PERFECTLY!
HO HO HO HO.
BUT RIT-CHAN, I REALLY THOUGHT YOU AND I WERE IN THE SAME GROUP...
HO-HO-HO-HO.
AND WHO WAS IT EXACTLY WHO CAME CRYING TO ME THE DAY BEFORE THE TEST, SAYING SHE DIDN'T UNDERSTAND ANYTHING ...?
にや GRIN にや GRIN
UH!? DON'T RAT ME OUT!!
NOW THAT'S THE RIT-CHAN WE ALL KNOW!!
GRAB
I DON'T WANNA HEAR THAT FROM SOMEONE WHO FLUNKED!!
ACTIN' ALL COOL ABOUT IT...!

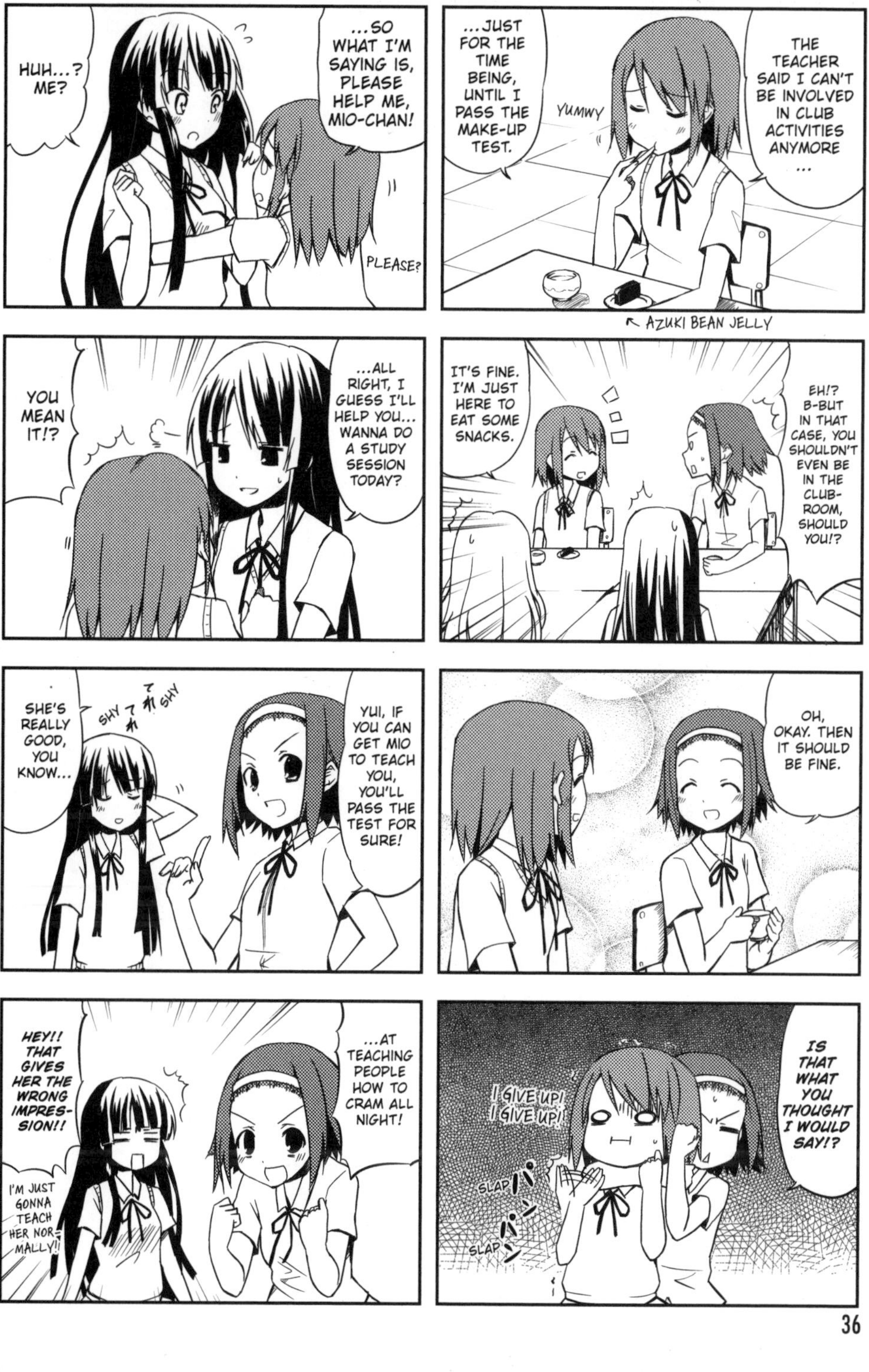
THE TEACHER SAID I CAN'T BE INVOLVED IN CLUB ACTIVITIES ANYMORE ...
YUMWY
...JUST FOR THE TIME BEING, UNTIL I PASS THE MAKE-UP TEST.
← AZUKI BEAN JELLY
EH!? B-BUT IN THAT CASE, YOU SHOULDN'T EVEN BE IN THE CLUB-ROOM, SHOULD YOU!?
IT'S FINE. I'M JUST HERE TO EAT SOME SNACKS.
OH, OKAY. THEN IT SHOULD BE FINE.
IS THAT WHAT YOU THOUGHT I WOULD SAY!?
I GIVE UP! I GIVE UP!
SLAP パン
SLAP パン
...SO WHAT I'M SAYING IS, PLEASE HELP ME, MIO-CHAN!
HUH...? ME?
PLEASE?
...ALL RIGHT, I GUESS I'LL HELP YOU... WANNA DO A STUDY SESSION TODAY?
YOU MEAN IT!?
YUI, IF YOU CAN GET MIO TO TEACH YOU, YOU'LL PASS THE TEST FOR SURE!
SHY てれ SHY
SHE'S REALLY GOOD, YOU KNOW...
...AT TEACHING PEOPLE HOW TO CRAM ALL NIGHT!
HEY!! THAT GIVES HER THE WRONG IMPRESSION!!
I'M JUST GONNA TEACH HER NOR-MALLY!!

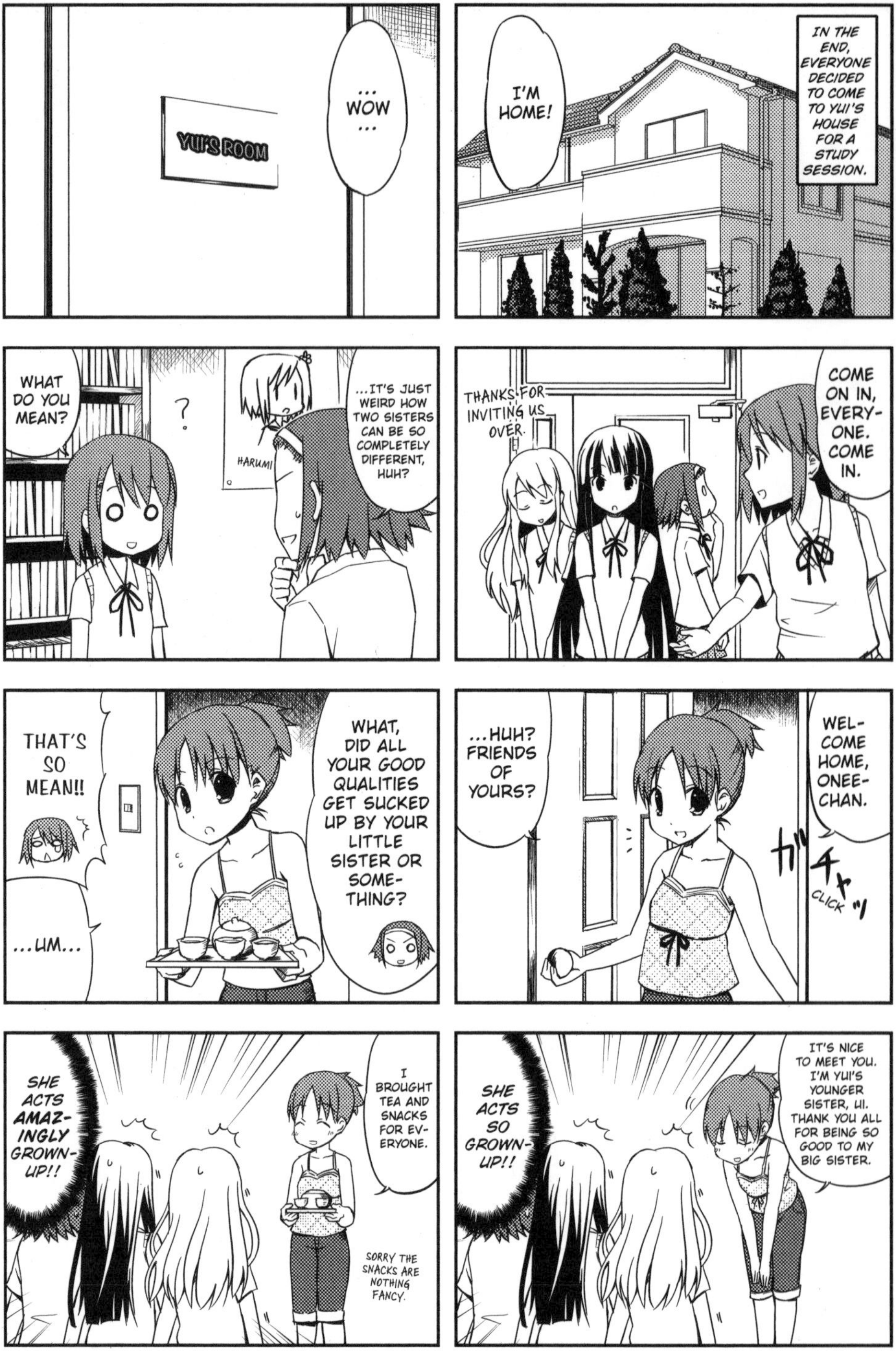
IN THE END, EVERYONE DECIDED TO COME TO YUI'S HOUSE FOR A STUDY SESSION.
I'M HOME!
COME ON IN, EVERYONE. COME IN.
THANKS FOR INVITING US OVER.
WELCOME HOME, ONEE-CHAN.
CLICK
...HUH? FRIENDS OF YOURS?
IT'S NICE TO MEET YOU. I'M YUI'S YOUNGER SISTER, UI. THANK YOU ALL FOR BEING SO GOOD TO MY BIG SISTER.
SHE ACTS SO GROWN-UP!!
...WOW...
YUI'S ROOM
...IT'S JUST WEIRD HOW TWO SISTERS CAN BE SO COMPLETELY DIFFERENT, HUH?
?
HARUMI
WHAT DO YOU MEAN?
WHAT, DID ALL YOUR GOOD QUALITIES GET SUCKED UP BY YOUR LITTLE SISTER OR SOMETHING?
THAT'S SO MEAN!!
...UM...
I BROUGHT TEA AND SNACKS FOR EVERYONE.
SORRY THE SNACKS ARE NOTHING FANCY.
SHE ACTS AMAZINGLY GROWN-UP!!

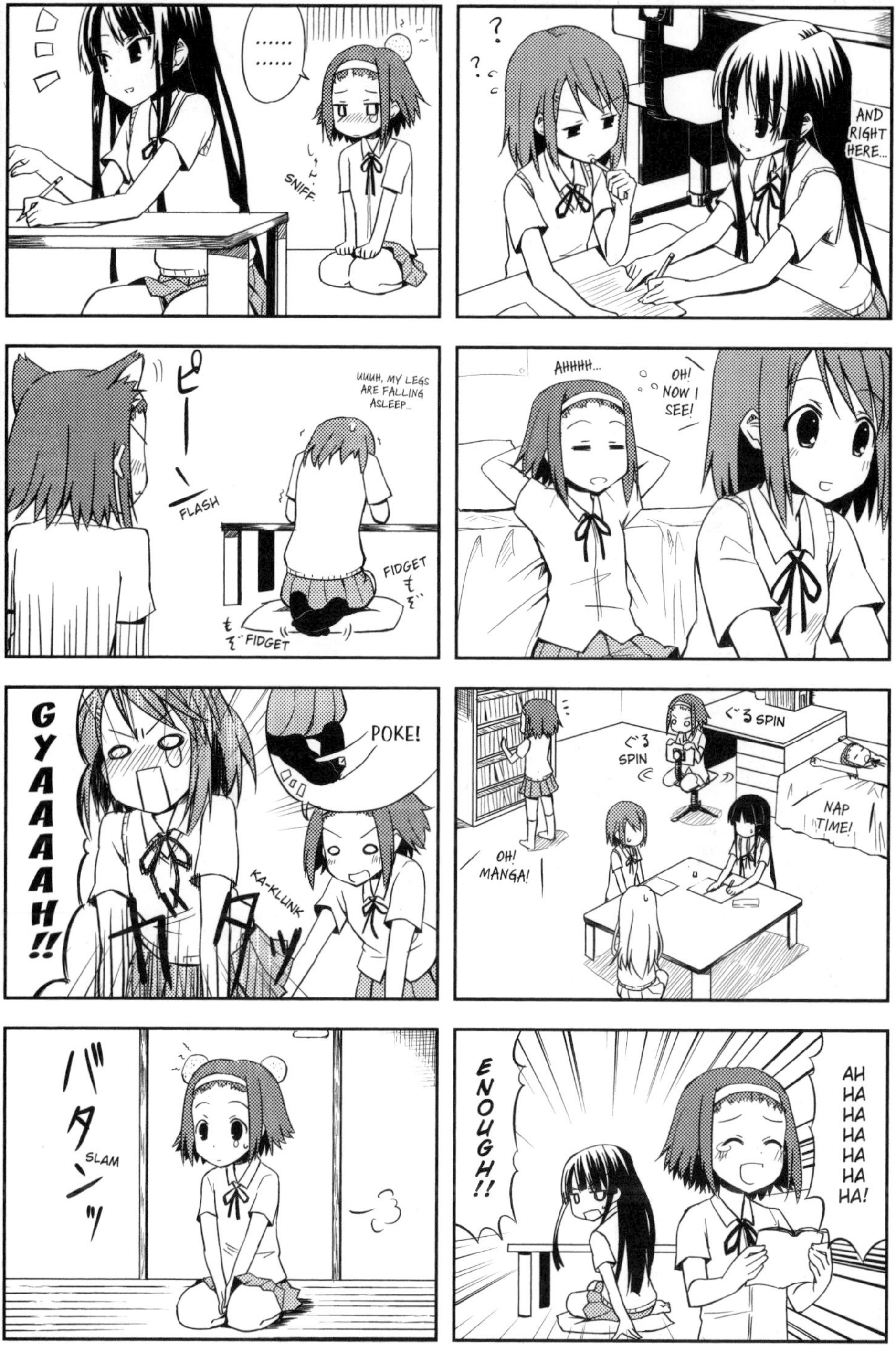
AND RIGHT HERE...
AHHHH...
OH! NOW I SEE!
ぐる SPIN
ぐる SPIN
NAP TIME!
OH! MANGA!
AH HA HA HA HA HA HA!
ENOUGH!!
......
......
SNIFF
UUUH, MY LEGS ARE FALLING ASLEEP...
ピーン
FLASH
もぞ FIDGET
もぞ FIDGET
POKE!
KA-KLUNK
GYAAAAAH!!
バタンッ
SLAM

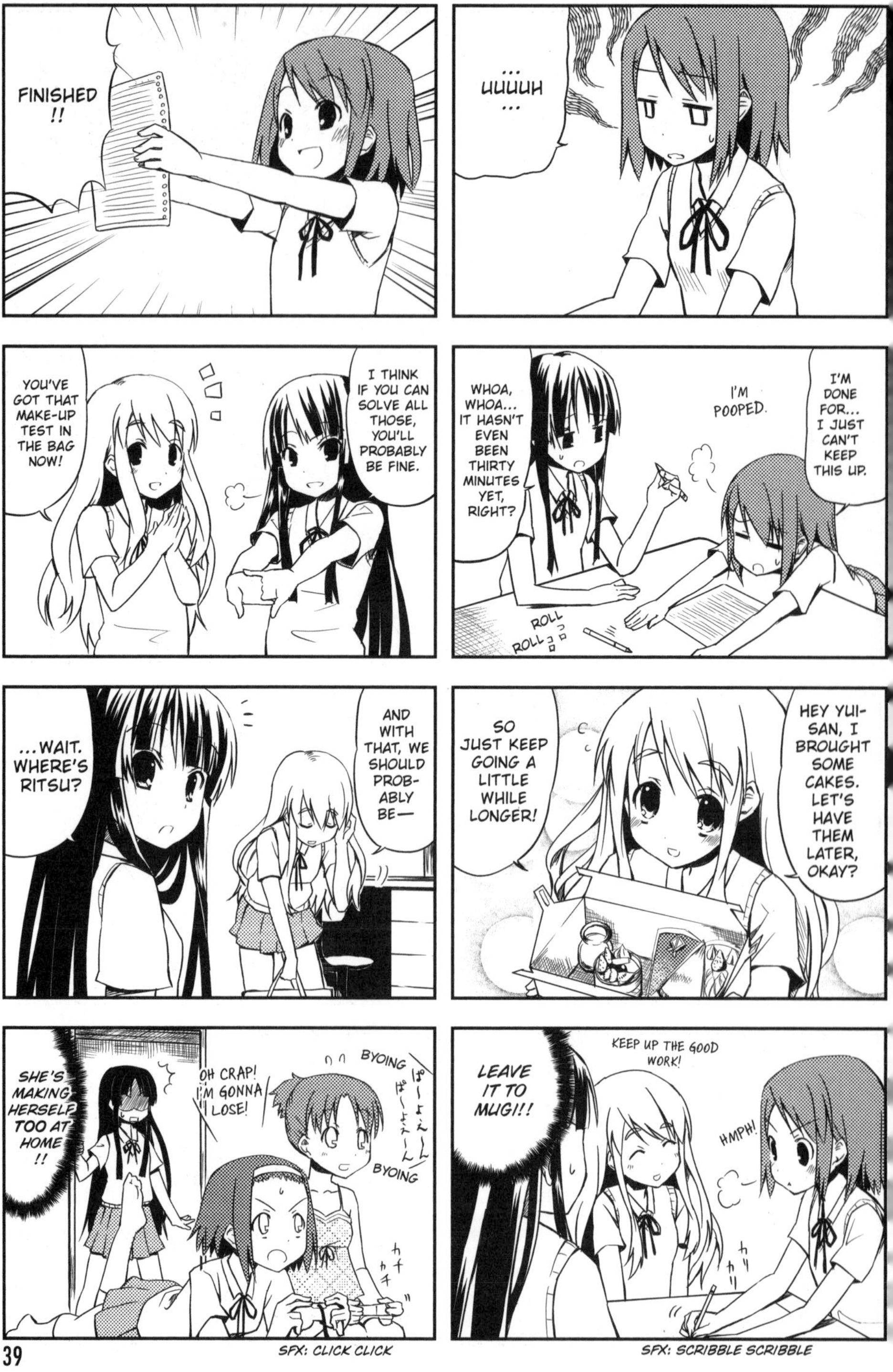
...UUUUH...
I'M DONE FOR... I JUST CAN'T KEEP THIS UP.
I'M POOPED.
WHOA, WHOA... IT HASN'T EVEN BEEN THIRTY MINUTES YET, RIGHT?
ROLL ROLL
HEY YUI-SAN, I BROUGHT SOME CAKES. LET'S HAVE THEM LATER, OKAY?
SO JUST KEEP GOING A LITTLE WHILE LONGER!
KEEP UP THE GOOD WORK!
HMPH!
カリ カリ
LEAVE IT TO MUGI!!
FINISHED!!
I THINK IF YOU CAN SOLVE ALL THOSE, YOU'LL PROBABLY BE FINE.
YOU'VE GOT THAT MAKE-UP TEST IN THE BAG NOW!
AND WITH THAT, WE SHOULD PROBABLY BE—
...WAIT. WHERE'S RITSU?
BYOING
ぱーよえーん
BYOING
OH CRAP! I'M GONNA LOSE!
カチ カチ
SHE'S MAKING HERSELF TOO AT HOME!!

SFX: SCRIBBLE SCRIBBLE

SFX: CLICK CLICK

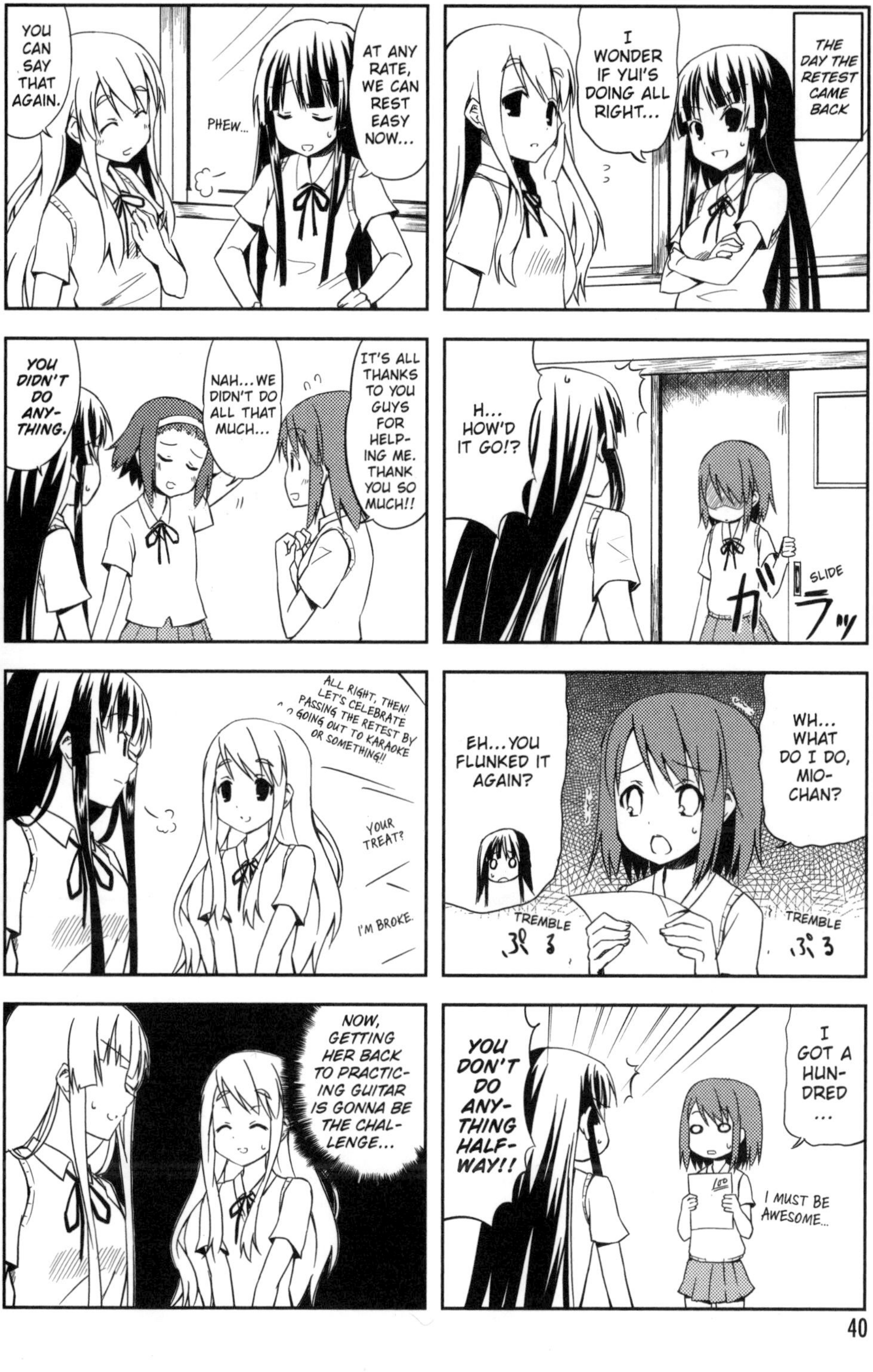
THE DAY THE RETEST CAME BACK
I WONDER IF YUI'S DOING ALL RIGHT...
H... HOW'D IT GO!?
SLIDE
ガラッ
WH... WHAT DO I DO, MIO-CHAN?
EH... YOU FLUNKED IT AGAIN?
TREMBLE
ぷる
TREMBLE
ぷる
I GOT A HUNDRED...
YOU DON'T DO ANYTHING HALFWAY!!
I MUST BE AWESOME...
AT ANY RATE, WE CAN REST EASY NOW...
PHEW...
YOU CAN SAY THAT AGAIN.
IT'S ALL THANKS TO YOU GUYS FOR HELPING ME. THANK YOU SO MUCH!!
NAH... WE DIDN'T DO ALL THAT MUCH...
YOU DIDN'T DO ANYTHING.
ALL RIGHT, THEN! LET'S CELEBRATE PASSING THE RETEST BY GOING OUT TO KARAOKE OR SOMETHING!!
YOUR TREAT?
I'M BROKE.
NOW, GETTING HER BACK TO PRACTICING GUITAR IS GONNA BE THE CHALLENGE...

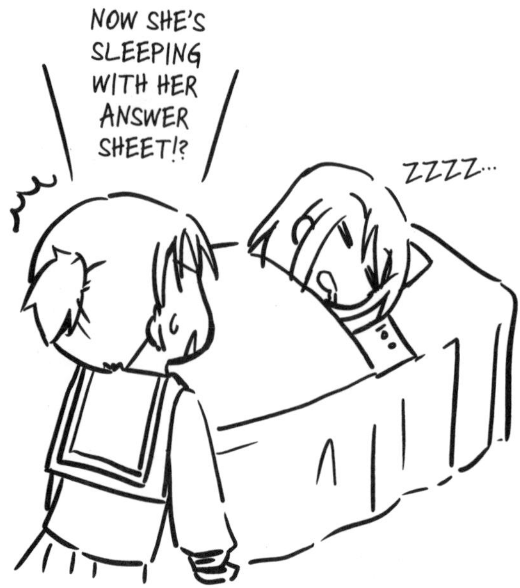
NOW SHE'S SLEEPING WITH HER ANSWER SHEET!?
ZZZZ...

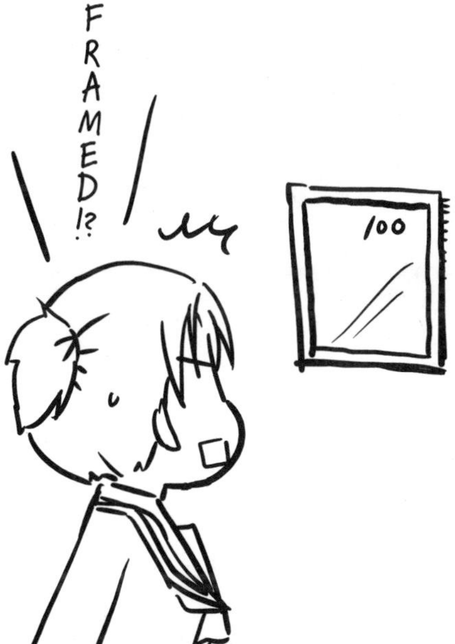
FRAMED!?
100

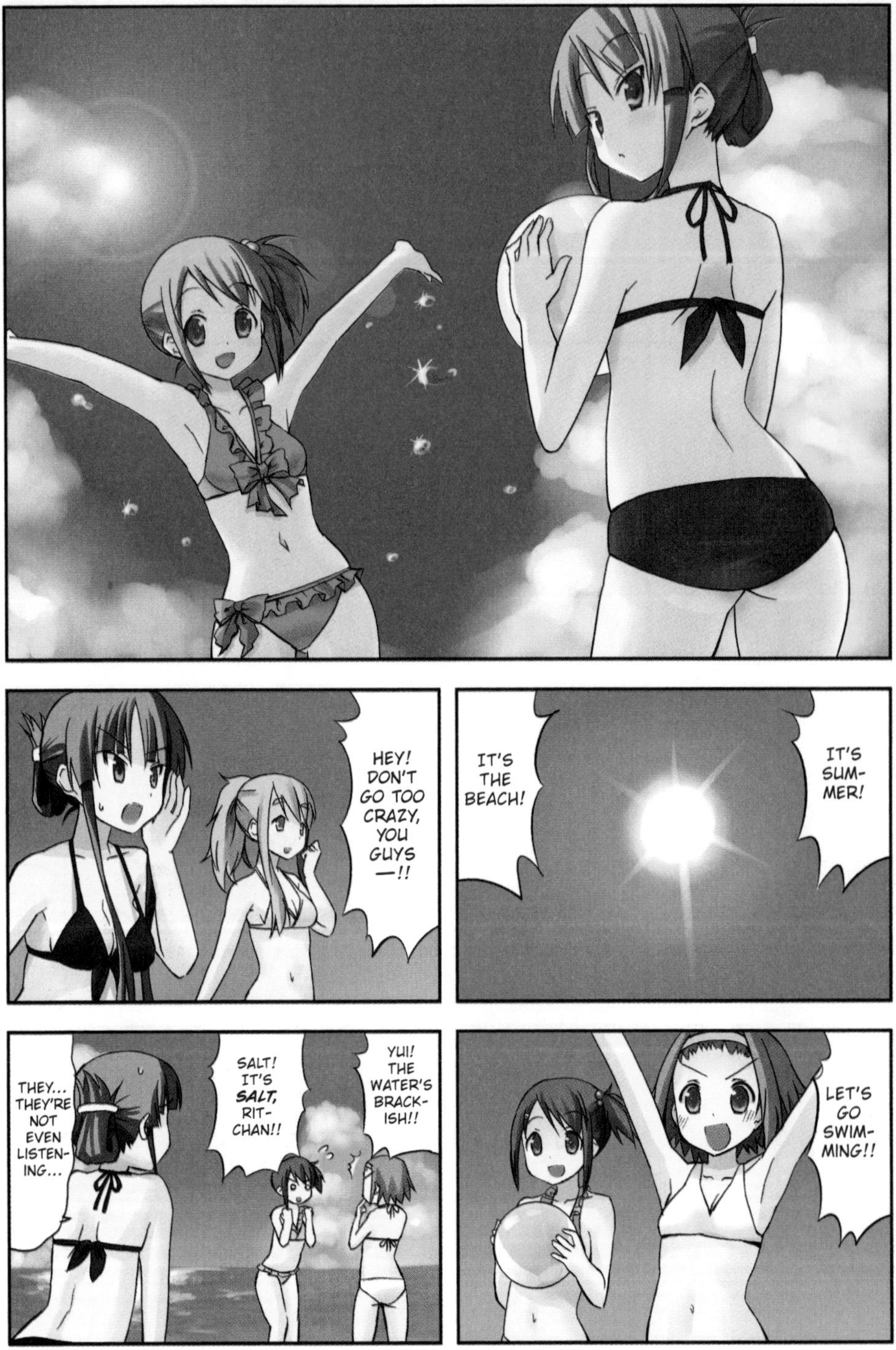
IT'S SUMMER!
IT'S THE BEACH!
HEY! DON'T GO TOO CRAZY, YOU GUYS—!!
LET'S GO SWIMMING!!
YUI! THE WATER'S BRACKISH!!
SALT! IT'S **SALT,** RITCHAN!!
THEY... THEY'RE NOT EVEN LISTENING...

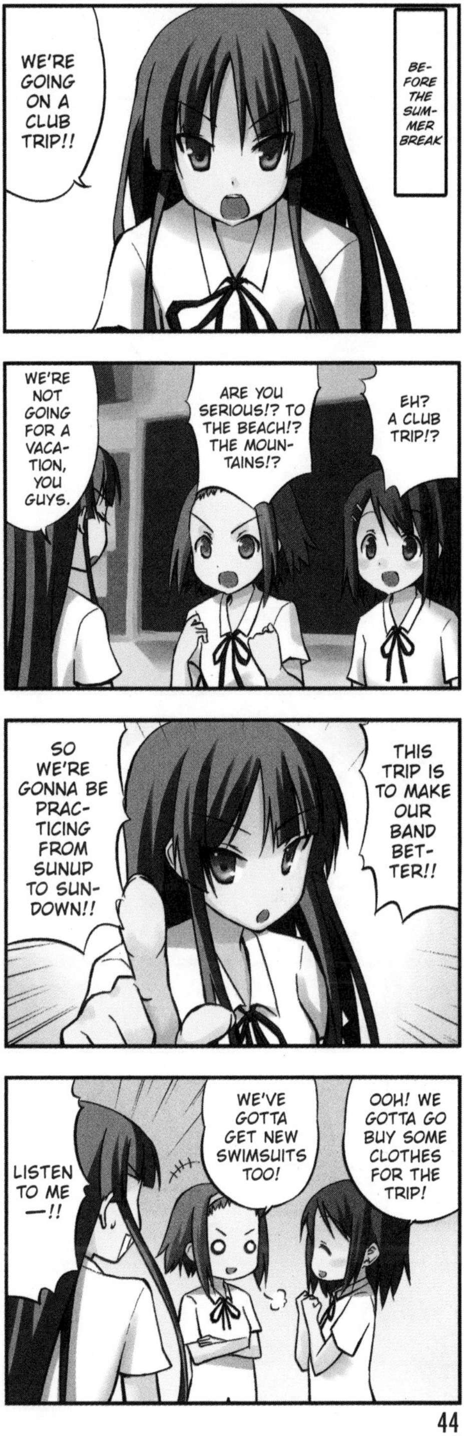
BEFORE THE SUMMER BREAK
WE'RE GOING ON A CLUB TRIP!!
EH? A CLUB TRIP!?
ARE YOU SERIOUS!? TO THE BEACH!? THE MOUNTAINS!?
WE'RE NOT GOING FOR A VACATION, YOU GUYS.
THIS TRIP IS TO MAKE OUR BAND BETTER!!
SO WE'RE GONNA BE PRACTICING FROM SUNUP TO SUNDOWN!!
OOH! WE GOTTA GO BUY SOME CLOTHES FOR THE TRIP!
WE'VE GOTTA GET NEW SWIMSUITS TOO!
LISTEN TO ME—!!

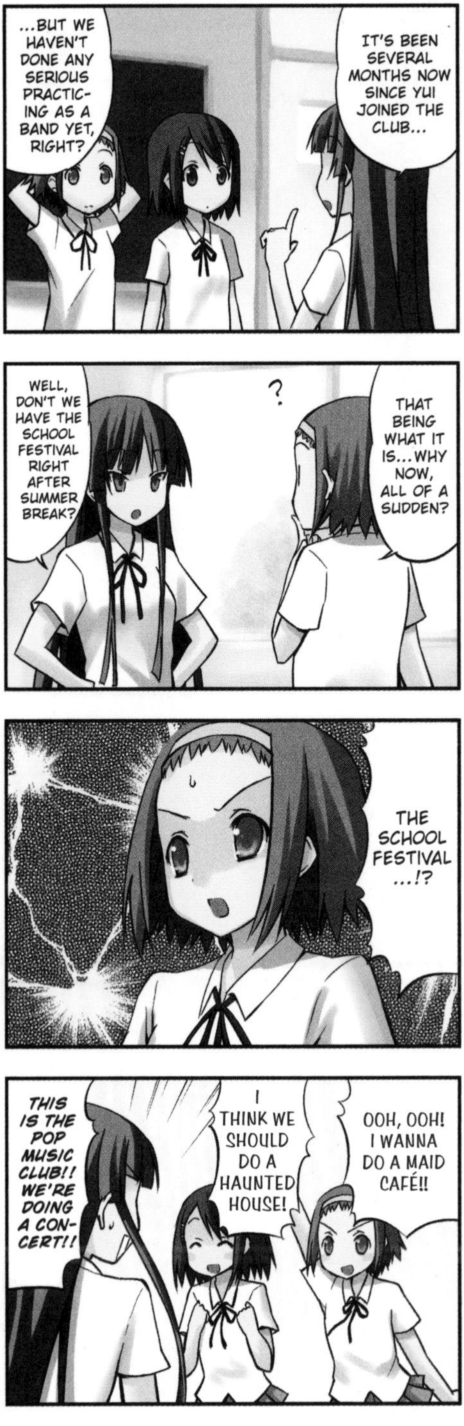
IT'S BEEN SEVERAL MONTHS NOW SINCE YUI JOINED THE CLUB...
...BUT WE HAVEN'T DONE ANY SERIOUS PRACTICING AS A BAND YET, RIGHT?
THAT BEING WHAT IT IS...WHY NOW, ALL OF A SUDDEN?
?
WELL, DON'T WE HAVE THE SCHOOL FESTIVAL RIGHT AFTER SUMMER BREAK?
THE SCHOOL FESTIVAL...!?
OOH, OOH! I WANNA DO A MAID CAFÉ!!
I THINK WE SHOULD DO A HAUNTED HOUSE!
THIS IS THE POP MUSIC CLUB!! WE'RE DOING A CONCERT!!

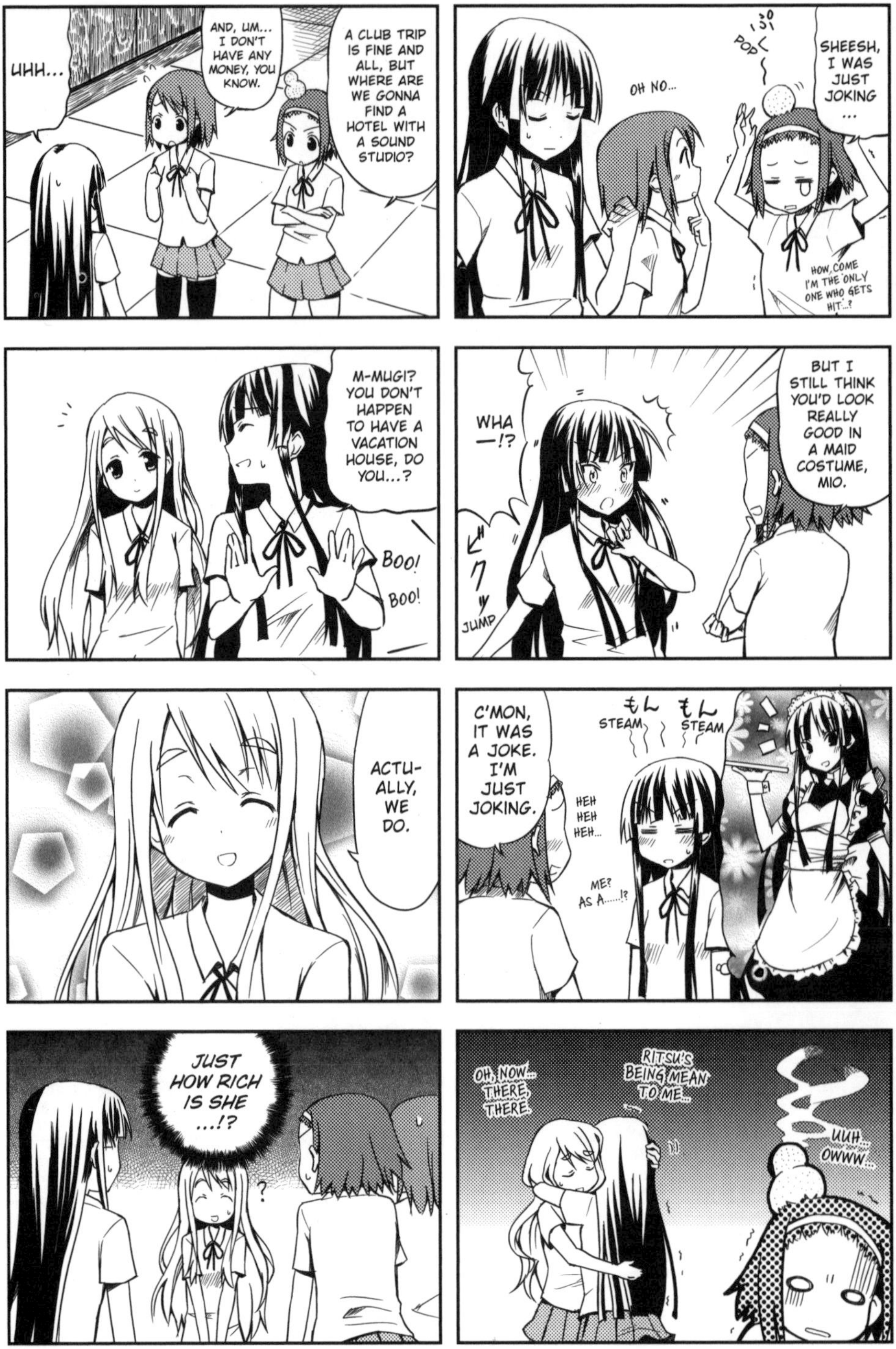
SHEESH, I WAS JUST JOKING ...
POP
OH NO...
HOW COME I'M THE ONLY ONE WHO GETS HIT...?
BUT I STILL THINK YOU'D LOOK REALLY GOOD IN A MAID COSTUME, MIO.
WHA —!?
ビクッ
JUMP
もん もん
STEAM STEAM
C'MON, IT WAS A JOKE. I'M JUST JOKING.
HEH HEH HEH...
ME? AS A......!?
UUH... OWWW...
RITSU'S BEING MEAN TO ME...
OH, NOW... THERE, THERE.
A CLUB TRIP IS FINE AND ALL, BUT WHERE ARE WE GONNA FIND A HOTEL WITH A SOUND STUDIO?
AND, UM... I DON'T HAVE ANY MONEY, YOU KNOW.
UHH...
M-MUGI? YOU DON'T HAPPEN TO HAVE A VACATION HOUSE, DO YOU...?
BOO! BOO!
ACTU-ALLY, WE DO.
JUST HOW RICH IS SHE ...!?

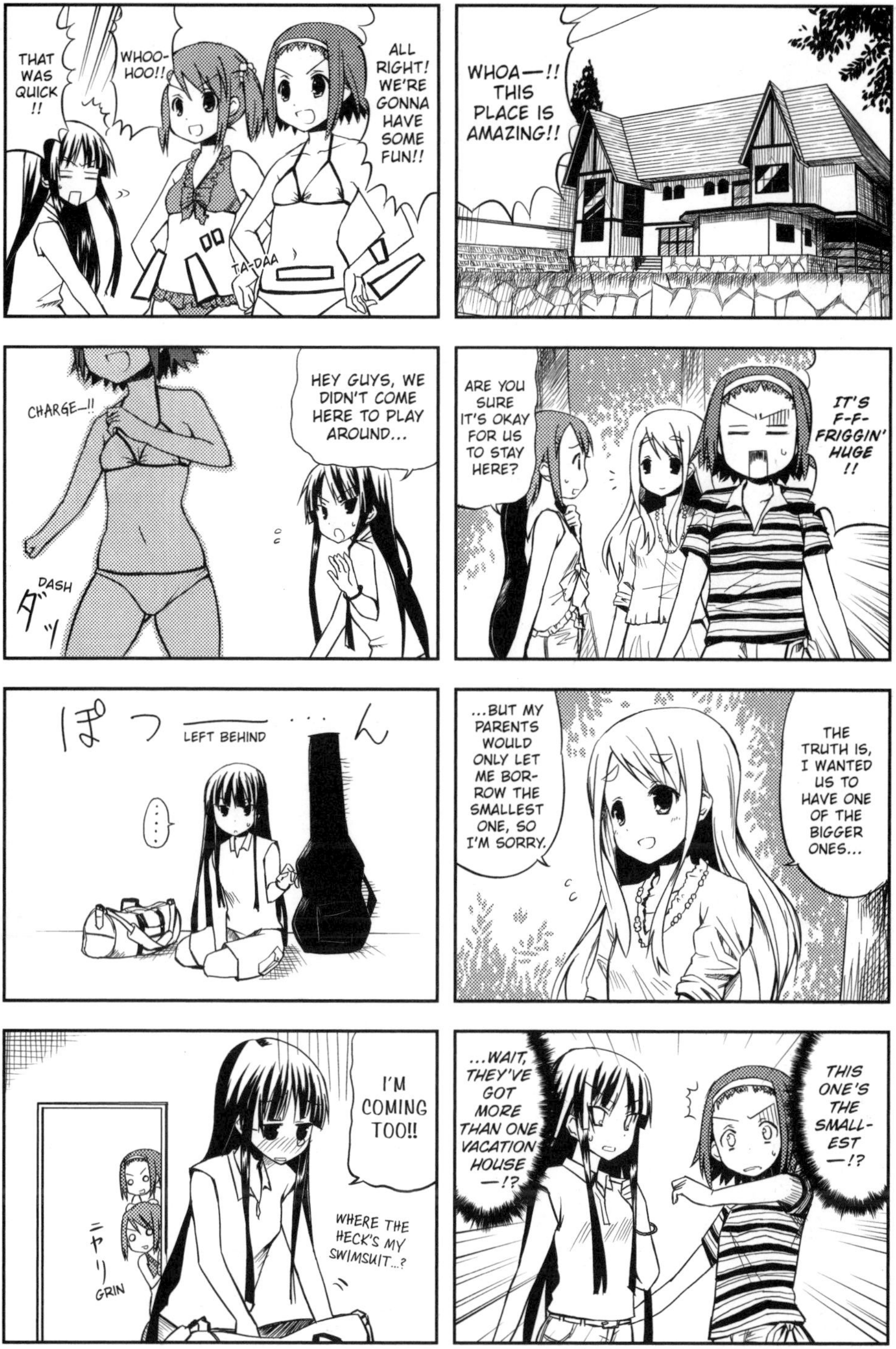
WHOA—!! THIS PLACE IS AMAZING!!
IT'S F-F-FRIGGIN' HUGE!!
ARE YOU SURE IT'S OKAY FOR US TO STAY HERE?
THE TRUTH IS, I WANTED US TO HAVE ONE OF THE BIGGER ONES...
...BUT MY PARENTS WOULD ONLY LET ME BOR-ROW THE SMALLEST ONE, SO I'M SORRY.
THIS ONE'S THE SMALL-EST—!?
...WAIT, THEY'VE GOT MORE THAN ONE VACATION HOUSE—!?
ALL RIGHT! WE'RE GONNA HAVE SOME FUN!!
WHOO-HOO!!
THAT WAS QUICK!!
TA-DAA
HEY GUYS, WE DIDN'T COME HERE TO PLAY AROUND...
CHARGE—!!
ダッ
DASH
ぽつ———…ん
LEFT BEHIND
I'M COMING TOO!!
WHERE THE HECK'S MY SWIMSUIT...?
ニヤリ
GRIN

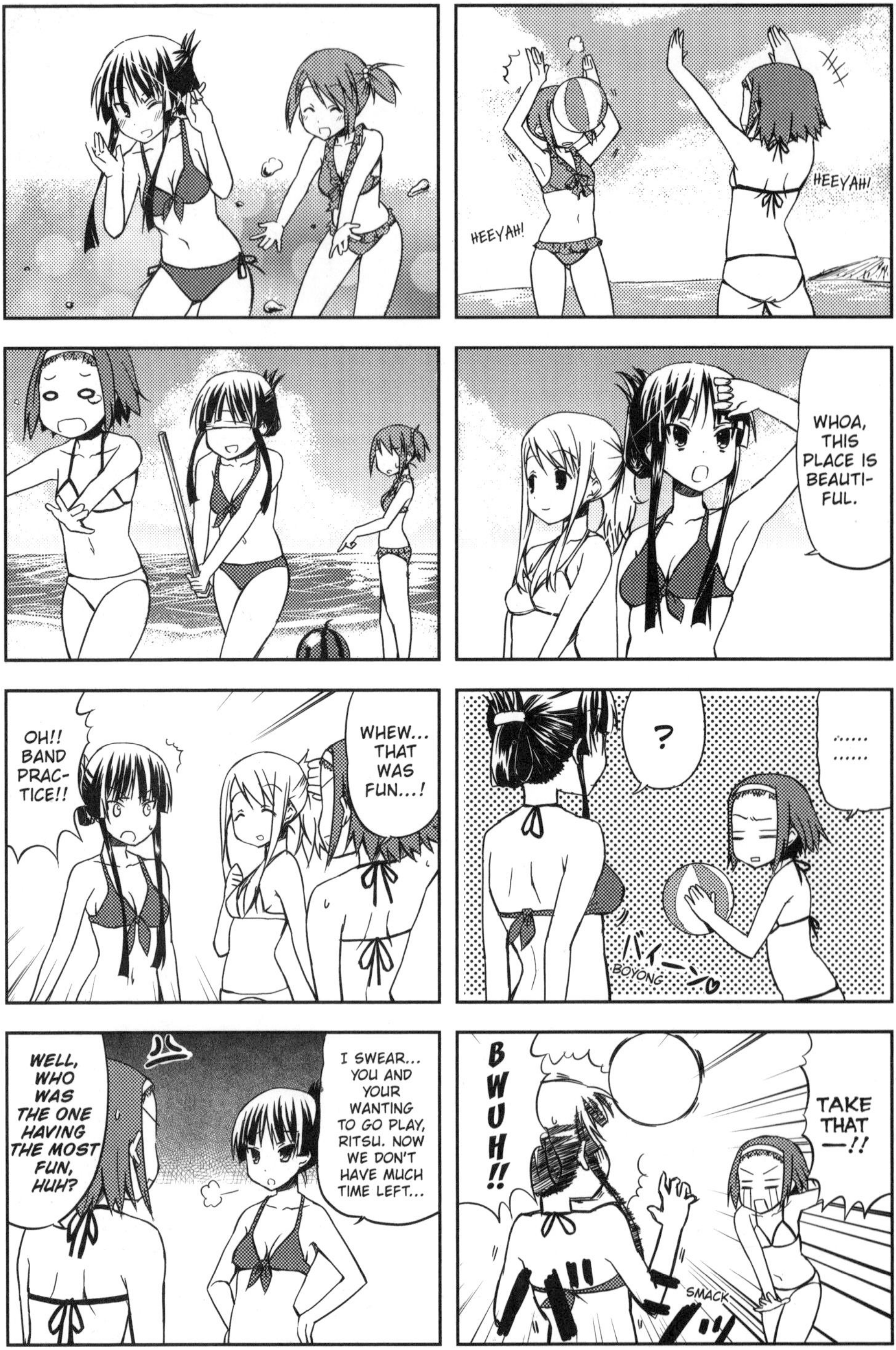
HEEYAH!
HEEYAH!
WHOA, THIS PLACE IS BEAUTI-FUL.
?
......
......
バイーン♥
BOYONG
TAKE THAT—!!
BWUH!!
SMACK
WHEW... THAT WAS FUN...!
OH!! BAND PRAC-TICE!!
I SWEAR... YOU AND YOUR WANTING TO GO PLAY, RITSU. NOW WE DON'T HAVE MUCH TIME LEFT...
WELL, WHO WAS THE ONE HAVING THE MOST FUN, HUH?

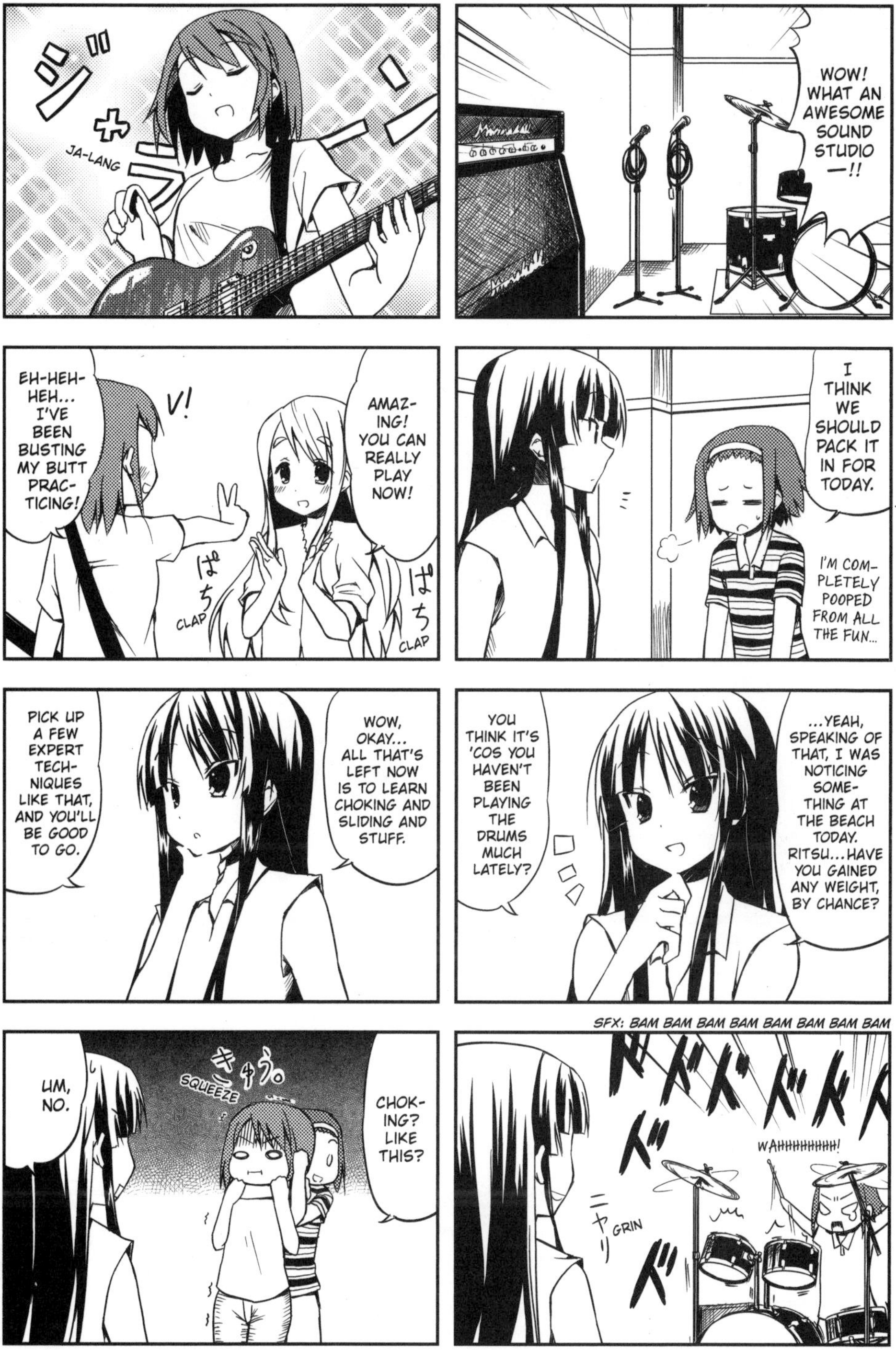
WOW! WHAT AN AWESOME SOUND STUDIO—!!
I THINK WE SHOULD PACK IT IN FOR TODAY.
I'M COMPLETELY POOPED FROM ALL THE FUN...
...YEAH, SPEAKING OF THAT, I WAS NOTICING SOMETHING AT THE BEACH TODAY. RITSU...HAVE YOU GAINED ANY WEIGHT, BY CHANCE?
YOU THINK IT'S 'COS YOU HAVEN'T BEEN PLAYING THE DRUMS MUCH LATELY?
SFX: BAM BAM BAM BAM BAM BAM BAM BAM
WAHHHHHHHH!
ニヤリ GRIN
ジャラーン JA-LANG
AMAZING! YOU CAN REALLY PLAY NOW!
EH-HEH-HEH... I'VE BEEN BUSTING MY BUTT PRACTICING!
V!
ぱち CLAP
ぱち CLAP
WOW, OKAY... ALL THAT'S LEFT NOW IS TO LEARN CHOKING AND SLIDING AND STUFF.
PICK UP A FEW EXPERT TECHNIQUES LIKE THAT, AND YOU'LL BE GOOD TO GO.
CHOKING? LIKE THIS?
きゅう。 SQUEEZE
UM, NO.

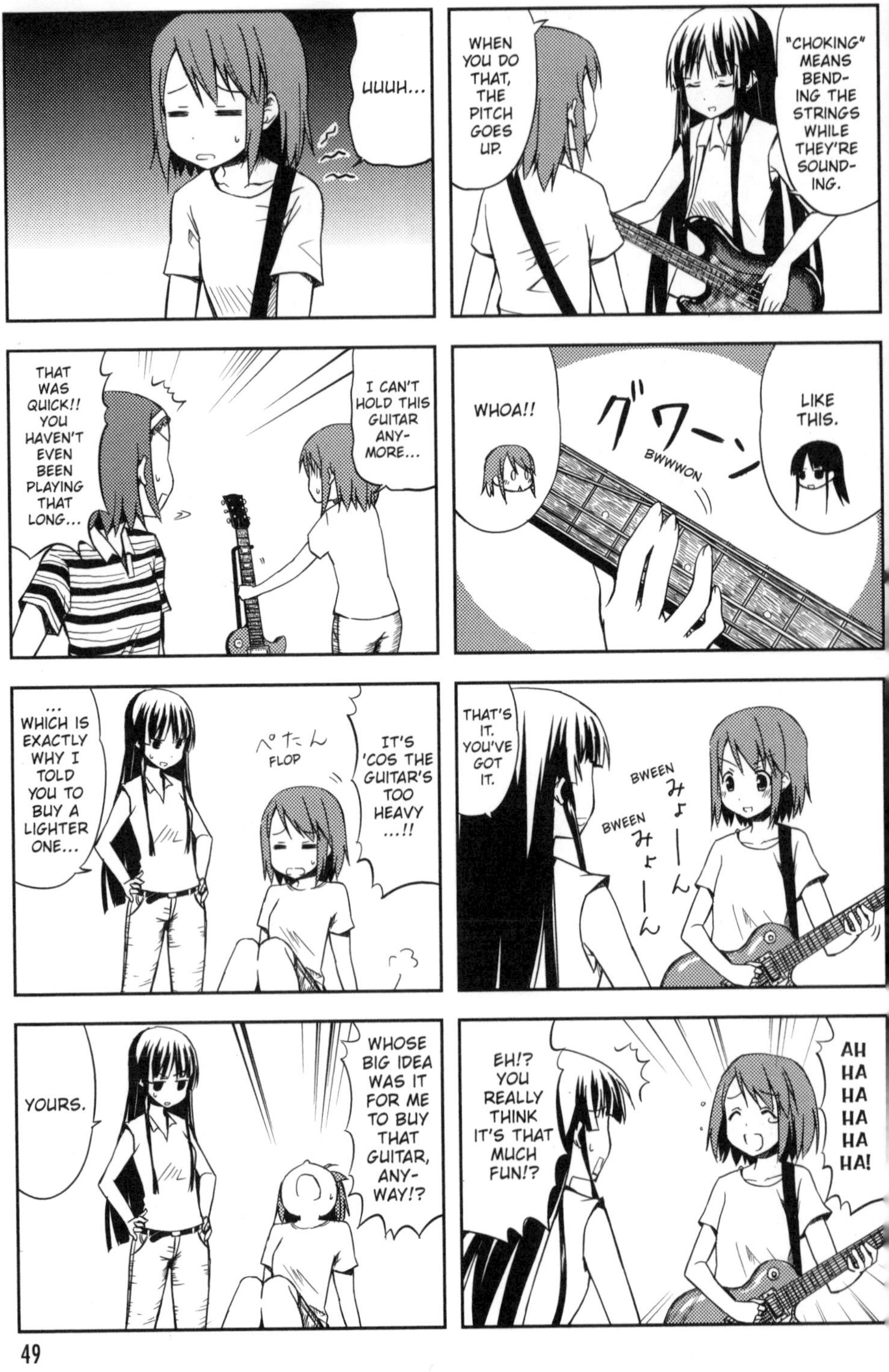
"CHOKING" MEANS BENDING THE STRINGS WHILE THEY'RE SOUNDING.
WHEN YOU DO THAT, THE PITCH GOES UP.
LIKE THIS.
グワーン
BWWWON
WHOA!!
THAT'S IT. YOU'VE GOT IT.
みょーん
BWEEN
みょーん
BWEEN
AH HA HA HA HA HA!
EH!? YOU REALLY THINK IT'S THAT MUCH FUN!?
UUUH...
I CAN'T HOLD THIS GUITAR ANYMORE...
THAT WAS QUICK!! YOU HAVEN'T EVEN BEEN PLAYING THAT LONG...
IT'S 'COS THE GUITAR'S TOO HEAVY ...!!
ぺたん
FLOP
... WHICH IS EXACTLY WHY I TOLD YOU TO BUY A LIGHTER ONE...
WHOSE BIG IDEA WAS IT FOR ME TO BUY THAT GUITAR, ANYWAY!?
YOURS.

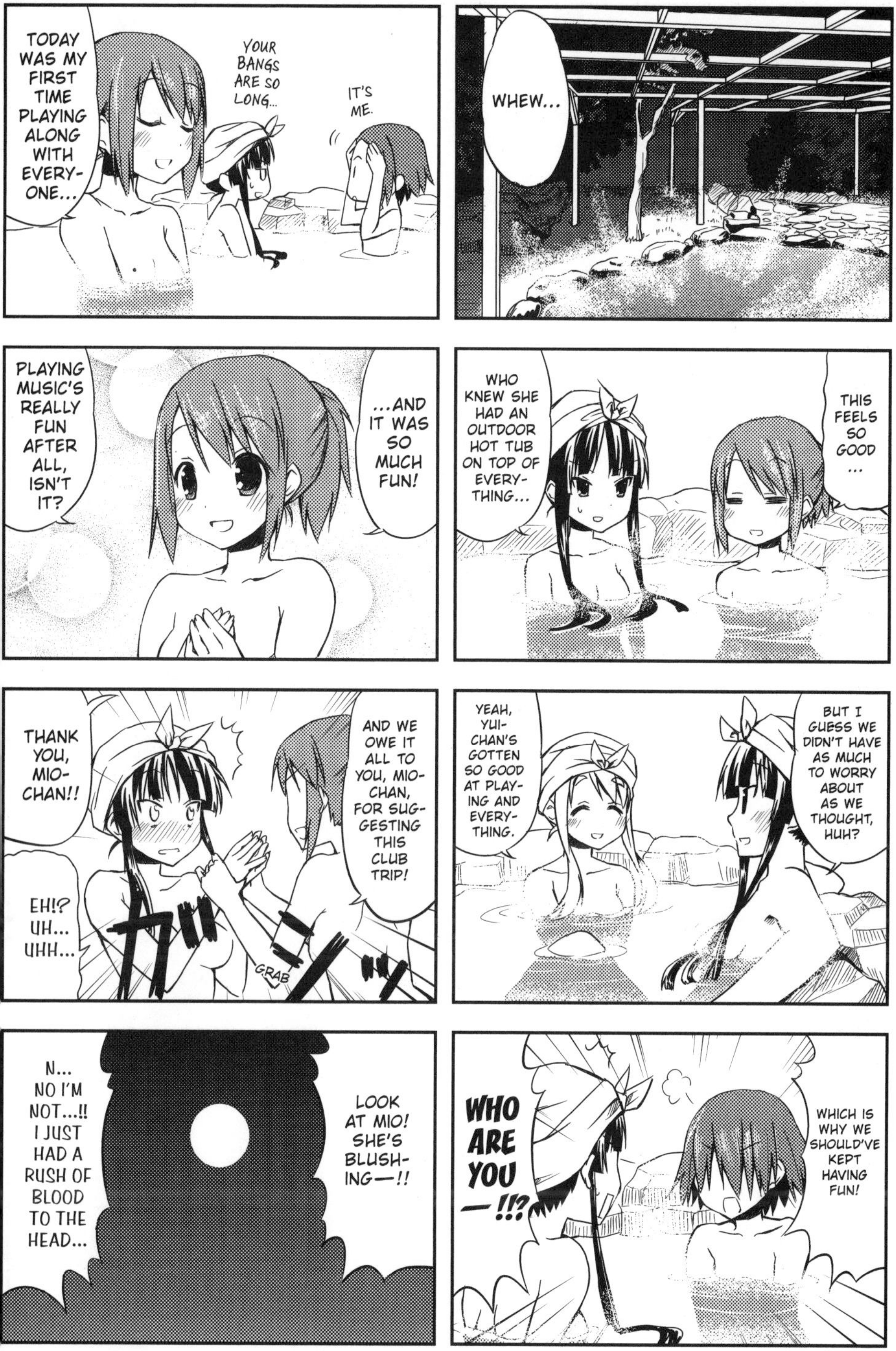
WHEW...
THIS FEELS SO GOOD...
WHO KNEW SHE HAD AN OUTDOOR HOT TUB ON TOP OF EVERYTHING...
BUT I GUESS WE DIDN'T HAVE AS MUCH TO WORRY ABOUT AS WE THOUGHT, HUH?
YEAH, YUI-CHAN'S GOTTEN SO GOOD AT PLAYING AND EVERYTHING.
WHICH IS WHY WE SHOULD'VE KEPT HAVING FUN!
WHO ARE YOU—!!?
IT'S ME.
YOUR BANGS ARE SO LONG...
TODAY WAS MY FIRST TIME PLAYING ALONG WITH EVERYONE...
...AND IT WAS SO MUCH FUN!
PLAYING MUSIC'S REALLY FUN AFTER ALL, ISN'T IT?
AND WE OWE IT ALL TO YOU, MIO-CHAN, FOR SUGGESTING THIS CLUB TRIP!
THANK YOU, MIO-CHAN!!
GRAB
EH!? UH... UHH...
LOOK AT MIO! SHE'S BLUSHING—!!
N... NO I'M NOT...!! I JUST HAD A RUSH OF BLOOD TO THE HEAD...

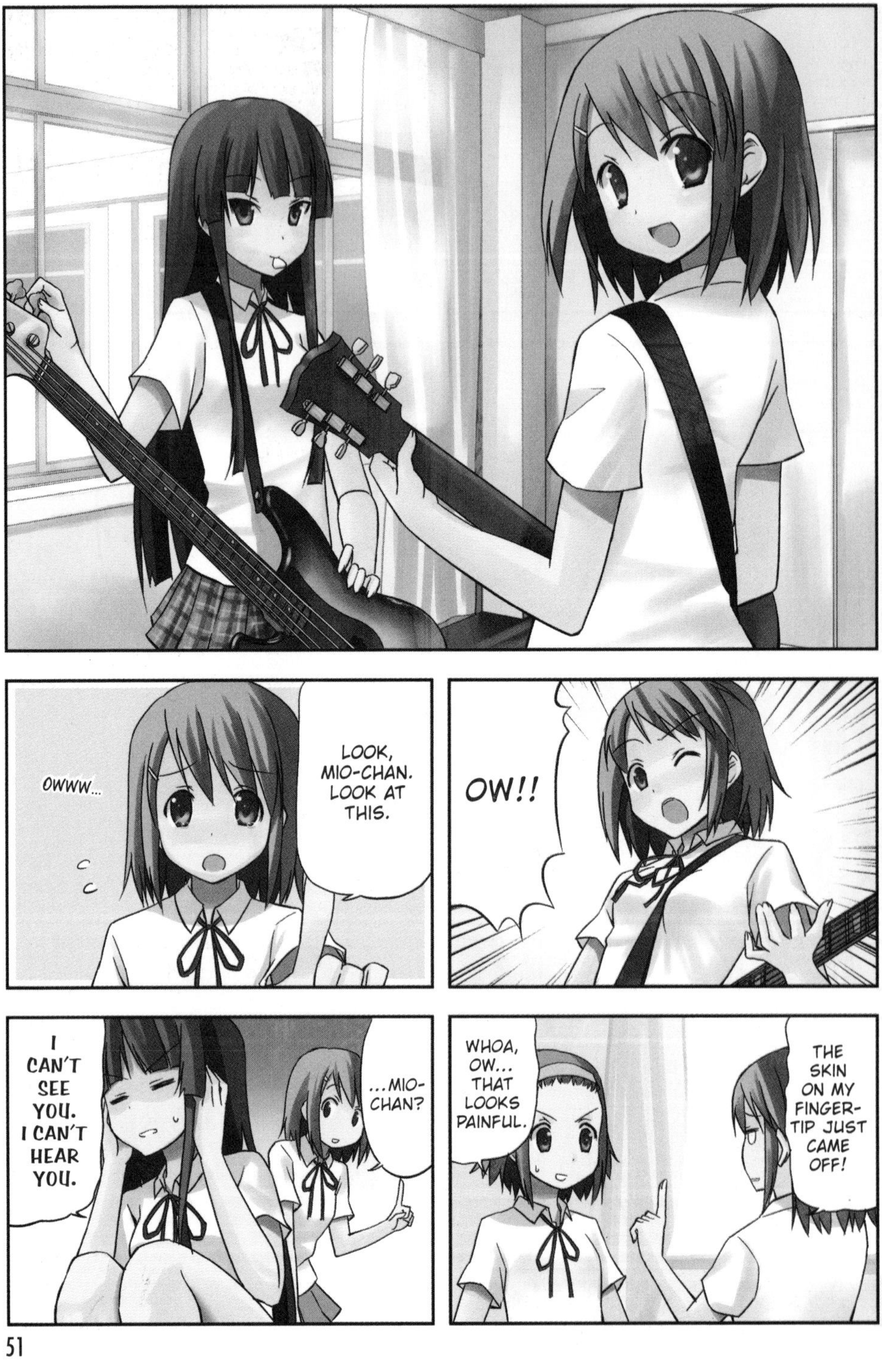
OW!!
LOOK, MIO-CHAN. LOOK AT THIS.
OWWW...
THE SKIN ON MY FINGER-TIP JUST CAME OFF!
WHOA, OW... THAT LOOKS PAINFUL.
...MIO-CHAN?
I CAN'T SEE YOU. I CAN'T HEAR YOU.

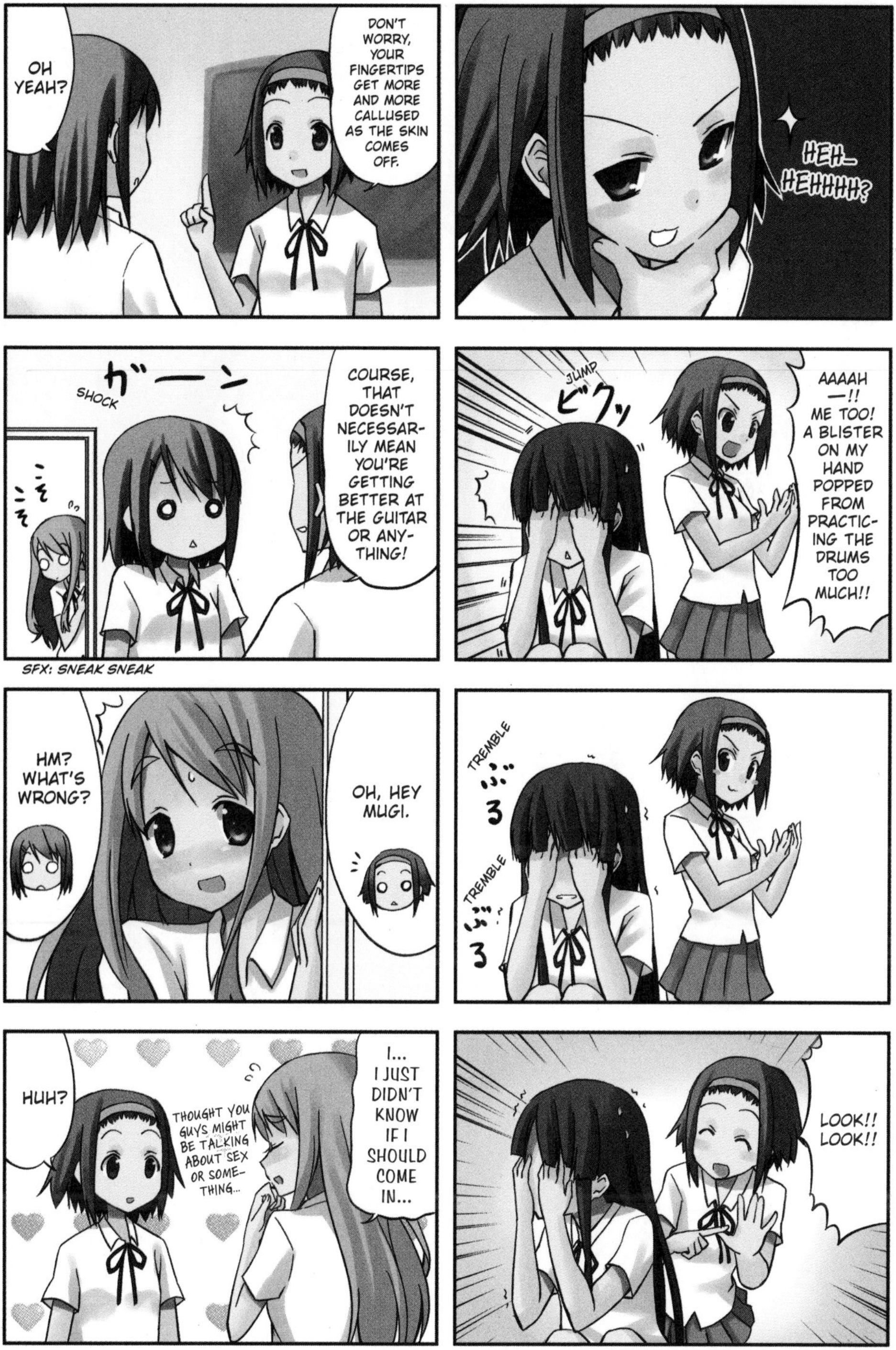
HEH-HEHHHH?
AAAAH—!! ME TOO! A BLISTER ON MY HAND POPPED FROM PRACTICING THE DRUMS TOO MUCH!!
JUMP
ビクッ
TREMBLE
ぷる
TREMBLE
ぷる
LOOK!! LOOK!!
DON'T WORRY, YOUR FINGERTIPS GET MORE AND MORE CALLUSED AS THE SKIN COMES OFF.
OH YEAH?
COURSE, THAT DOESN'T NECESSARILY MEAN YOU'RE GETTING BETTER AT THE GUITAR OR ANYTHING!
ガーン
SHOCK
こそこそ
SFX: SNEAK SNEAK
OH, HEY MUGI.
HM? WHAT'S WRONG?
I... I JUST DIDN'T KNOW IF I SHOULD COME IN...
THOUGHT YOU GUYS MIGHT BE TALKING ABOUT SEX OR SOMETHING...
HUH?

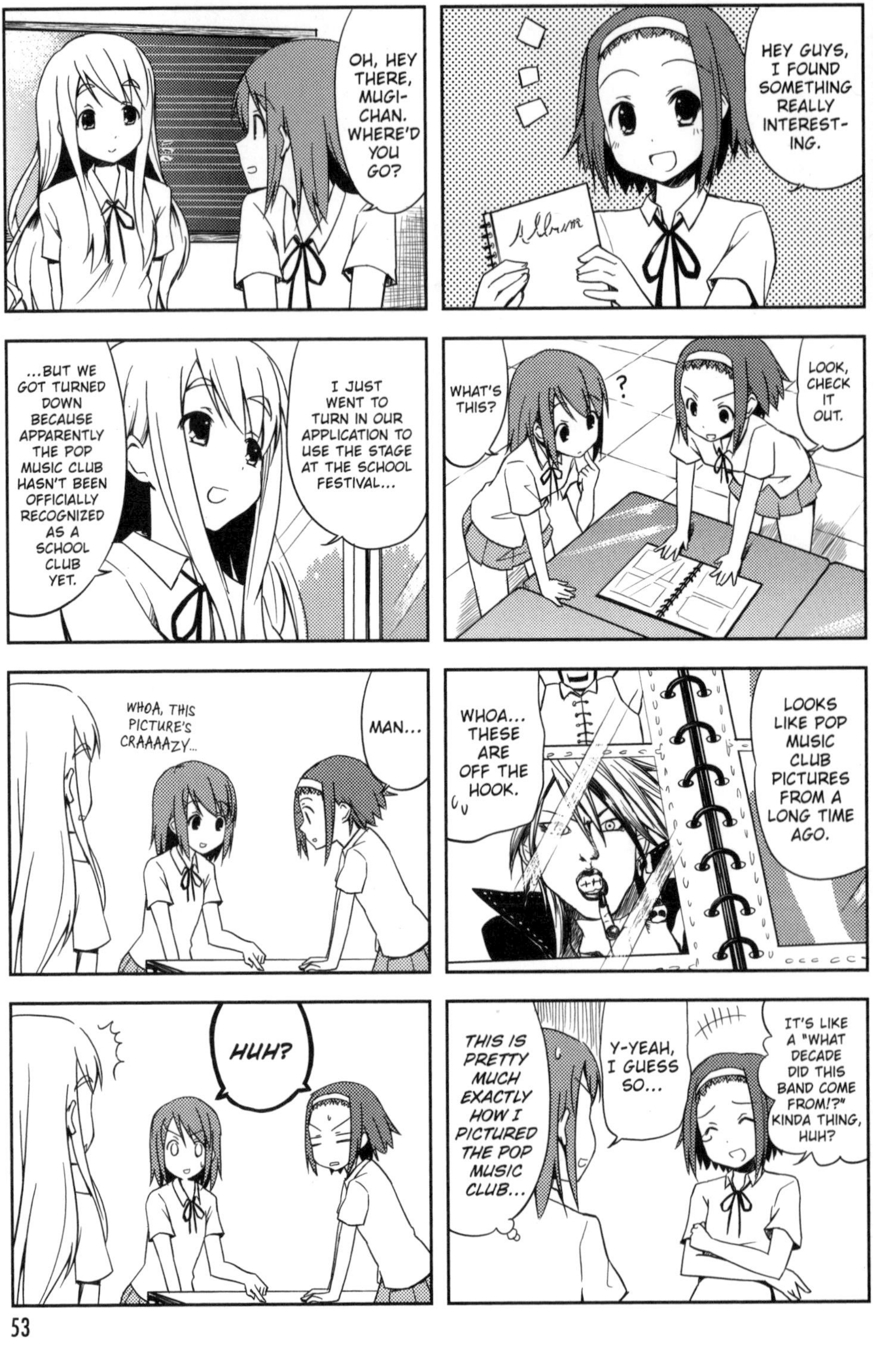
HEY GUYS, I FOUND SOMETHING REALLY INTEREST-ING.
Album
LOOK, CHECK IT OUT.
?
WHAT'S THIS?
LOOKS LIKE POP MUSIC CLUB PICTURES FROM A LONG TIME AGO.
WHOA... THESE ARE OFF THE HOOK.
IT'S LIKE A "WHAT DECADE DID THIS BAND COME FROM!?" KINDA THING, HUH?
Y-YEAH, I GUESS SO...
THIS IS PRETTY MUCH EXACTLY HOW I PICTURED THE POP MUSIC CLUB...
OH, HEY THERE, MUGI-CHAN. WHERE'D YOU GO?
I JUST WENT TO TURN IN OUR APPLICATION TO USE THE STAGE AT THE SCHOOL FESTIVAL...
...BUT WE GOT TURNED DOWN BECAUSE APPARENTLY THE POP MUSIC CLUB HASN'T BEEN OFFICIALLY RECOGNIZED AS A SCHOOL CLUB YET.
MAN...
WHOA, THIS PICTURE'S CRAAAAZY...
HUH?

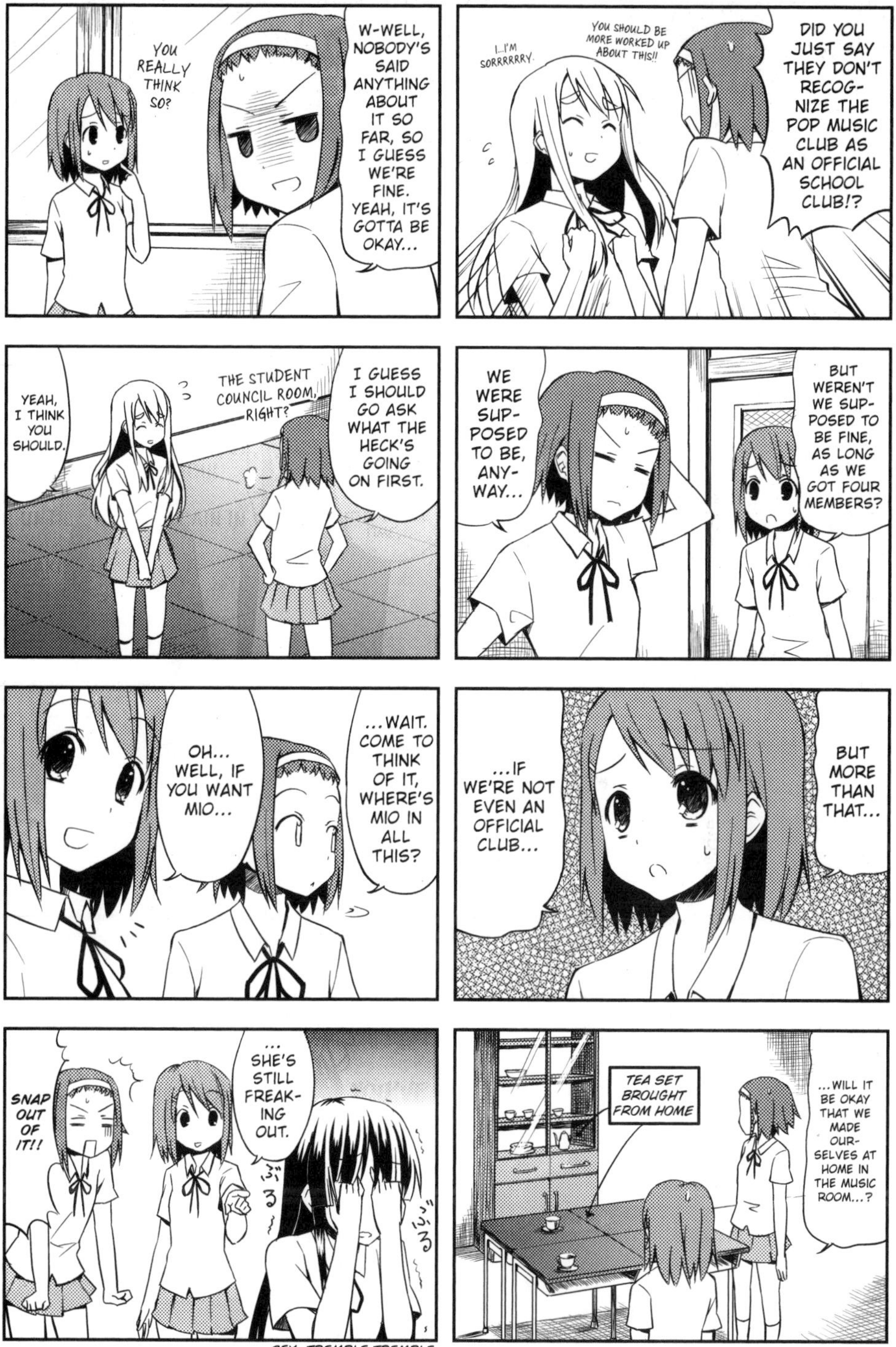
DID YOU JUST SAY THEY DON'T RECOG-NIZE THE POP MUSIC CLUB AS AN OFFICIAL SCHOOL CLUB!?
YOU SHOULD BE MORE WORKED UP ABOUT THIS!!
I...I'M SORRRRRRY.
BUT WEREN'T WE SUP-POSED TO BE FINE, AS LONG AS WE GOT FOUR MEMBERS?
WE WERE SUP-POSED TO BE, ANY-WAY...
BUT MORE THAN THAT...
...IF WE'RE NOT EVEN AN OFFICIAL CLUB...
...WILL IT BE OKAY THAT WE MADE OUR-SELVES AT HOME IN THE MUSIC ROOM...?
TEA SET BROUGHT FROM HOME
W-WELL, NOBODY'S SAID ANYTHING ABOUT IT SO FAR, SO I GUESS WE'RE FINE. YEAH, IT'S GOTTA BE OKAY...
YOU REALLY THINK SO?
I GUESS I SHOULD GO ASK WHAT THE HECK'S GOING ON FIRST.
THE STUDENT COUNCIL ROOM, RIGHT?
YEAH, I THINK YOU SHOULD.
...WAIT. COME TO THINK OF IT, WHERE'S MIO IN ALL THIS?
OH... WELL, IF YOU WANT MIO...
...SHE'S STILL FREAK-ING OUT.
ぶる
ぶる
SNAP OUT OF IT!!
SFX: TREMBLE TREMBLE

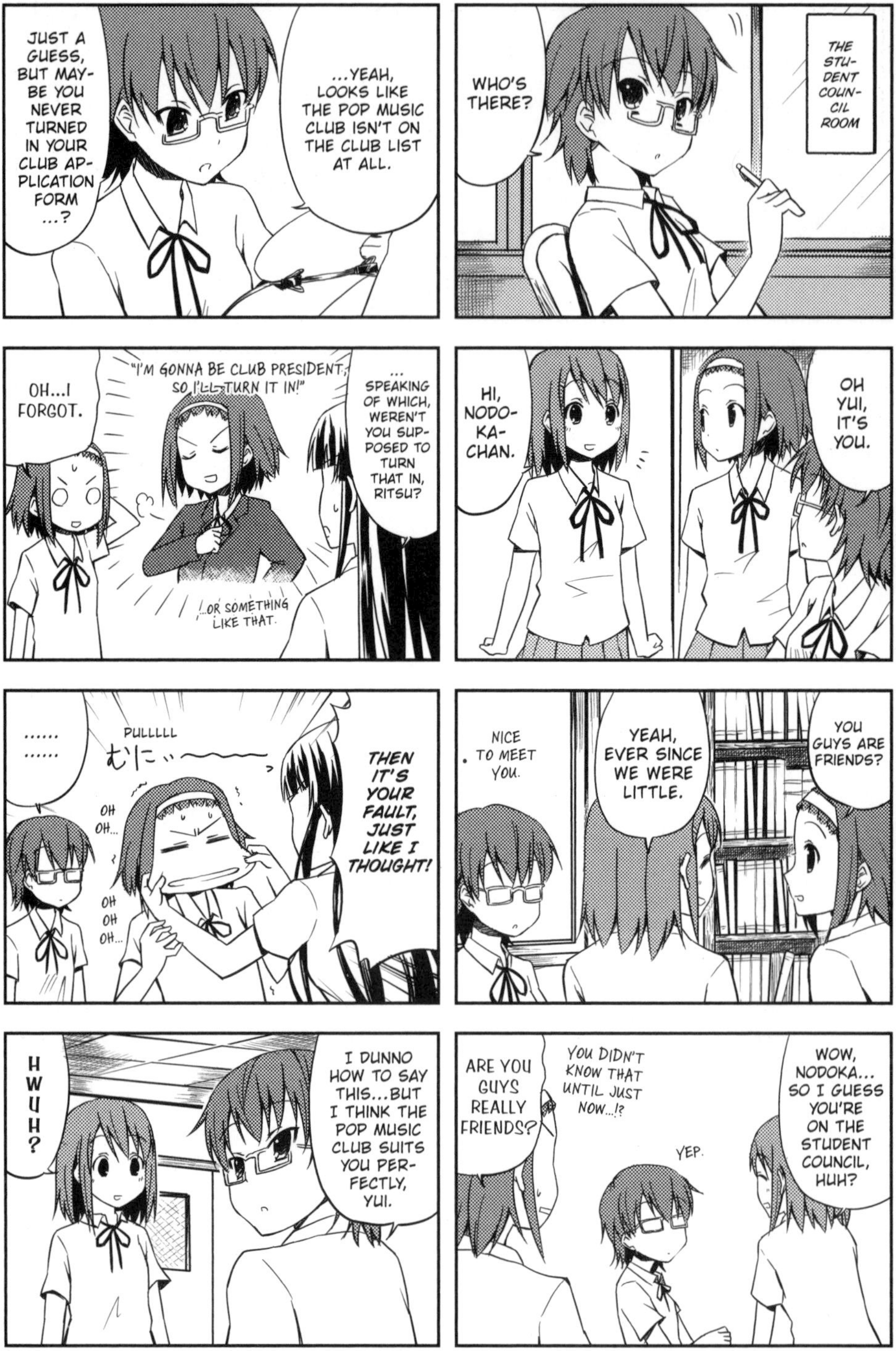
THE STUDENT COUNCIL ROOM
WHO'S THERE?
OH YUI, IT'S YOU.
HI, NODOKA-CHAN.
YOU GUYS ARE FRIENDS?
YEAH, EVER SINCE WE WERE LITTLE.
NICE TO MEET YOU.
WOW, NODOKA... SO I GUESS YOU'RE ON THE STUDENT COUNCIL, HUH?
YEP.
YOU DIDN'T KNOW THAT UNTIL JUST NOW...!?
ARE YOU GUYS REALLY FRIENDS?
...YEAH, LOOKS LIKE THE POP MUSIC CLUB ISN'T ON THE CLUB LIST AT ALL.
JUST A GUESS, BUT MAYBE YOU NEVER TURNED IN YOUR CLUB APPLICATION FORM ...?
...SPEAKING OF WHICH, WEREN'T YOU SUPPOSED TO TURN THAT IN, RITSU?
"I'M GONNA BE CLUB PRESIDENT, SO I'LL TURN IT IN!"
...OR SOMETHING LIKE THAT.
OH...I FORGOT.
THEN IT'S YOUR FAULT, JUST LIKE I THOUGHT!
PULLLLL
むに
OH OH...
OH OH OH...
......
......
I DUNNO HOW TO SAY THIS...BUT I THINK THE POP MUSIC CLUB SUITS YOU PERFECTLY, YUI.
HWUH?

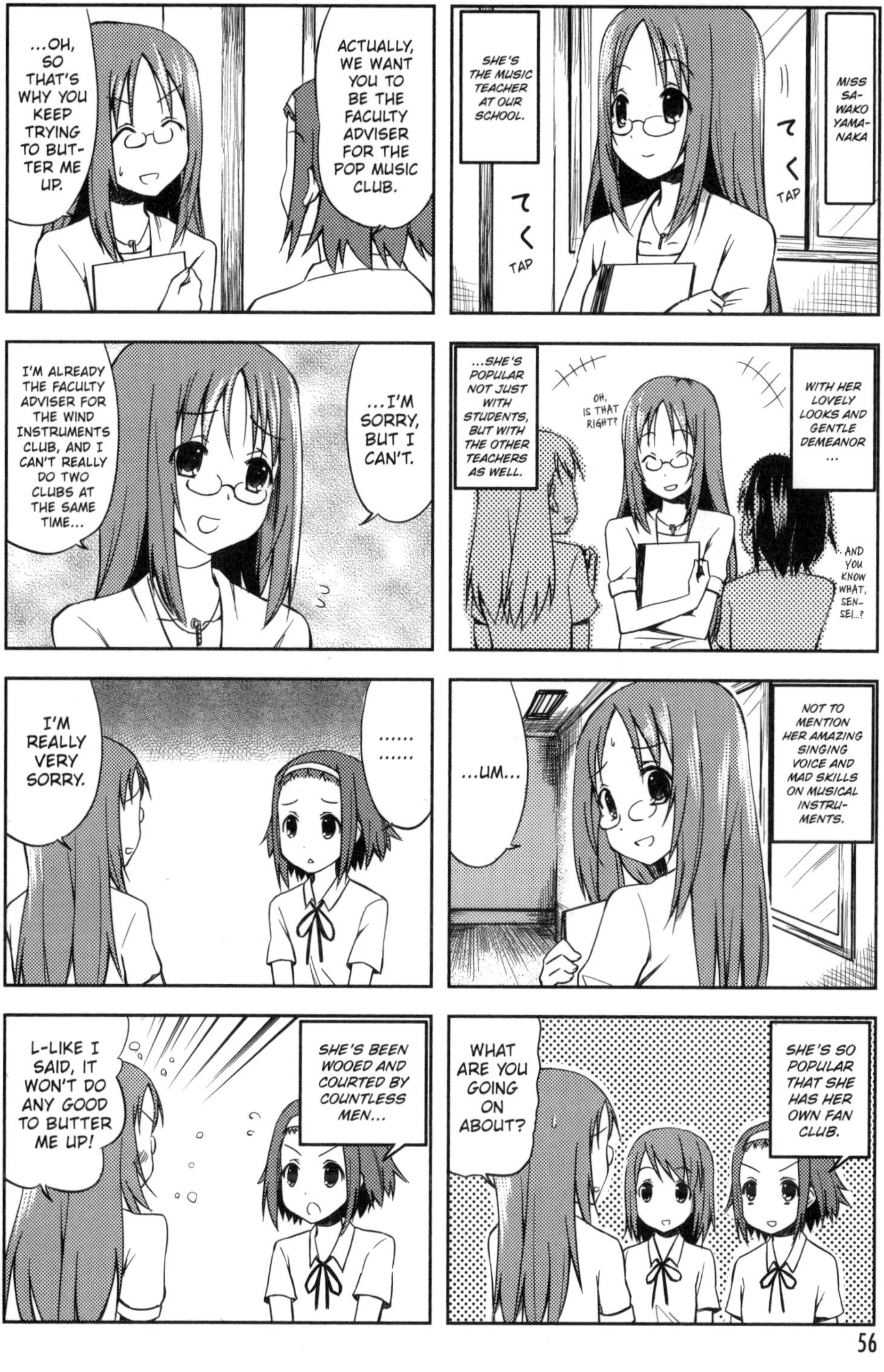
MISS SAWAKO YAMANAKA
てく TAP
SHE'S THE MUSIC TEACHER AT OUR SCHOOL.
てく TAP
ACTUALLY, WE WANT YOU TO BE THE FACULTY ADVISER FOR THE POP MUSIC CLUB.
...OH, SO THAT'S WHY YOU KEEP TRYING TO BUTTER ME UP.
WITH HER LOVELY LOOKS AND GENTLE DEMEANOR...
AND YOU KNOW WHAT, SENSEI...?
OH, IS THAT RIGHT?
...SHE'S POPULAR NOT JUST WITH STUDENTS, BUT WITH THE OTHER TEACHERS AS WELL.
...I'M SORRY, BUT I CAN'T.
I'M ALREADY THE FACULTY ADVISER FOR THE WIND INSTRUMENTS CLUB, AND I CAN'T REALLY DO TWO CLUBS AT THE SAME TIME...
NOT TO MENTION HER AMAZING SINGING VOICE AND MAD SKILLS ON MUSICAL INSTRUMENTS.
...UM...
......
......
I'M REALLY VERY SORRY.
SHE'S SO POPULAR THAT SHE HAS HER OWN FAN CLUB.
WHAT ARE YOU GOING ON ABOUT?
SHE'S BEEN WOOED AND COURTED BY COUNTLESS MEN...
L-LIKE I SAID, IT WON'T DO ANY GOOD TO BUTTER ME UP!

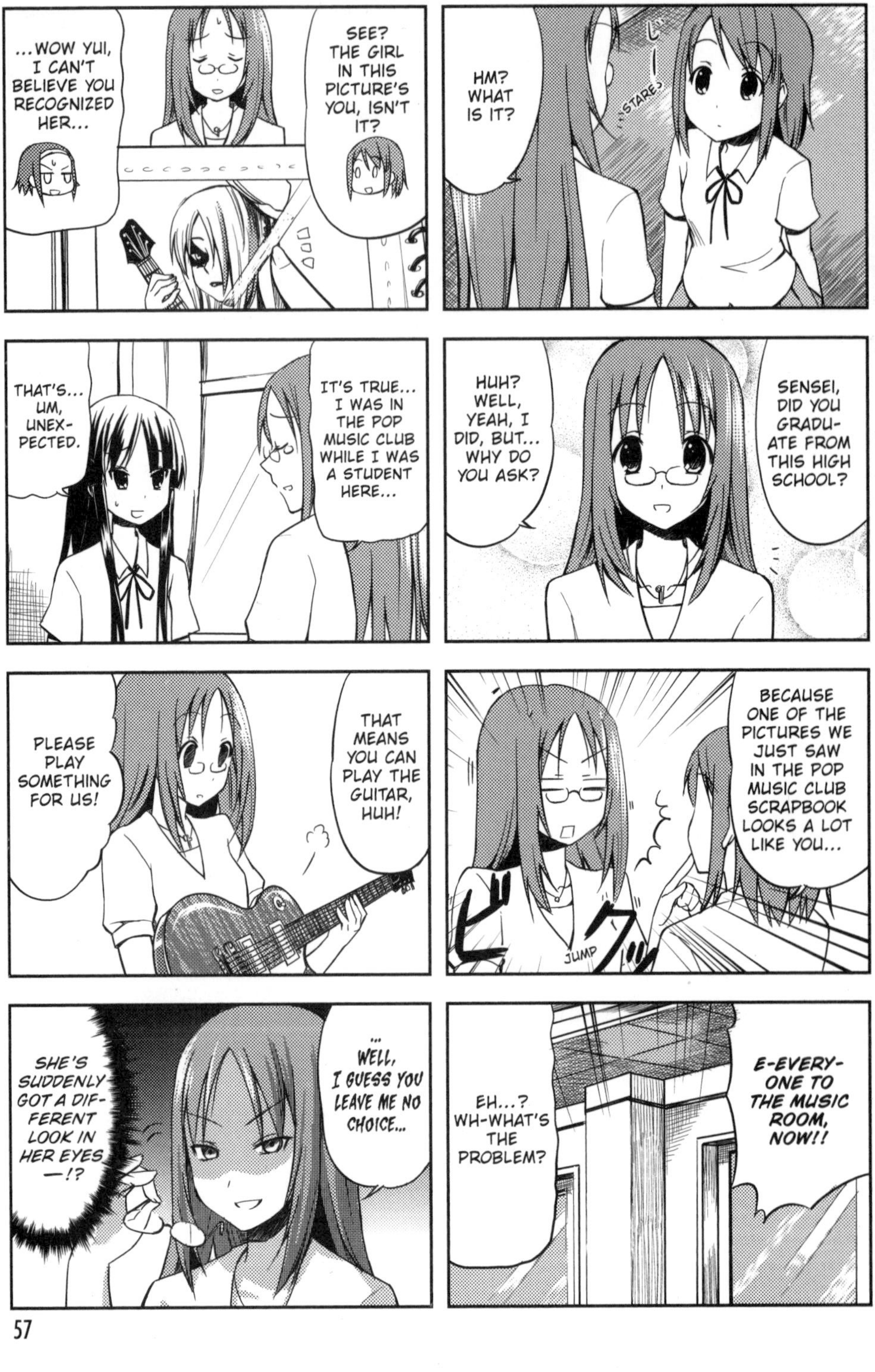
HM? WHAT IS IT?
じー
STARE
SEE? THE GIRL IN THIS PICTURE'S YOU, ISN'T IT?
...WOW YUI, I CAN'T BELIEVE YOU RECOGNIZED HER...
SENSEI, DID YOU GRADUATE FROM THIS HIGH SCHOOL?
HUH? WELL, YEAH, I DID, BUT... WHY DO YOU ASK?
IT'S TRUE... I WAS IN THE POP MUSIC CLUB WHILE I WAS A STUDENT HERE...
THAT'S... UM, UNEXPECTED.
BECAUSE ONE OF THE PICTURES WE JUST SAW IN THE POP MUSIC CLUB SCRAPBOOK LOOKS A LOT LIKE YOU...
ビクッ
JUMP
THAT MEANS YOU CAN PLAY THE GUITAR, HUH!
PLEASE PLAY SOMETHING FOR US!
E-EVERYONE TO THE MUSIC ROOM, NOW!!
EH...? WH-WHAT'S THE PROBLEM?
... WELL, I GUESS YOU LEAVE ME NO CHOICE...
SHE'S SUDDENLY GOT A DIFFERENT LOOK IN HER EYES—!?

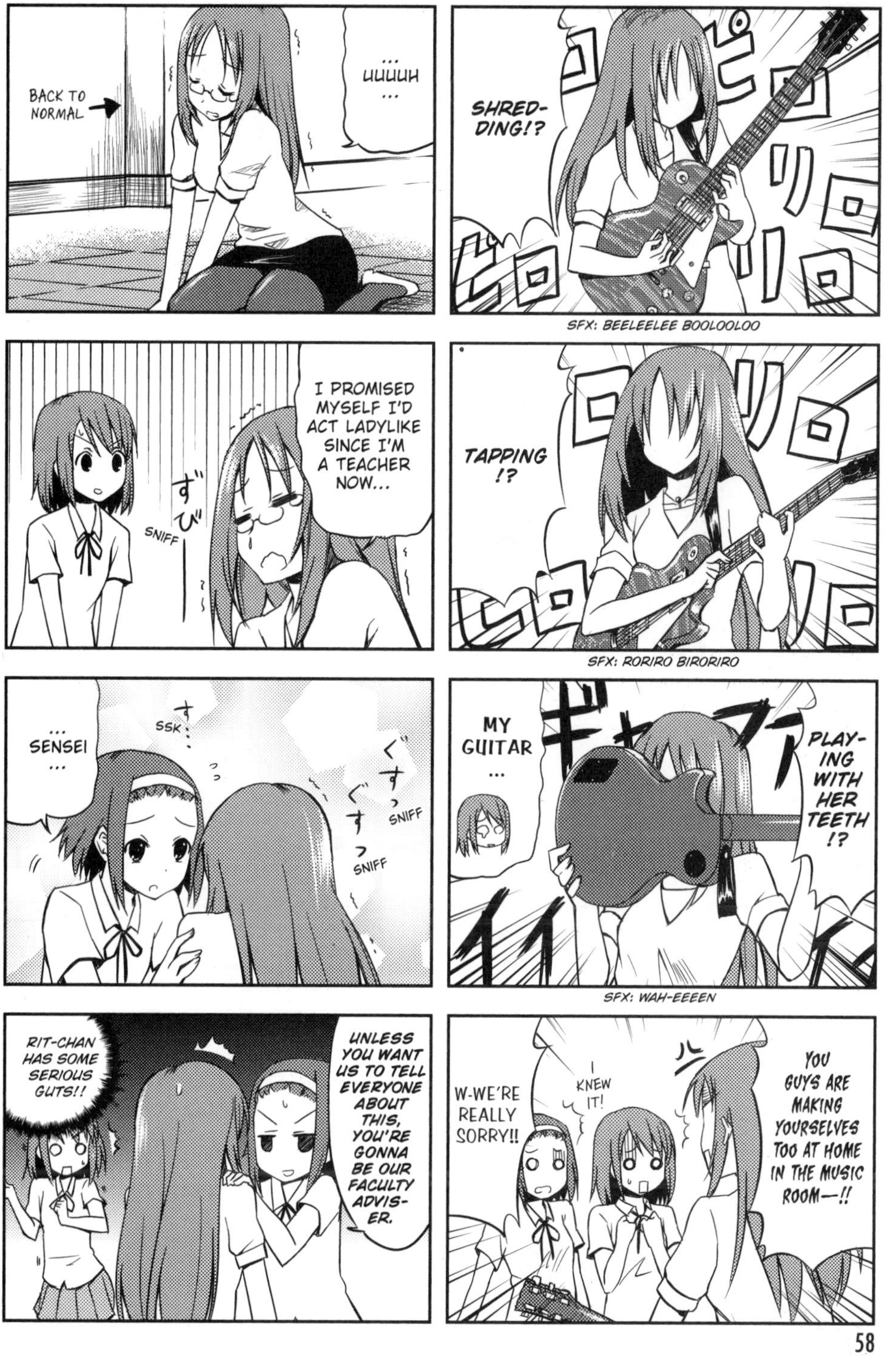
SHRED-DING!?
SFX: BEELEELEE BOOLOOLOO
TAPPING!?
SFX: RORIRO BIRORIRO
PLAY-ING WITH HER TEETH!?
MY GUITAR...
SFX: WAH-EEEEN
YOU GUYS ARE MAKING YOURSELVES TOO AT HOME IN THE MUSIC ROOM—!!
I KNEW IT!
W-WE'RE REALLY SORRY!!
...UUUUH...
BACK TO NORMAL
I PROMISED MYSELF I'D ACT LADYLIKE SINCE I'M A TEACHER NOW...
ずび
SNIFF
ぐすっ SNIFF
ぐすっ SNIFF
す SSK
...SENSEI...
UNLESS YOU WANT US TO TELL EVERYONE ABOUT THIS, YOU'RE GONNA BE OUR FACULTY ADVIS-ER.
RIT-CHAN HAS SOME SERIOUS GUTS!!

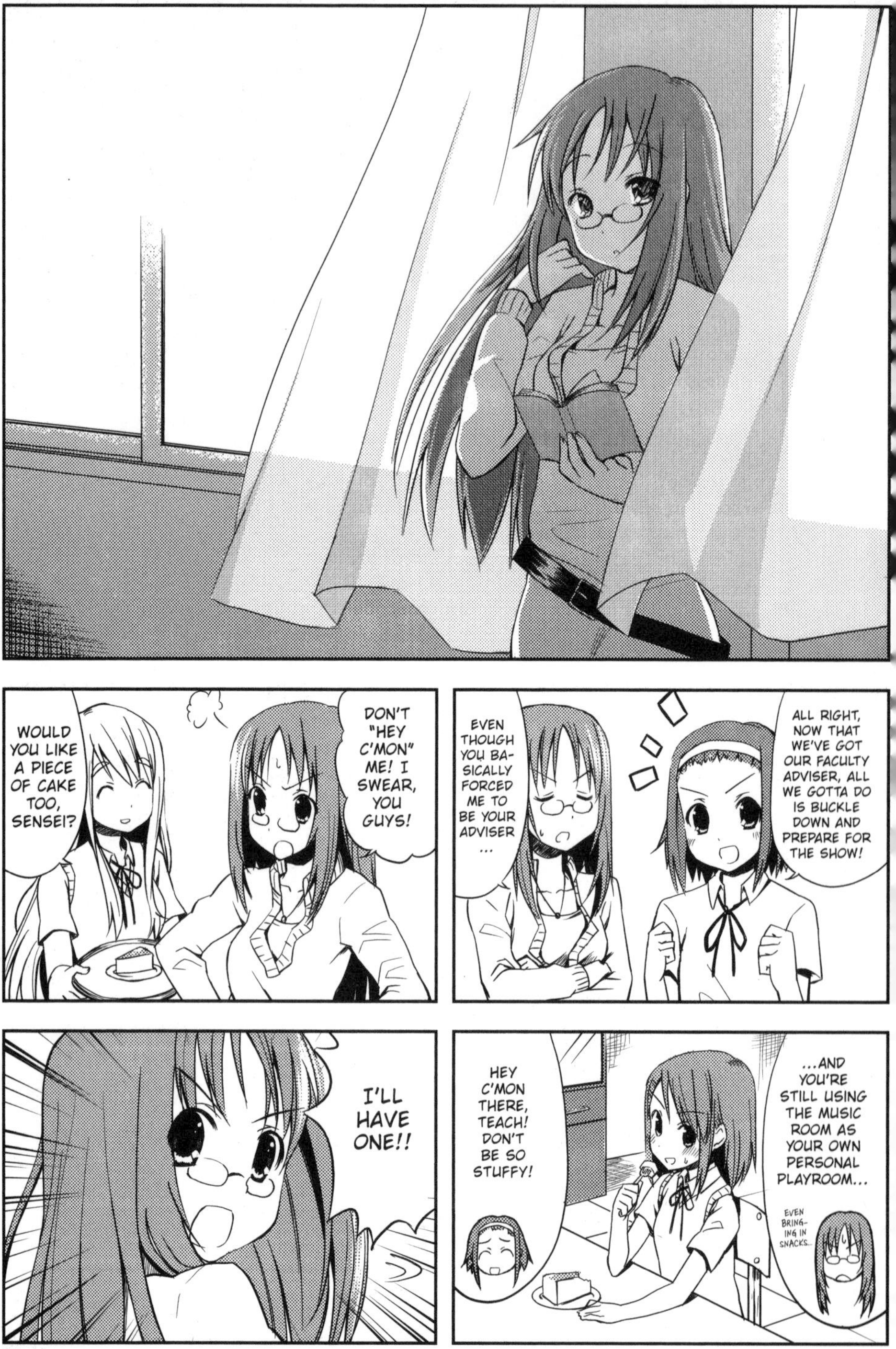
ALL RIGHT, NOW THAT WE'VE GOT OUR FACULTY ADVISER, ALL WE GOTTA DO IS BUCKLE DOWN AND PREPARE FOR THE SHOW!
EVEN THOUGH YOU BASICALLY FORCED ME TO BE YOUR ADVISER ...
...AND YOU'RE STILL USING THE MUSIC ROOM AS YOUR OWN PERSONAL PLAYROOM...
EVEN BRINGING IN SNACKS...
HEY C'MON THERE, TEACH! DON'T BE SO STUFFY!
DON'T "HEY C'MON" ME! I SWEAR, YOU GUYS!
WOULD YOU LIKE A PIECE OF CAKE TOO, SENSEI?
I'LL HAVE ONE!!

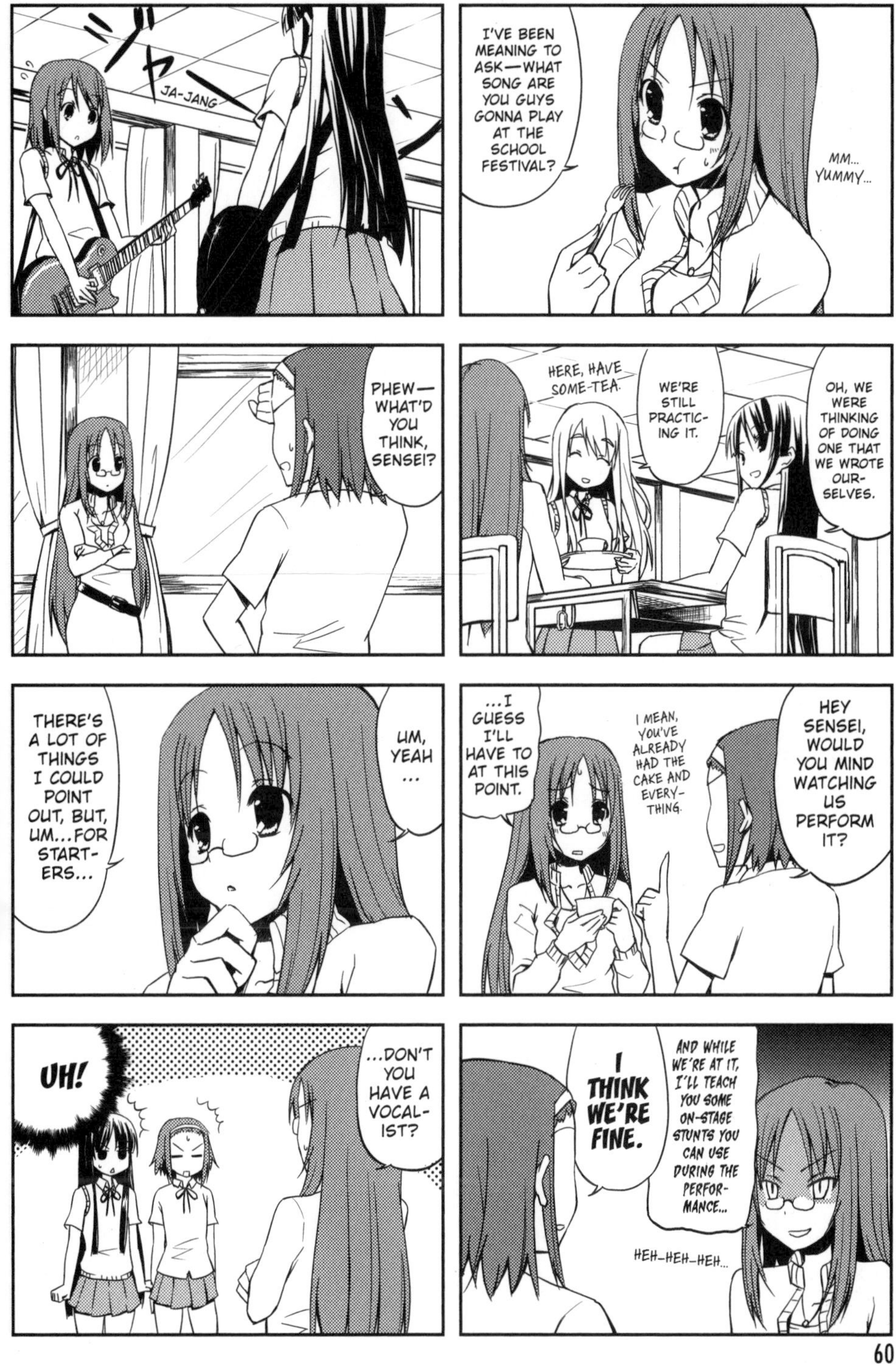
MM... YUMMY...
I'VE BEEN MEANING TO ASK—WHAT SONG ARE YOU GUYS GONNA PLAY AT THE SCHOOL FESTIVAL?
OH, WE WERE THINKING OF DOING ONE THAT WE WROTE OURSELVES.
WE'RE STILL PRACTICING IT.
HERE, HAVE SOME TEA.
HEY SENSEI, WOULD YOU MIND WATCHING US PERFORM IT?
I MEAN, YOU'VE ALREADY HAD THE CAKE AND EVERYTHING.
...I GUESS I'LL HAVE TO AT THIS POINT.
AND WHILE WE'RE AT IT, I'LL TEACH YOU SOME ON-STAGE STUNTS YOU CAN USE DURING THE PERFORMANCE...
I THINK WE'RE FINE.
HEH-HEH-HEH...
JA-JANG
PHEW—WHAT'D YOU THINK, SENSEI?
UM, YEAH...
THERE'S A LOT OF THINGS I COULD POINT OUT, BUT, UM...FOR STARTERS...
...DON'T YOU HAVE A VOCALIST?
UH!

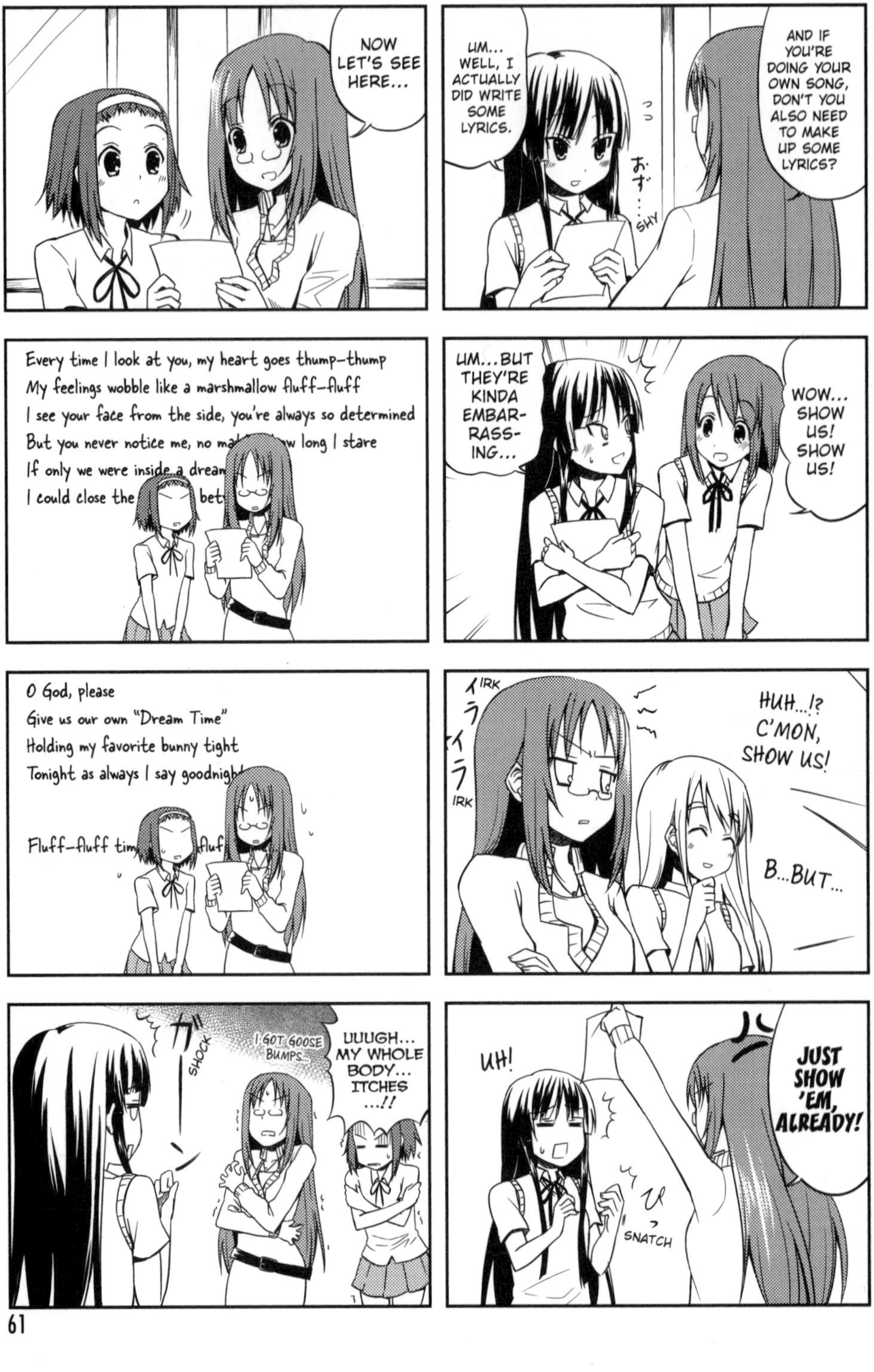
AND IF YOU'RE DOING YOUR OWN SONG, DON'T YOU ALSO NEED TO MAKE UP SOME LYRICS?
UM... WELL, I ACTUALLY DID WRITE SOME LYRICS.
おず…
SHY
WOW... SHOW US! SHOW US!
UM...BUT THEY'RE KINDA EMBARRASSING...
HUH...!? C'MON, SHOW US!
イラ IRK
イラ IRK
B...BUT...
JUST SHOW 'EM, ALREADY!
UH!
ひっ
SNATCH
NOW LET'S SEE HERE...
Every time I look at you, my heart goes thump-thump
My feelings wobble like a marshmallow fluff-fluff
I see your face from the side, you're always so determined
But you never notice me, no ma ow long I stare
If only we were inside a drean
I could close the bet
O God, please
Give us our own "Dream Time"
Holding my favorite bunny tight
Tonight as always I say goodnig
Fluff-fluff tim fluf
ガ
SHOCK
UUUGH... MY WHOLE BODY... ITCHES ...!!
I GOT GOOSE BUMPS...

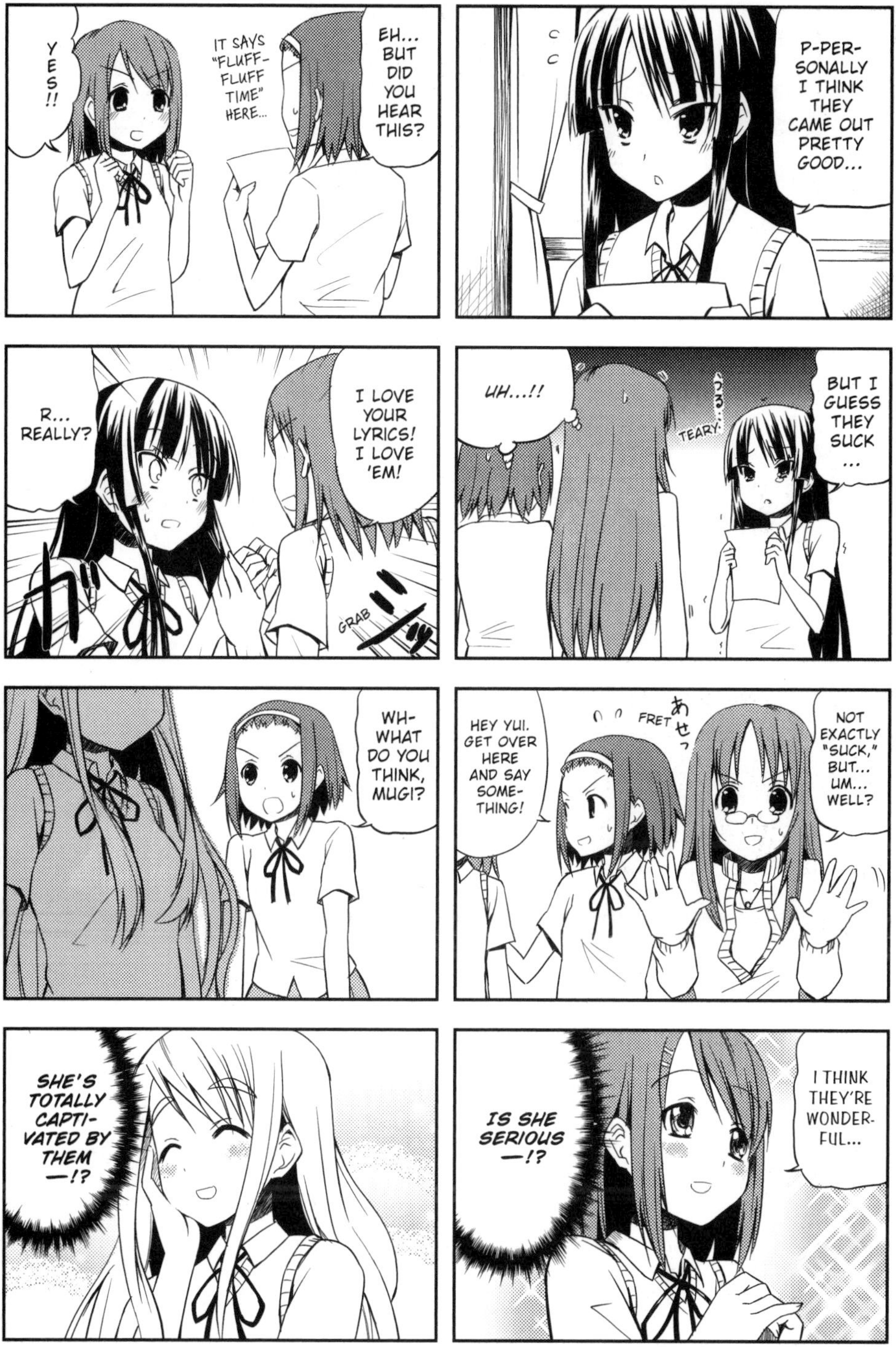
P-PERSONALLY I THINK THEY CAME OUT PRETTY GOOD...
BUT I GUESS THEY SUCK...
TEARY
UH...!!
NOT EXACTLY "SUCK," BUT... UM... WELL?
FRET
HEY YUI. GET OVER HERE AND SAY SOMETHING!
I THINK THEY'RE WONDERFUL...
IS SHE SERIOUS—!?
EH... BUT DID YOU HEAR THIS?
IT SAYS "FLUFF-FLUFF TIME" HERE...
YES!!
I LOVE YOUR LYRICS! I LOVE 'EM!
R... REALLY?
GRAB
WH-WHAT DO YOU THINK, MUGI?
SHE'S TOTALLY CAPTIVATED BY THEM—!?

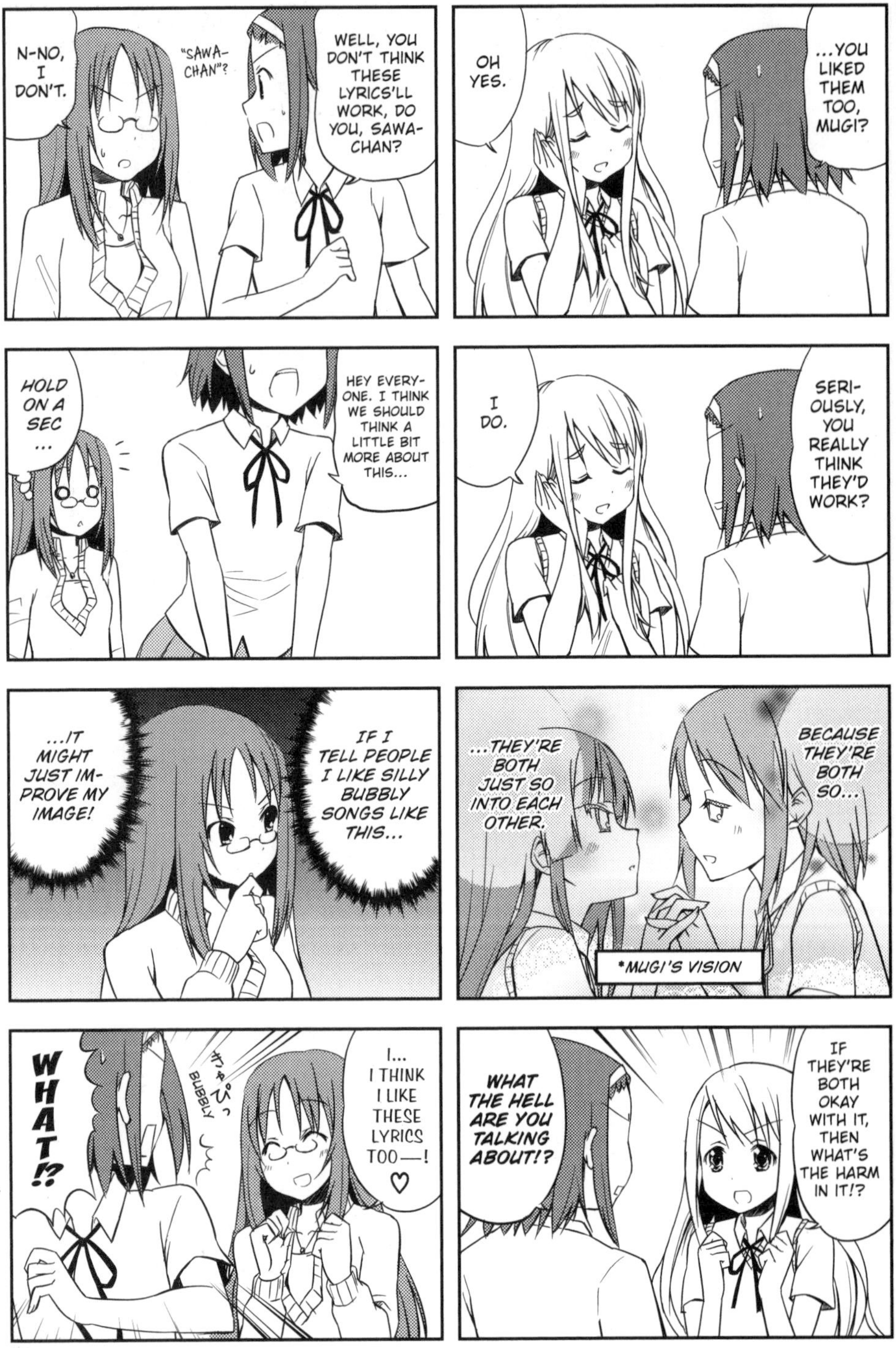
WELL, YOU DON'T THINK THESE LYRICS'LL WORK, DO YOU, SAWA-CHAN?
"SAWA-CHAN"?
N-NO, I DON'T.
HEY EVERY-ONE. I THINK WE SHOULD THINK A LITTLE BIT MORE ABOUT THIS...
HOLD ON A SEC...
IF I TELL PEOPLE I LIKE SILLY BUBBLY SONGS LIKE THIS...
...IT MIGHT JUST IM-PROVE MY IMAGE!
I... I THINK I LIKE THESE LYRICS TOO—! ♥
BUBBLY
WHAT!?
...YOU LIKED THEM TOO, MUGI?
OH YES.
SERI-OUSLY, YOU REALLY THINK THEY'D WORK?
I DO.
BECAUSE THEY'RE BOTH SO...
...THEY'RE BOTH JUST SO INTO EACH OTHER.
*MUGI'S VISION
IF THEY'RE BOTH OKAY WITH IT, THEN WHAT'S THE HARM IN IT!?
WHAT THE HELL ARE YOU TALKING ABOUT!?

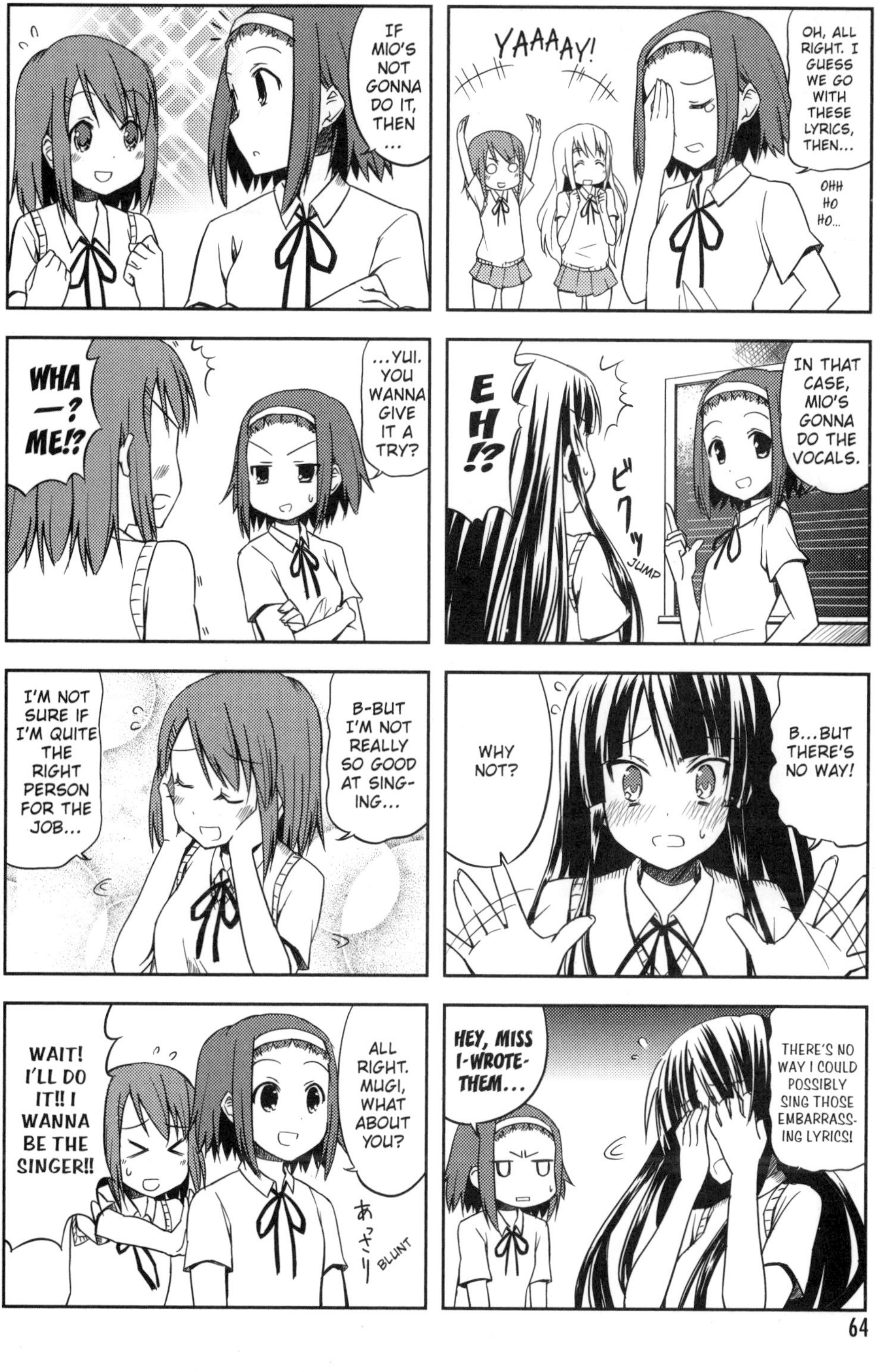
OH, ALL RIGHT. I GUESS WE GO WITH THESE LYRICS, THEN...
YAAAAY!
OHH HO HO...
IN THAT CASE, MIO'S GONNA DO THE VOCALS.
EH!?
ビクッ
JUMP
B...BUT THERE'S NO WAY!
WHY NOT?
THERE'S NO WAY I COULD POSSIBLY SING THOSE EMBARRASS-ING LYRICS!
HEY, MISS I-WROTE-THEM...
IF MIO'S NOT GONNA DO IT, THEN...
...YUI. YOU WANNA GIVE IT A TRY?
WHA—? ME!?
B-BUT I'M NOT REALLY SO GOOD AT SING-ING...
I'M NOT SURE IF I'M QUITE THE RIGHT PERSON FOR THE JOB...
ALL RIGHT. MUGI, WHAT ABOUT YOU?
WAIT! I'LL DO IT!! I WANNA BE THE SINGER!!
あっさり
BLUNT

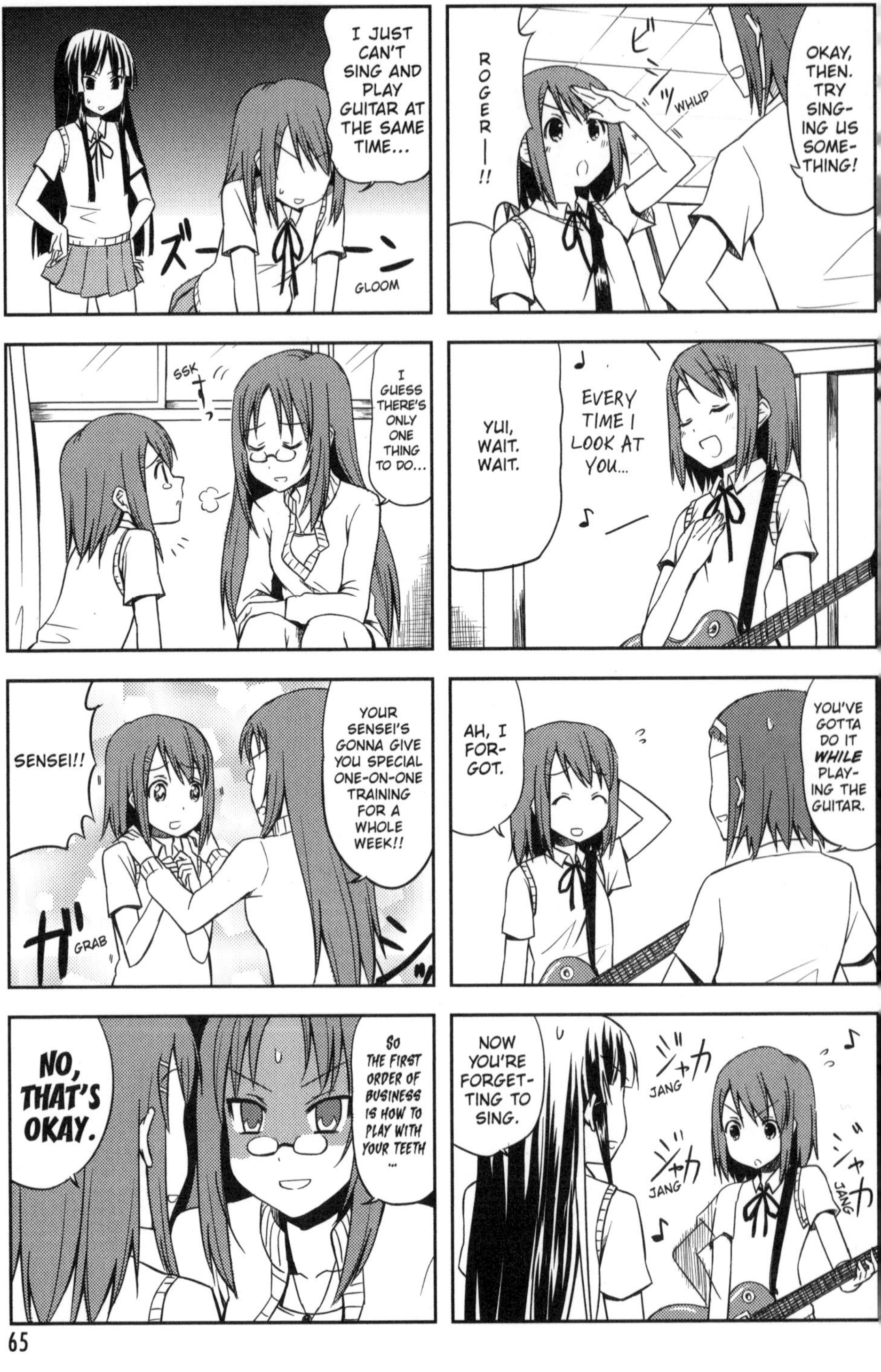

OKAY, THEN. TRY SINGING US SOMETHING!
ROGER—!!
WHUP
EVERY TIME I LOOK AT YOU...
YUI, WAIT. WAIT.
YOU'VE GOTTA DO IT *WHILE* PLAYING THE GUITAR.
AH, I FORGOT.
JANG
JANG
JANG
NOW YOU'RE FORGETTING TO SING.
I JUST CAN'T SING AND PLAY GUITAR AT THE SAME TIME...
GLOOM
SSK
I GUESS THERE'S ONLY ONE THING TO DO...
YOUR SENSEI'S GONNA GIVE YOU SPECIAL ONE-ON-ONE TRAINING FOR A WHOLE WEEK!!
SENSEI!!
GRAB
SO THE FIRST ORDER OF BUSINESS IS HOW TO PLAY WITH YOUR TEETH...
NO, THAT'S OKAY.

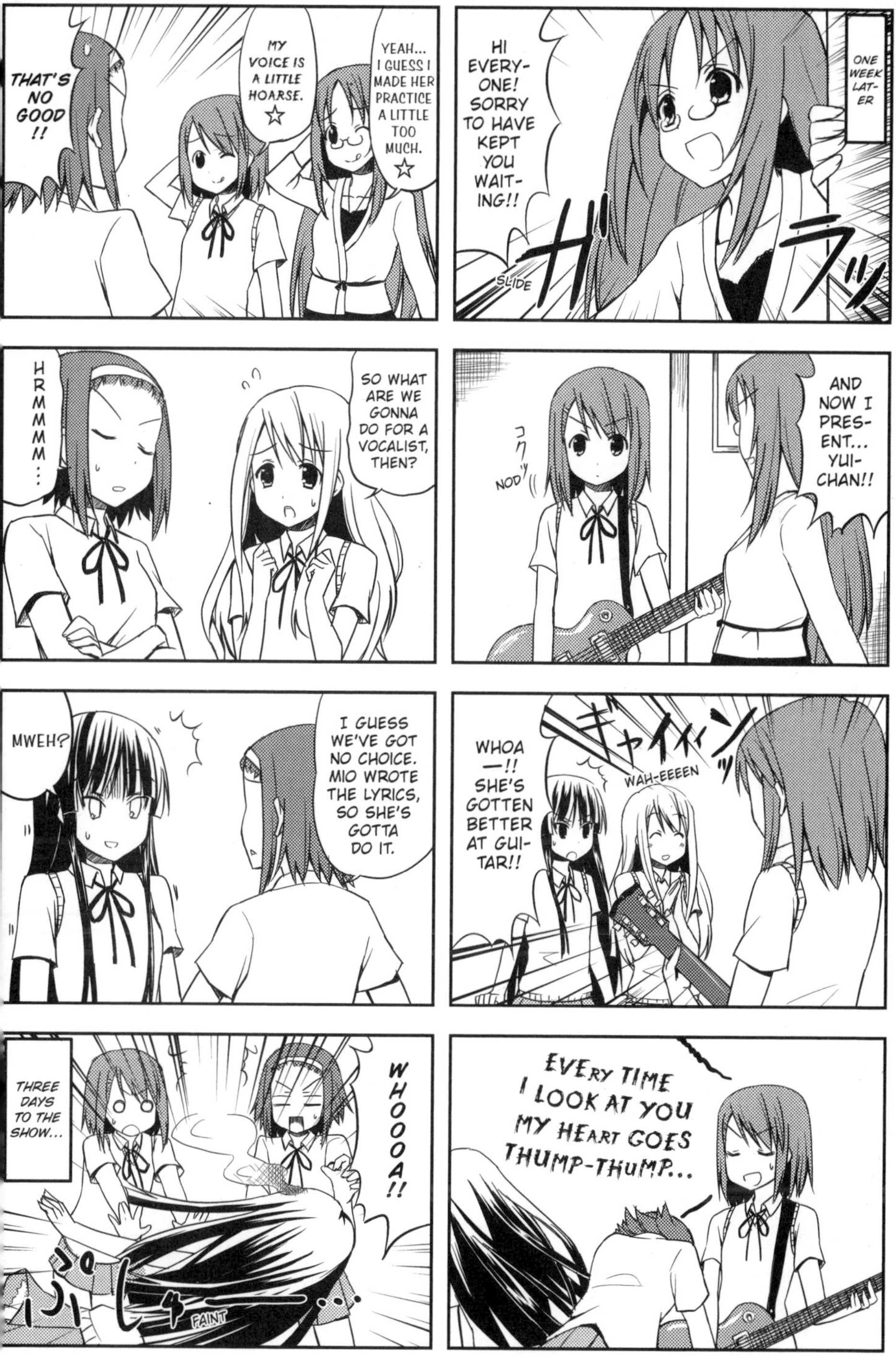
ONE WEEK LATER
HI EVERY-ONE! SORRY TO HAVE KEPT YOU WAIT-ING!!
ガラッ
SLIDE
AND NOW I PRES-ENT... YUI-CHAN!!
コクッ
NOD
ギャイィンッ
WAH-EEEEN
WHOA —!! SHE'S GOTTEN BETTER AT GUI-TAR!!
EVERY TIME I LOOK AT YOU MY HEART GOES THUMP-THUMP...
YEAH... I GUESS I MADE HER PRACTICE A LITTLE TOO MUCH. ☆
MY VOICE IS A LITTLE HOARSE. ☆
THAT'S NO GOOD!!
SO WHAT ARE WE GONNA DO FOR A VOCALIST, THEN?
HRMMMM...
I GUESS WE'VE GOT NO CHOICE. MIO WROTE THE LYRICS, SO SHE'S GOTTA DO IT.
MWEH?
THREE DAYS TO THE SHOW...
WHOOOOA!!
ぷしゅー...
FAINT

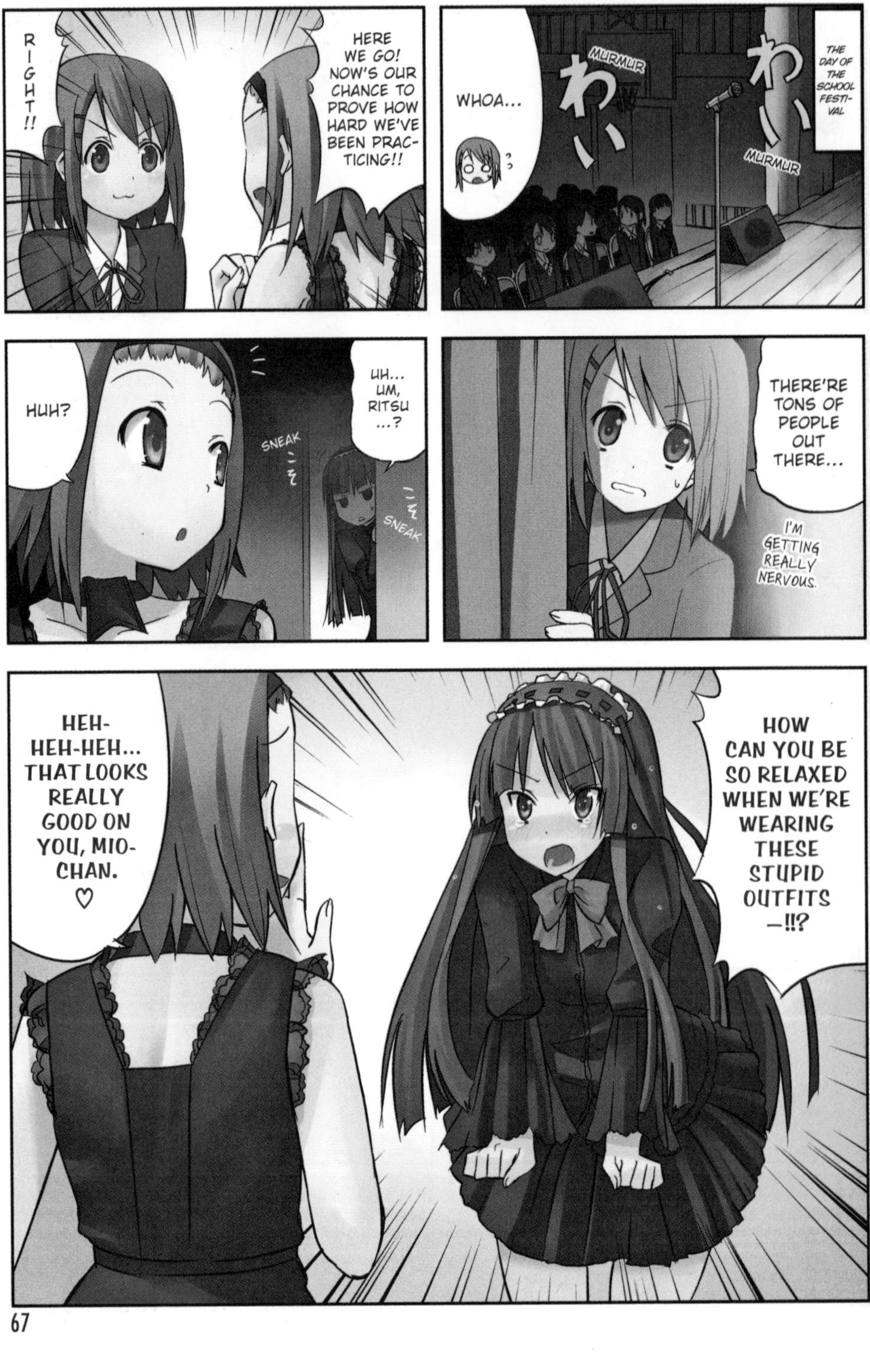
THE DAY OF THE SCHOOL FESTIVAL
わい
MURMUR
わい
MURMUR
WHOA...
HERE WE GO! NOW'S OUR CHANCE TO PROVE HOW HARD WE'VE BEEN PRACTICING!!
RIGHT!!
THERE'RE TONS OF PEOPLE OUT THERE...
I'M GETTING REALLY NERVOUS.
UH... UM, RITSU...?
SNEAK
SNEAK
HUH?
HOW CAN YOU BE SO RELAXED WHEN WE'RE WEARING THESE STUPID OUTFITS—!!?
HEH-HEH-HEH... THAT LOOKS REALLY GOOD ON YOU, MIO-CHAN. ♡

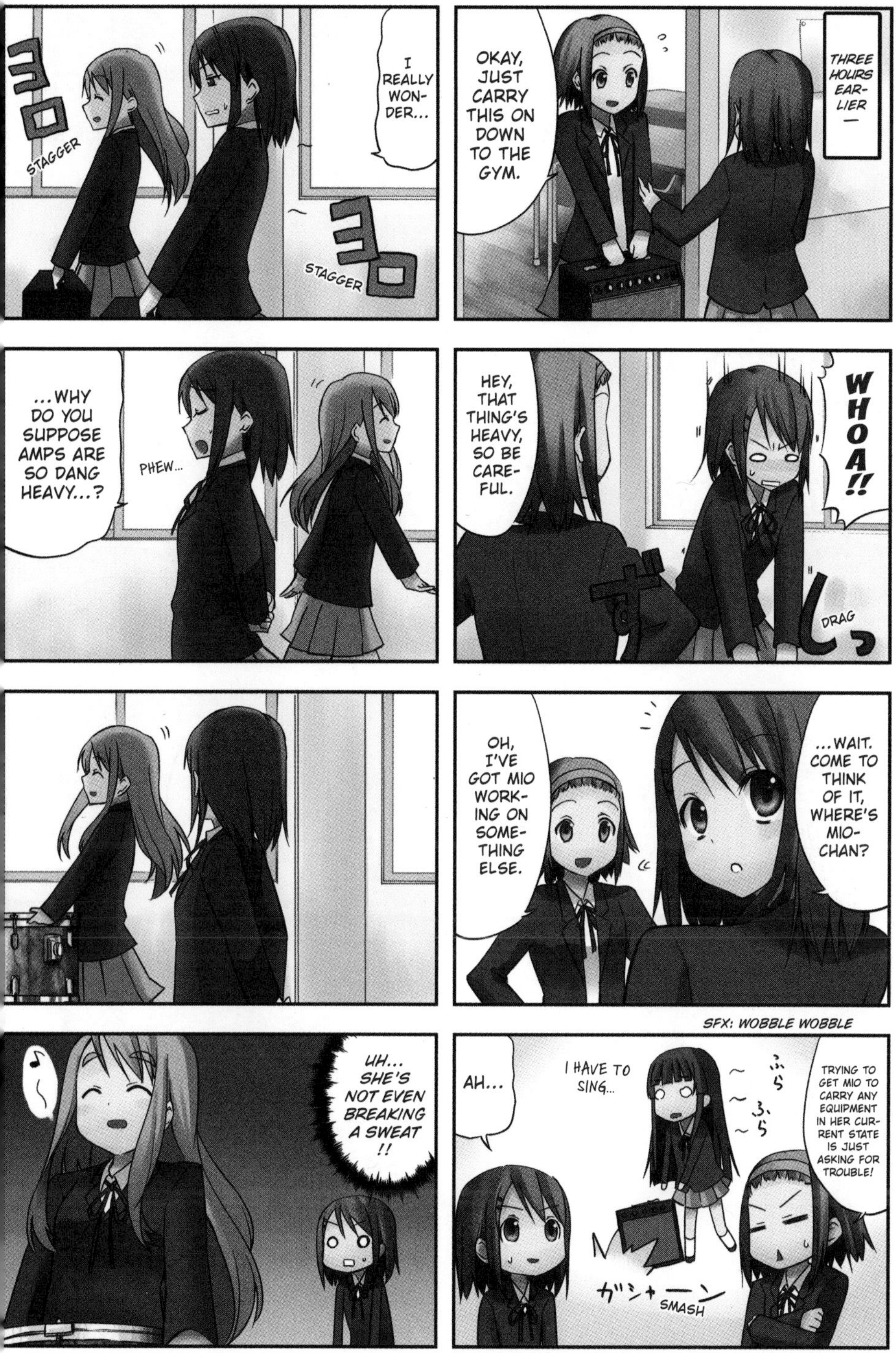
THREE HOURS EARLIER—
OKAY, JUST CARRY THIS ON DOWN TO THE GYM.
WHOA!!
HEY, THAT THING'S HEAVY, SO BE CAREFUL.
DRAG
...WAIT. COME TO THINK OF IT, WHERE'S MIO-CHAN?
OH, I'VE GOT MIO WORKING ON SOMETHING ELSE.
SFX: WOBBLE WOBBLE
TRYING TO GET MIO TO CARRY ANY EQUIPMENT IN HER CURRENT STATE IS JUST ASKING FOR TROUBLE!
ふら ふら
I HAVE TO SING...
AH...
ガシャーン
SMASH
I REALLY WONDER...
ヨロ
STAGGER
ヨロ
STAGGER
PHEW...
...WHY DO YOU SUPPOSE AMPS ARE SO DANG HEAVY...?
UH... SHE'S NOT EVEN BREAKING A SWEAT!!

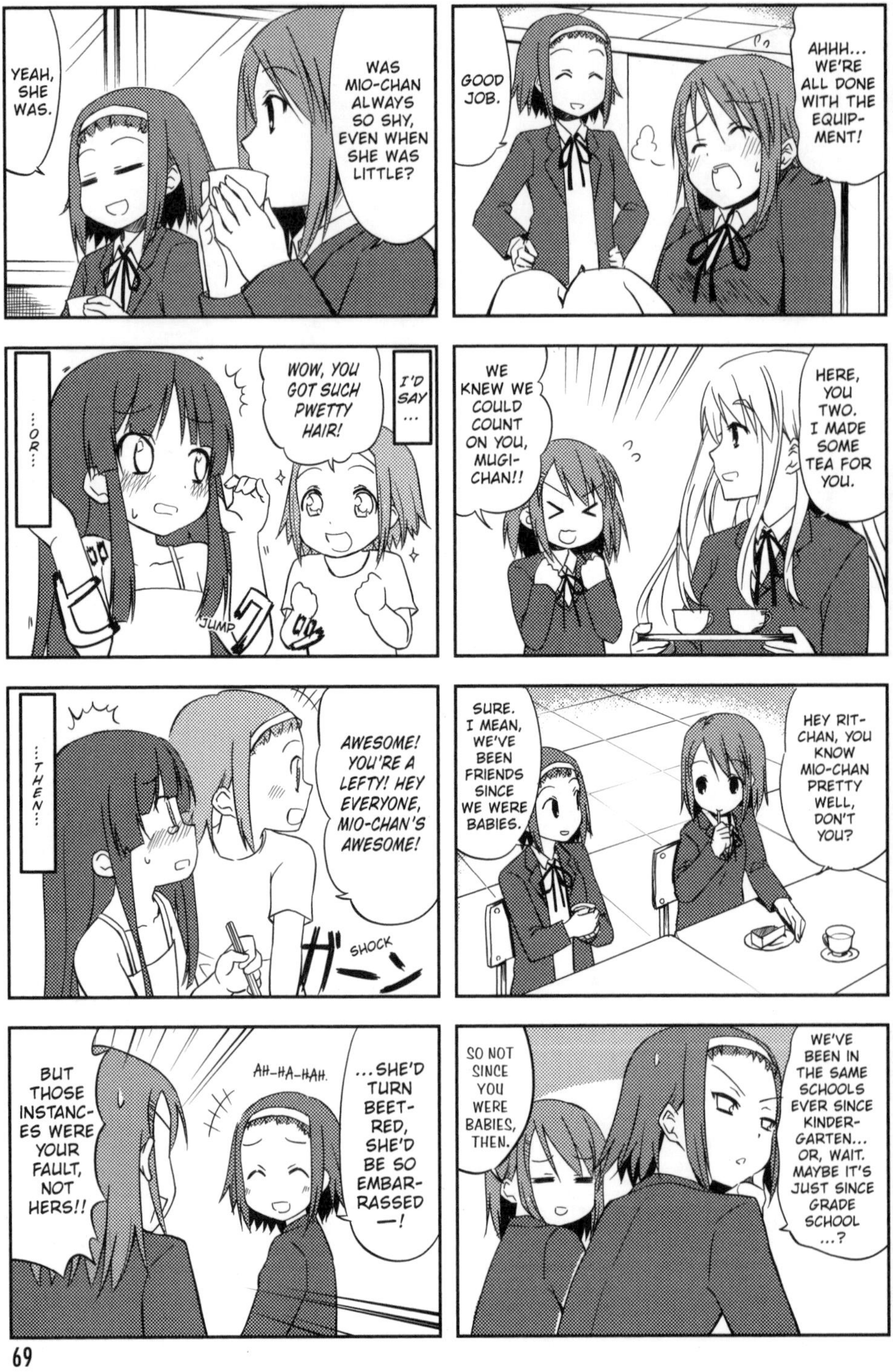
AHHH... WE'RE ALL DONE WITH THE EQUIP-MENT!
GOOD JOB.
HERE, YOU TWO. I MADE SOME TEA FOR YOU.
WE KNEW WE COULD COUNT ON YOU, MUGI-CHAN!!
HEY RIT-CHAN, YOU KNOW MIO-CHAN PRETTY WELL, DON'T YOU?
SURE. I MEAN, WE'VE BEEN FRIENDS SINCE WE WERE BABIES.
WE'VE BEEN IN THE SAME SCHOOLS EVER SINCE KINDER-GARTEN... OR, WAIT. MAYBE IT'S JUST SINCE GRADE SCHOOL ...?
SO NOT SINCE YOU WERE BABIES, THEN.
WAS MIO-CHAN ALWAYS SO SHY, EVEN WHEN SHE WAS LITTLE?
YEAH, SHE WAS.
I'D SAY...
WOW, YOU GOT SUCH PWETTY HAIR!
...OR...
JUMP
AWESOME! YOU'RE A LEFTY! HEY EVERYONE, MIO-CHAN'S AWESOME!
...THEN...
SHOCK
ガーン
...SHE'D TURN BEET-RED, SHE'D BE SO EMBAR-RASSED—!
AH-HA-HAH.
BUT THOSE INSTANC-ES WERE YOUR FAULT, NOT HERS!!

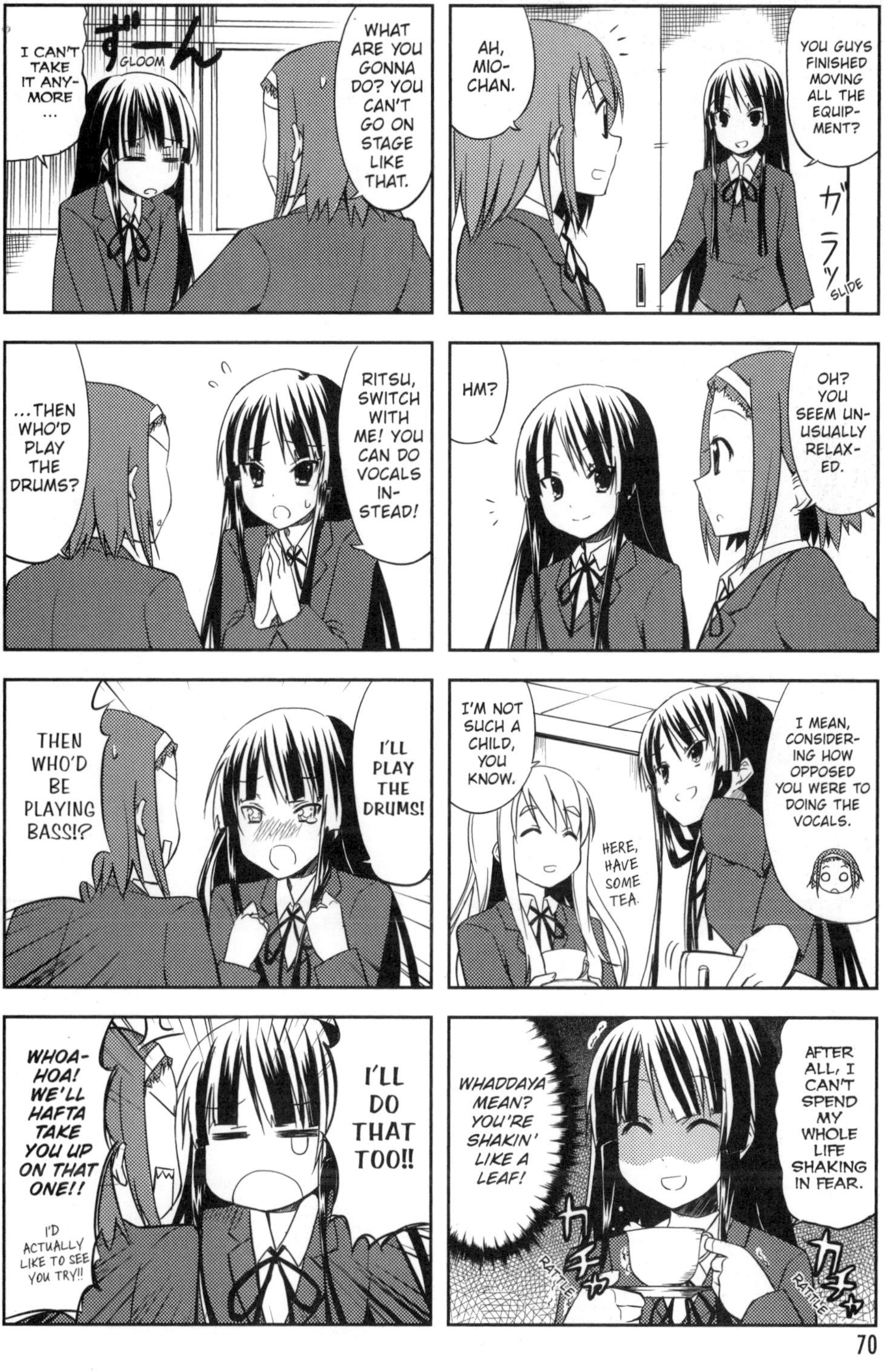
YOU GUYS FINISHED MOVING ALL THE EQUIP-MENT?
ガラッ
SLIDE
AH, MIO-CHAN.
OH? YOU SEEM UN-USUALLY RELAX-ED.
HM?
I MEAN, CONSIDER-ING HOW OPPOSED YOU WERE TO DOING THE VOCALS.
HERE, HAVE SOME TEA.
I'M NOT SUCH A CHILD, YOU KNOW.
AFTER ALL, I CAN'T SPEND MY WHOLE LIFE SHAKING IN FEAR.
WHADDAYA MEAN? YOU'RE SHAKIN' LIKE A LEAF!
カチャ
RATTLE
カチャ
RATTLE
ずーん
GLOOM
I CAN'T TAKE IT ANY-MORE ...
WHAT ARE YOU GONNA DO? YOU CAN'T GO ON STAGE LIKE THAT.
RITSU, SWITCH WITH ME! YOU CAN DO VOCALS IN-STEAD!
...THEN WHO'D PLAY THE DRUMS?
I'LL PLAY THE DRUMS!
THEN WHO'D BE PLAYING BASS!?
I'LL DO THAT TOO!!
WHOA-HOA! WE'LL HAFTA TAKE YOU UP ON THAT ONE!!
I'D ACTUALLY LIKE TO SEE YOU TRY!!

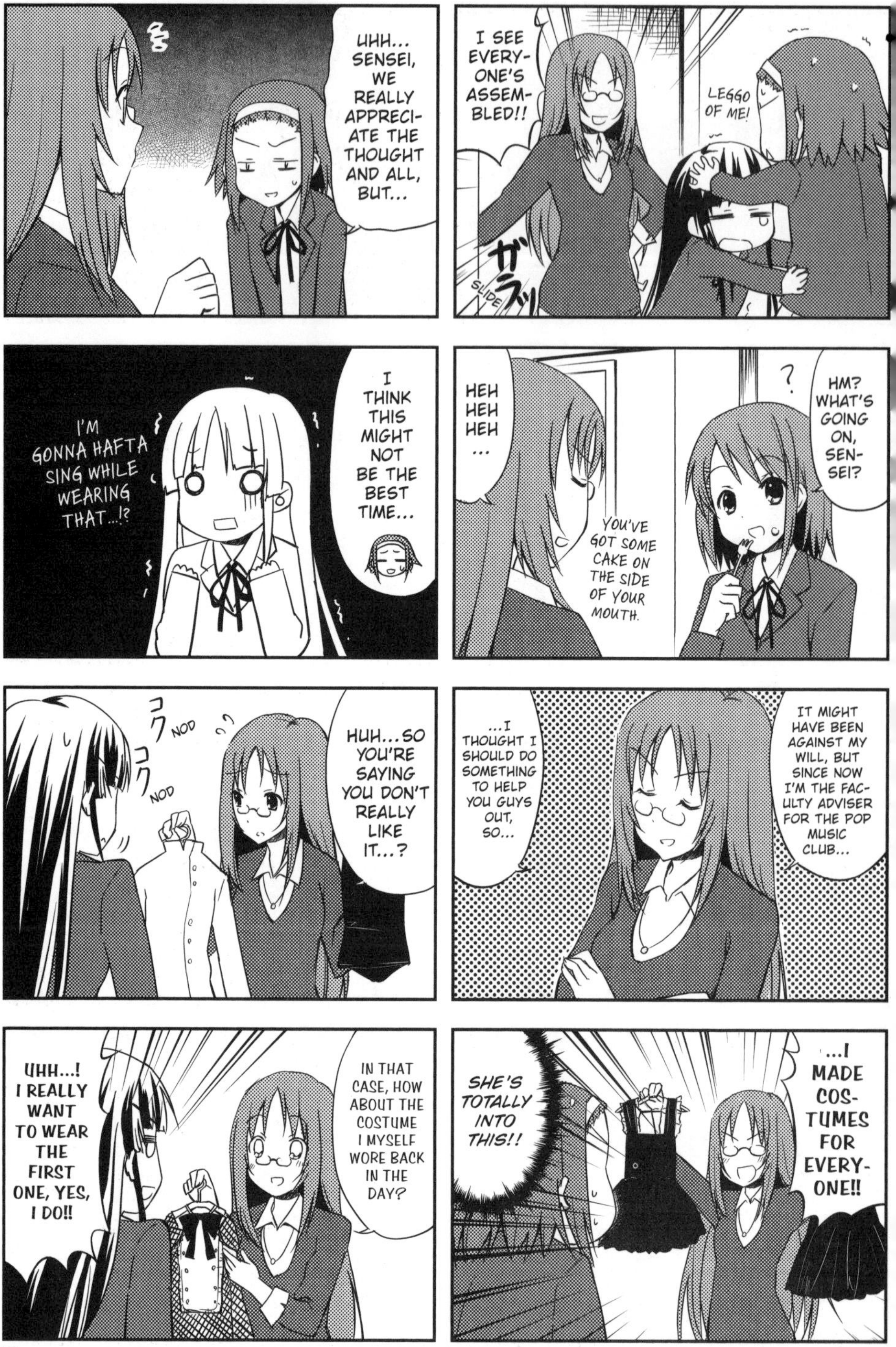
I SEE EVERY-ONE'S ASSEM-BLED!!
LEGGO OF ME!
ガラッ SLIDE
HM? WHAT'S GOING ON, SEN-SEI?
?
HEH HEH HEH ...
YOU'VE GOT SOME CAKE ON THE SIDE OF YOUR MOUTH.
IT MIGHT HAVE BEEN AGAINST MY WILL, BUT SINCE NOW I'M THE FAC-ULTY ADVISER FOR THE POP MUSIC CLUB...
...I THOUGHT I SHOULD DO SOMETHING TO HELP YOU GUYS OUT, SO...
...I MADE COS-TUMES FOR EVERY-ONE!!
SHE'S TOTALLY INTO THIS!!
UHH... SENSEI, WE REALLY APPRECI-ATE THE THOUGHT AND ALL, BUT...
I THINK THIS MIGHT NOT BE THE BEST TIME...
I'M GONNA HAFTA SING WHILE WEARING THAT...!?
HUH...SO YOU'RE SAYING YOU DON'T REALLY LIKE IT...?
コク NOD
コク NOD
IN THAT CASE, HOW ABOUT THE COSTUME I MYSELF WORE BACK IN THE DAY?
UHH...! I REALLY WANT TO WEAR THE FIRST ONE, YES, I DO!!

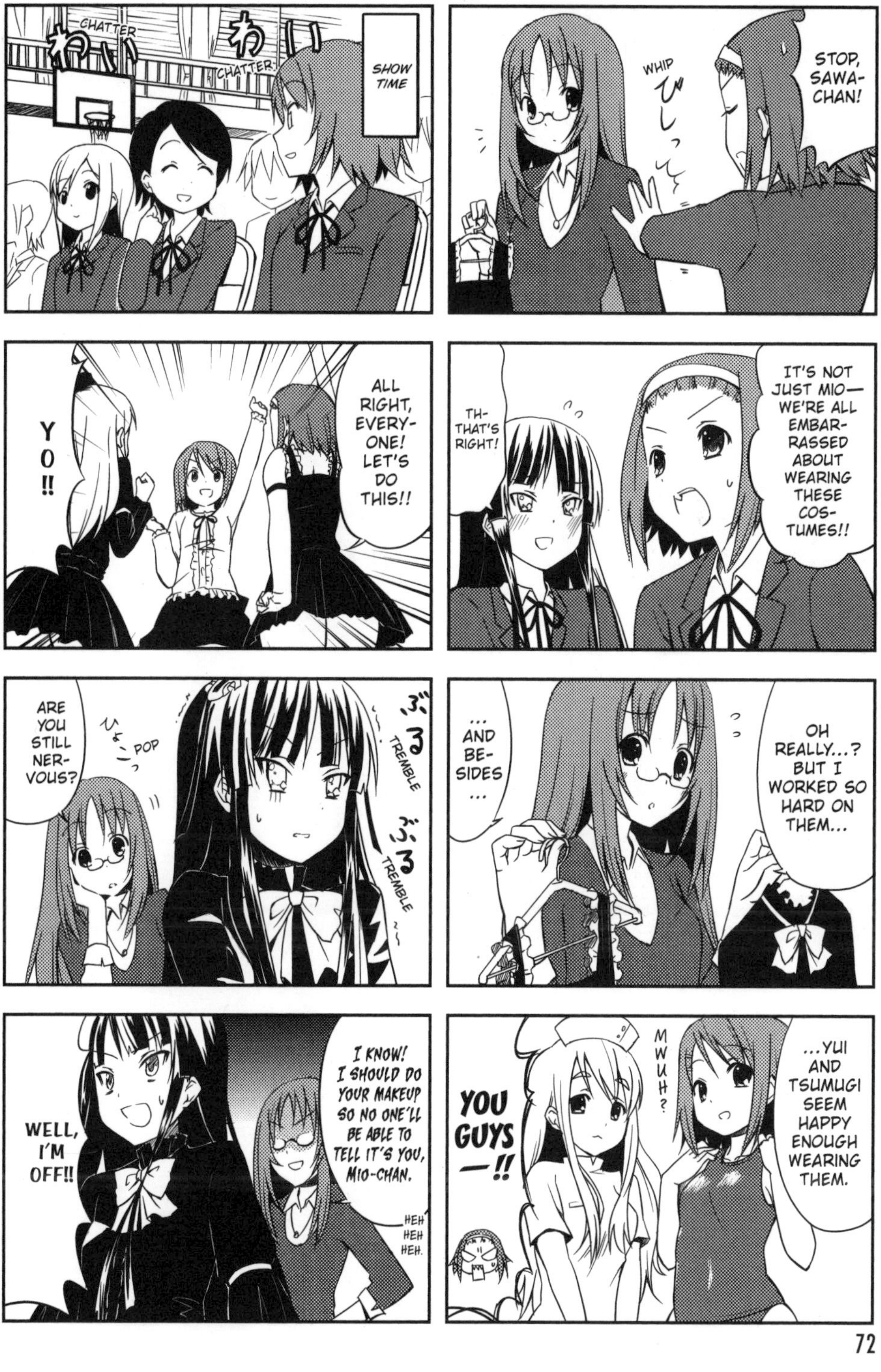
STOP, SAWA-CHAN!
WHIP
びしっ
IT'S NOT JUST MIO—WE'RE ALL EMBARRASSED ABOUT WEARING THESE COSTUMES!!
TH-THAT'S RIGHT!
OH REALLY...? BUT I WORKED SO HARD ON THEM...
...AND BESIDES...
...YUI AND TSUMUGI SEEM HAPPY ENOUGH WEARING THEM.
MWUH?
YOU GUYS—!!
SHOW TIME
わい CHATTER
わい CHATTER
ALL RIGHT, EVERYONE! LET'S DO THIS!!
YO!!
ARE YOU STILL NERVOUS?
POP
ぶる TREMBLE
ぶる TREMBLE
I KNOW! I SHOULD DO YOUR MAKEUP SO NO ONE'LL BE ABLE TO TELL IT'S YOU, MIO-CHAN.
WELL, I'M OFF!!
HEH HEH HEH.

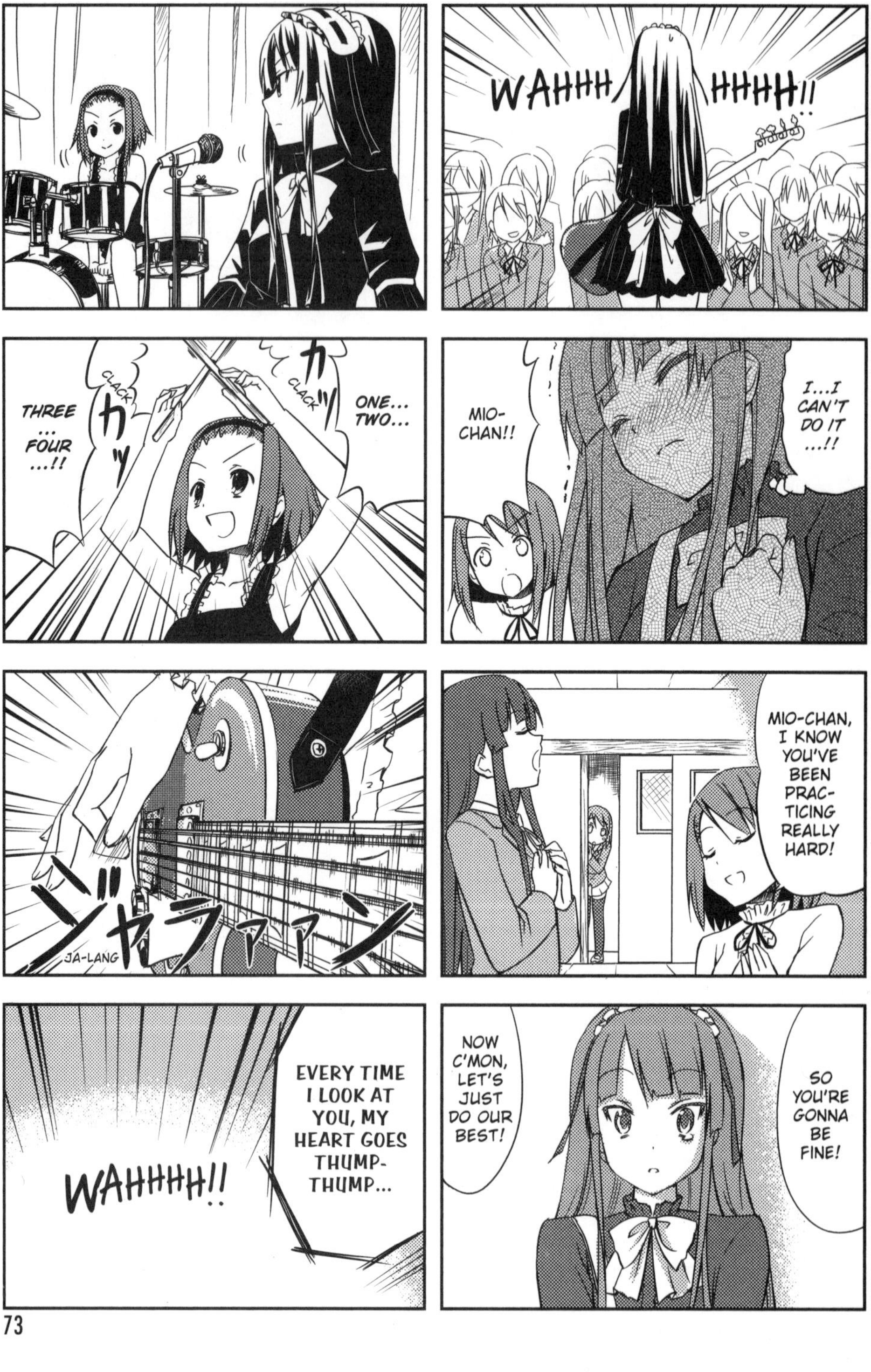
WAHHH HHHH!!
I...I CAN'T DO IT ...!!
MIO-CHAN!!
MIO-CHAN, I KNOW YOU'VE BEEN PRAC-TICING REALLY HARD!
SO YOU'RE GONNA BE FINE!
NOW C'MON, LET'S JUST DO OUR BEST!
ONE... TWO...
CLACK
カッ
CLACK
カッ
THREE ... FOUR ...!!
ジャラァァン
JA-LANG
EVERY TIME I LOOK AT YOU, MY HEART GOES THUMP-THUMP...
WAHHHH!!

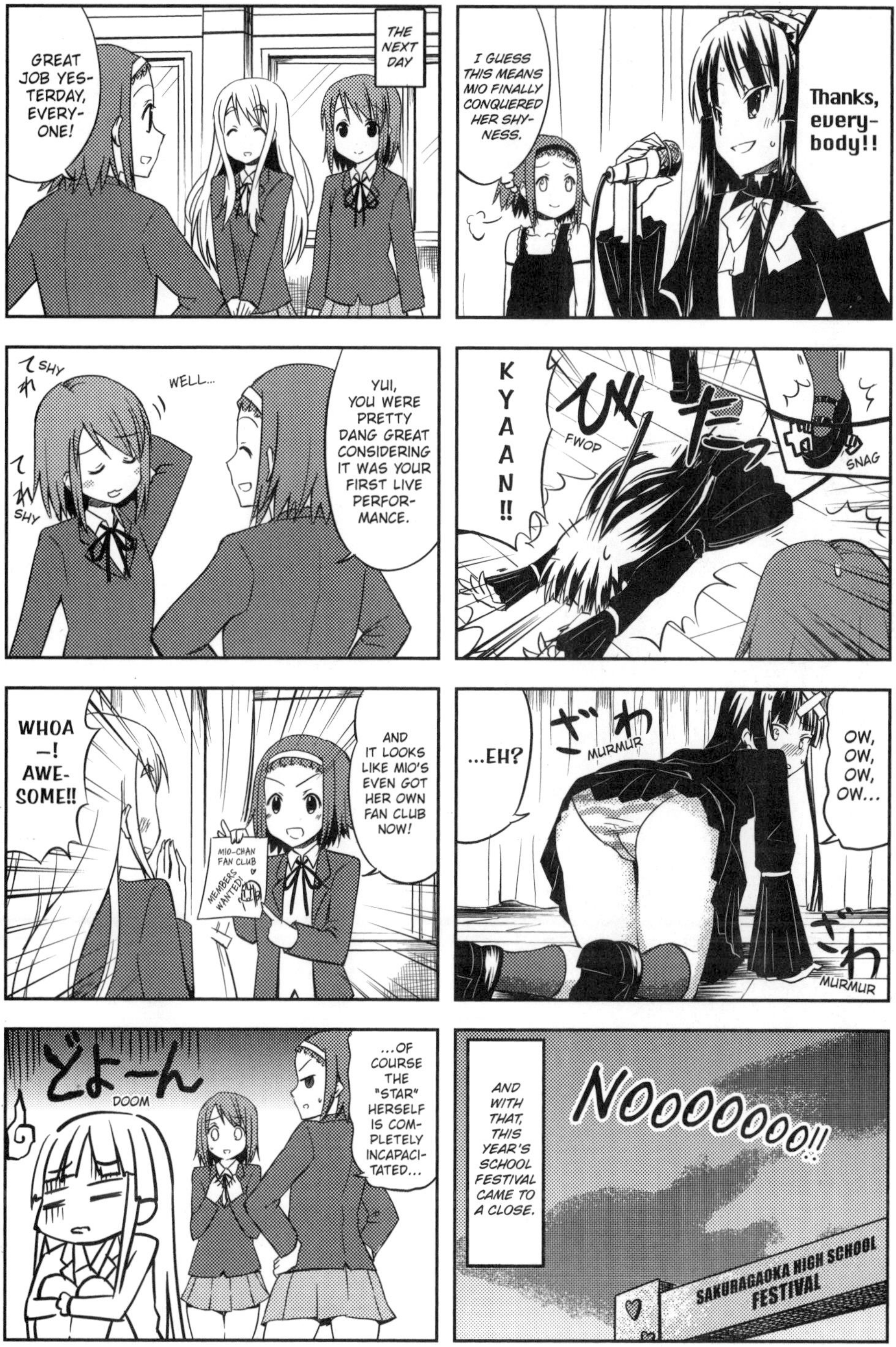
Thanks, everybody!!
I GUESS THIS MEANS MIO FINALLY CONQUERED HER SHYNESS.
SNAG
びたっ
FWOP
KYAAN!!
OW, OW, OW, OW...
ざわ
MURMUR
...EH?
ざわ
MURMUR
NOOOOOOO!!
AND WITH THAT, THIS YEAR'S SCHOOL FESTIVAL CAME TO A CLOSE.
SAKURAGAOKA HIGH SCHOOL FESTIVAL
THE NEXT DAY
GREAT JOB YESTERDAY, EVERYONE!
YUI, YOU WERE PRETTY DANG GREAT CONSIDERING IT WAS YOUR FIRST LIVE PERFORMANCE.
WELL...
てれ
SHY
てれ
SHY
AND IT LOOKS LIKE MIO'S EVEN GOT HER OWN FAN CLUB NOW!
MIO-CHAN FAN CLUB
MEMBERS WANTED!
WHOA—! AWESOME!!
...OF COURSE THE "STAR" HERSELF IS COMPLETELY INCAPACITATED...
どよーん
DOOM

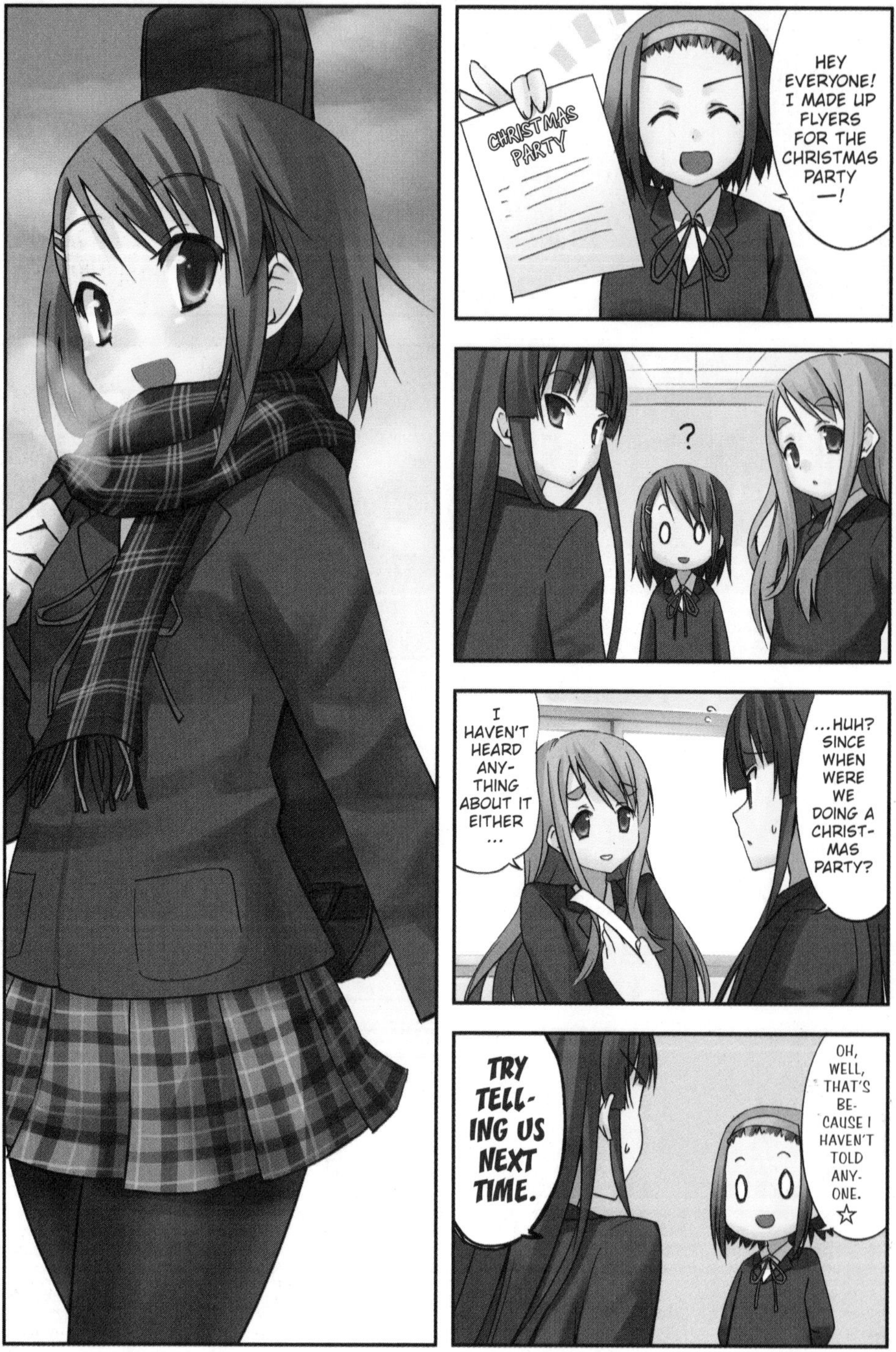
HEY EVERYONE! I MADE UP FLYERS FOR THE CHRISTMAS PARTY —!
CHRISTMAS PARTY
?
...HUH? SINCE WHEN WERE WE DOING A CHRISTMAS PARTY?
I HAVEN'T HEARD ANYTHING ABOUT IT EITHER...
OH, WELL, THAT'S BECAUSE I HAVEN'T TOLD ANYONE. ☆
TRY TELLING US NEXT TIME.

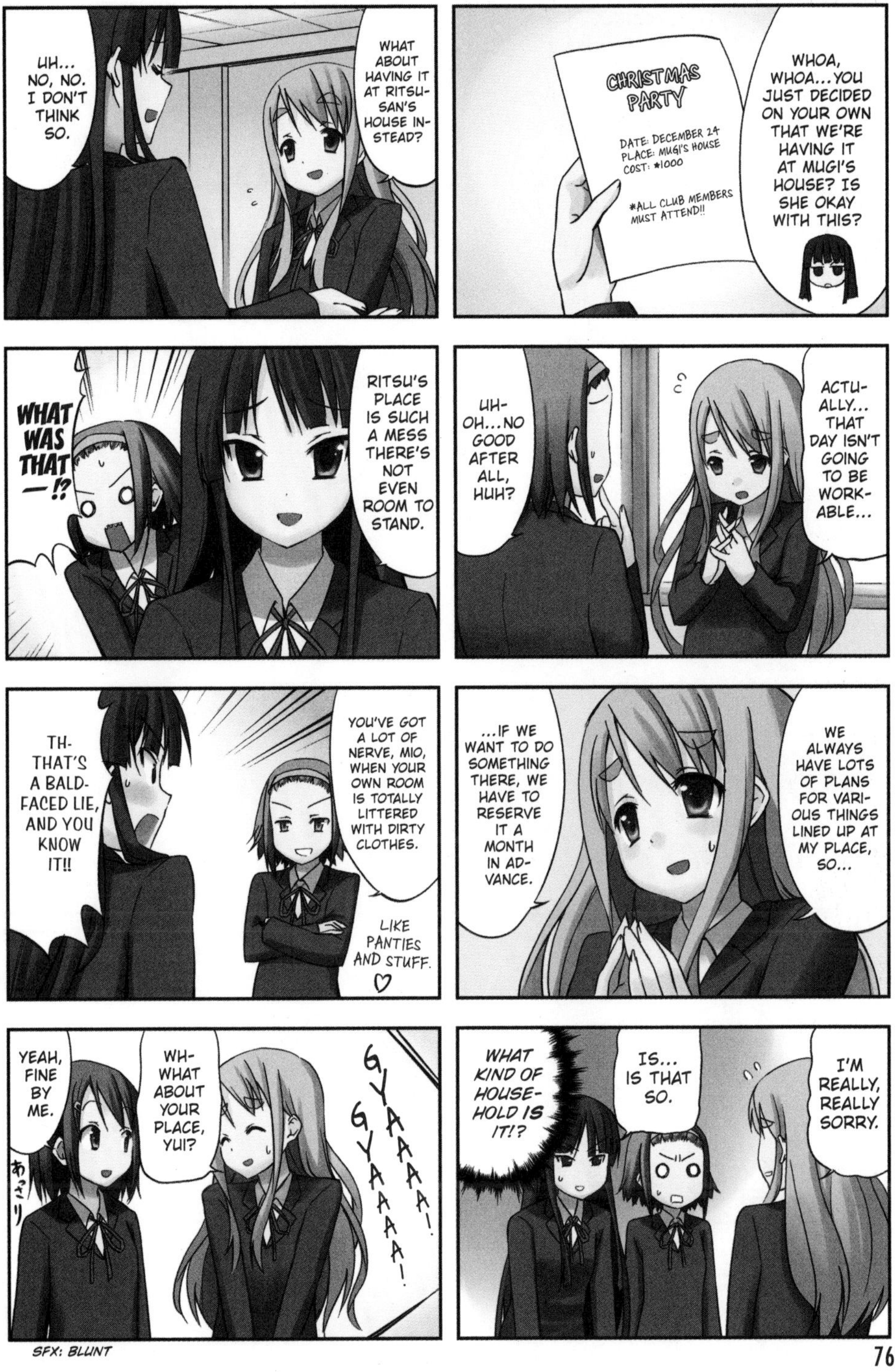
CHRISTMAS PARTY
DATE: DECEMBER 24
PLACE: MUGI'S HOUSE
COST: ¥1000
*ALL CLUB MEMBERS MUST ATTEND!!
WHOA, WHOA...YOU JUST DECIDED ON YOUR OWN THAT WE'RE HAVING IT AT MUGI'S HOUSE? IS SHE OKAY WITH THIS?
ACTU-ALLY... THAT DAY ISN'T GOING TO BE WORK-ABLE...
UH-OH...NO GOOD AFTER ALL, HUH?
WE ALWAYS HAVE LOTS OF PLANS FOR VARI-OUS THINGS LINED UP AT MY PLACE, SO...
...IF WE WANT TO DO SOMETHING THERE, WE HAVE TO RESERVE IT A MONTH IN AD-VANCE.
I'M REALLY, REALLY SORRY.
IS... IS THAT SO.
WHAT KIND OF HOUSE-HOLD IS IT!?
WHAT ABOUT HAVING IT AT RITSU-SAN'S HOUSE IN-STEAD?
UH... NO, NO. I DON'T THINK SO.
RITSU'S PLACE IS SUCH A MESS THERE'S NOT EVEN ROOM TO STAND.
WHAT WAS THAT—!?
YOU'VE GOT A LOT OF NERVE, MIO, WHEN YOUR OWN ROOM IS TOTALLY LITTERED WITH DIRTY CLOTHES.
LIKE PANTIES AND STUFF. ♡
TH-THAT'S A BALD-FACED LIE, AND YOU KNOW IT!!
GYAAAAA! GYAAAAAA!
WH-WHAT ABOUT YOUR PLACE, YUI?
YEAH, FINE BY ME.
あっさり

SFX: BLUNT

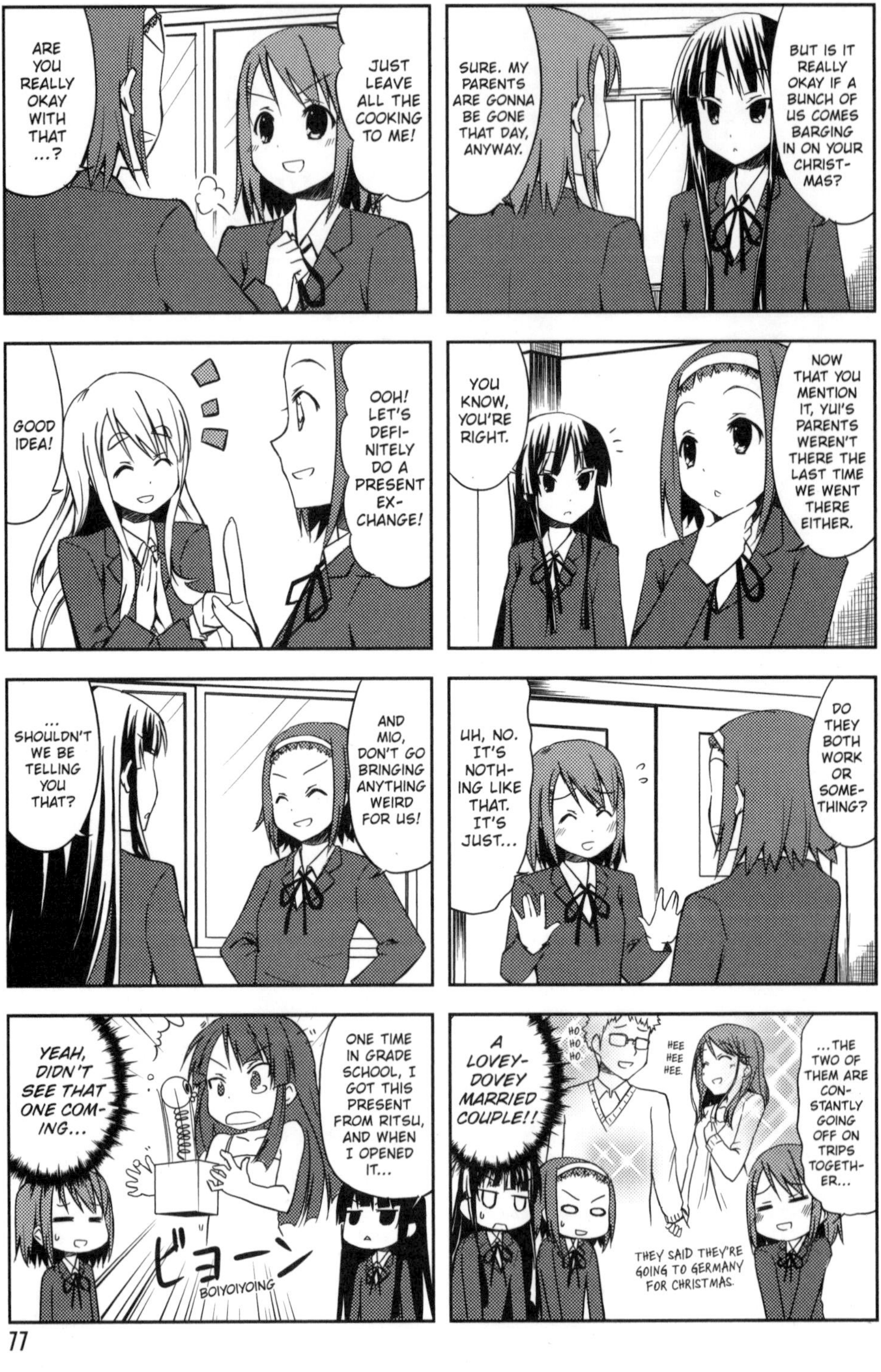
BUT IS IT REALLY OKAY IF A BUNCH OF US COMES BARGING IN ON YOUR CHRISTMAS?
SURE. MY PARENTS ARE GONNA BE GONE THAT DAY, ANYWAY.
NOW THAT YOU MENTION IT, YUI'S PARENTS WEREN'T THERE THE LAST TIME WE WENT THERE EITHER.
YOU KNOW, YOU'RE RIGHT.
DO THEY BOTH WORK OR SOMETHING?
UH, NO. IT'S NOTHING LIKE THAT. IT'S JUST...
...THE TWO OF THEM ARE CONSTANTLY GOING OFF ON TRIPS TOGETHER...
HEE HEE HEE.
HO HO HO.
A LOVEY-DOVEY MARRIED COUPLE!!
THEY SAID THEY'RE GOING TO GERMANY FOR CHRISTMAS.
JUST LEAVE ALL THE COOKING TO ME!
ARE YOU REALLY OKAY WITH THAT ...?
OOH! LET'S DEFINITELY DO A PRESENT EXCHANGE!
GOOD IDEA!
AND MIO, DON'T GO BRINGING ANYTHING WEIRD FOR US!
... SHOULDN'T WE BE TELLING YOU THAT?
ONE TIME IN GRADE SCHOOL, I GOT THIS PRESENT FROM RITSU, AND WHEN I OPENED IT...
YEAH, DIDN'T SEE THAT ONE COMING...
ビョーン
BOIYOIYOING

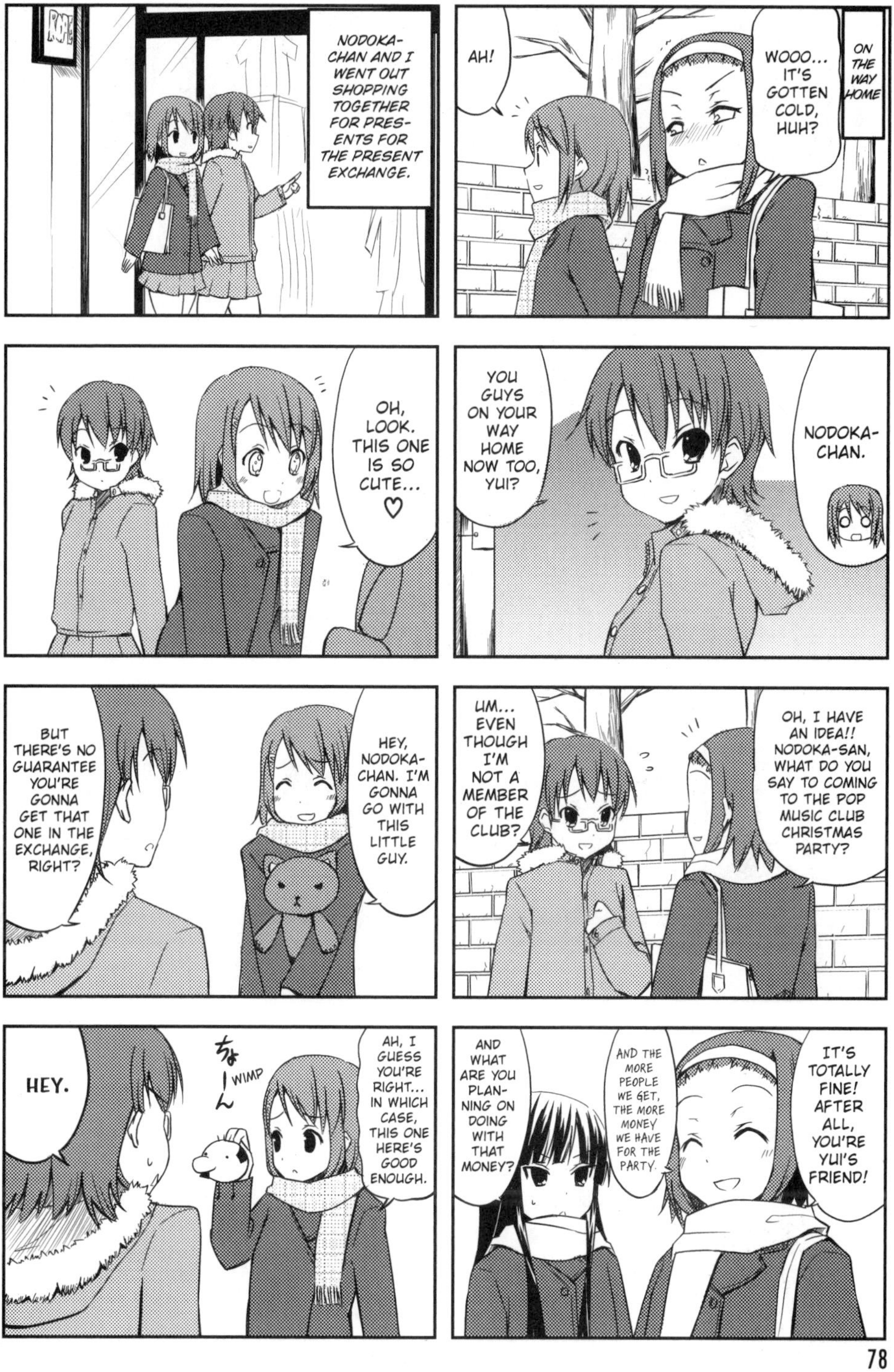
ON THE WAY HOME
WOOO... IT'S GOTTEN COLD, HUH?
AH!
NODOKA-CHAN.
YOU GUYS ON YOUR WAY HOME NOW TOO, YUI?
OH, I HAVE AN IDEA!! NODOKA-SAN, WHAT DO YOU SAY TO COMING TO THE POP MUSIC CLUB CHRISTMAS PARTY?
UM... EVEN THOUGH I'M NOT A MEMBER OF THE CLUB?
IT'S TOTALLY FINE! AFTER ALL, YOU'RE YUI'S FRIEND!
AND THE MORE PEOPLE WE GET, THE MORE MONEY WE HAVE FOR THE PARTY.
AND WHAT ARE YOU PLAN-NING ON DOING WITH THAT MONEY?
NODOKA-CHAN AND I WENT OUT SHOPPING TOGETHER FOR PRES-ENTS FOR THE PRESENT EXCHANGE.
OH, LOOK. THIS ONE IS SO CUTE... ♡
HEY, NODOKA-CHAN. I'M GONNA GO WITH THIS LITTLE GUY.
BUT THERE'S NO GUARANTEE YOU'RE GONNA GET THAT ONE IN THE EXCHANGE, RIGHT?
AH, I GUESS YOU'RE RIGHT... IN WHICH CASE, THIS ONE HERE'S GOOD ENOUGH.
ちょ～ん WIMP
HEY.

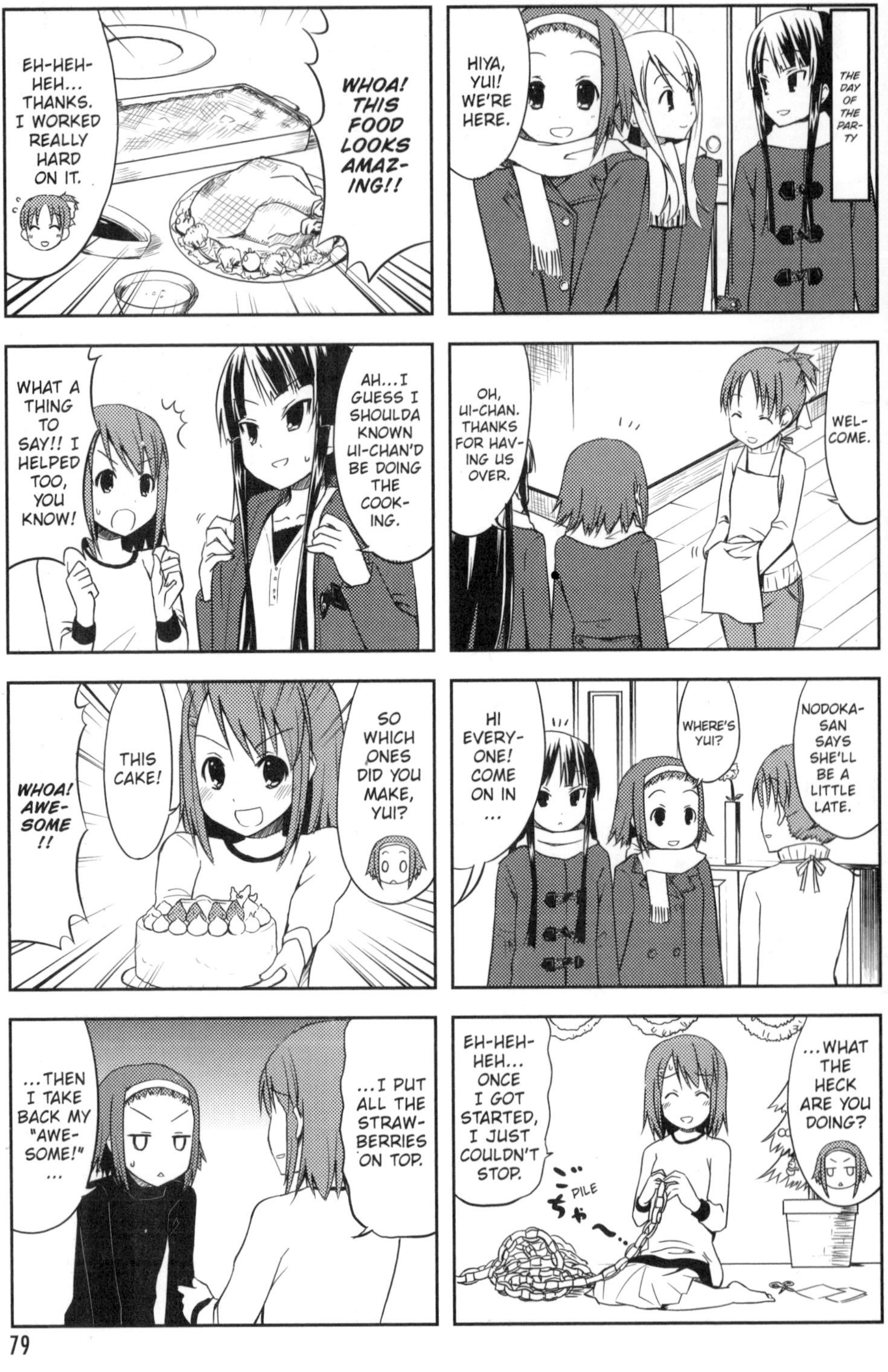
THE DAY OF THE PARTY
HIYA, YUI! WE'RE HERE.
WELCOME.
OH, UI-CHAN. THANKS FOR HAVING US OVER.
NODOKA-SAN SAYS SHE'LL BE A LITTLE LATE.
WHERE'S YUI?
HI EVERYONE! COME ON IN ...
...WHAT THE HECK ARE YOU DOING?
EH-HEH-HEH... ONCE I GOT STARTED, I JUST COULDN'T STOP.
PILE
WHOA! THIS FOOD LOOKS AMAZING!!
EH-HEH-HEH... THANKS. I WORKED REALLY HARD ON IT.
AH...I GUESS I SHOULDA KNOWN UI-CHAN'D BE DOING THE COOKING.
WHAT A THING TO SAY!! I HELPED TOO, YOU KNOW!
SO WHICH ONES DID YOU MAKE, YUI?
THIS CAKE!
WHOA! AWESOME!!
...I PUT ALL THE STRAWBERRIES ON TOP.
...THEN I TAKE BACK MY "AWESOME!" ...

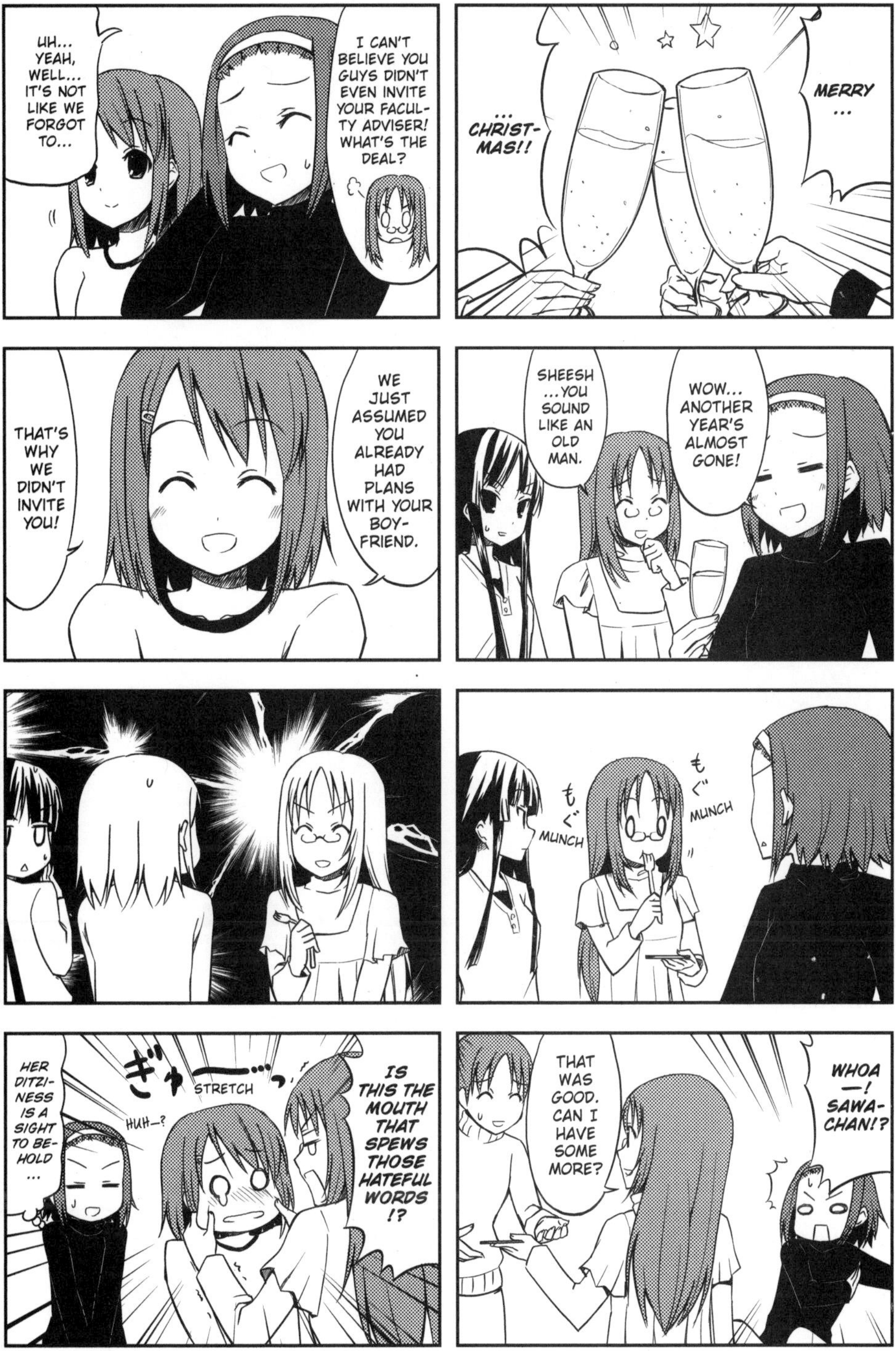
MERRY ...
... CHRIST-MAS!!
WOW... ANOTHER YEAR'S ALMOST GONE!
SHEESH ...YOU SOUND LIKE AN OLD MAN.
もぐ MUNCH
もぐ MUNCH
WHOA—! SAWA-CHAN!?
THAT WAS GOOD. CAN I HAVE SOME MORE?
I CAN'T BELIEVE YOU GUYS DIDN'T EVEN INVITE YOUR FACULTY ADVISER! WHAT'S THE DEAL?
UH... YEAH, WELL... IT'S NOT LIKE WE FORGOT TO...
WE JUST ASSUMED YOU ALREADY HAD PLANS WITH YOUR BOY-FRIEND.
THAT'S WHY WE DIDN'T INVITE YOU!
IS THIS THE MOUTH THAT SPEWS THOSE HATEFUL WORDS!?
ぎゅーーっ STRETCH
HUH—?
HER DITZINESS IS A SIGHT TO BE-HOLD ...

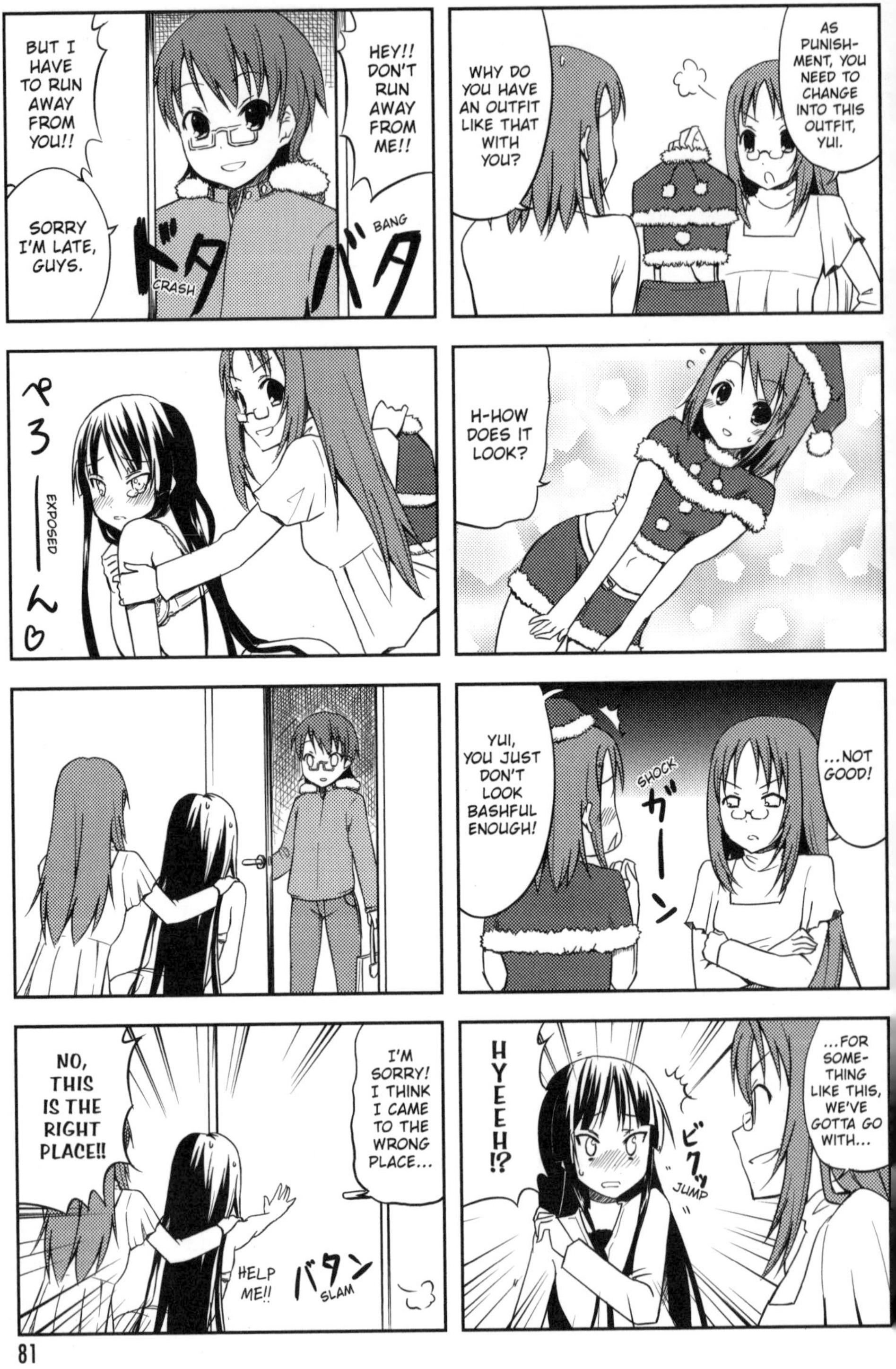
AS PUNISHMENT, YOU NEED TO CHANGE INTO THIS OUTFIT, YUI.
WHY DO YOU HAVE AN OUTFIT LIKE THAT WITH YOU?
H-HOW DOES IT LOOK?
...NOT GOOD!
SHOCK
ガーン
YUI, YOU JUST DON'T LOOK BASHFUL ENOUGH!
...FOR SOMETHING LIKE THIS, WE'VE GOTTA GO WITH...
ビクッ
JUMP
HYEEEH!?
HEY!! DON'T RUN AWAY FROM ME!!
BUT I HAVE TO RUN AWAY FROM YOU!!
バタ
BANG
ドタ
CRASH
SORRY I'M LATE, GUYS.
ぺろーん♡
EXPOSED
I'M SORRY! I THINK I CAME TO THE WRONG PLACE...
バタン
SLAM
NO, THIS IS THE RIGHT PLACE!!
HELP ME!!

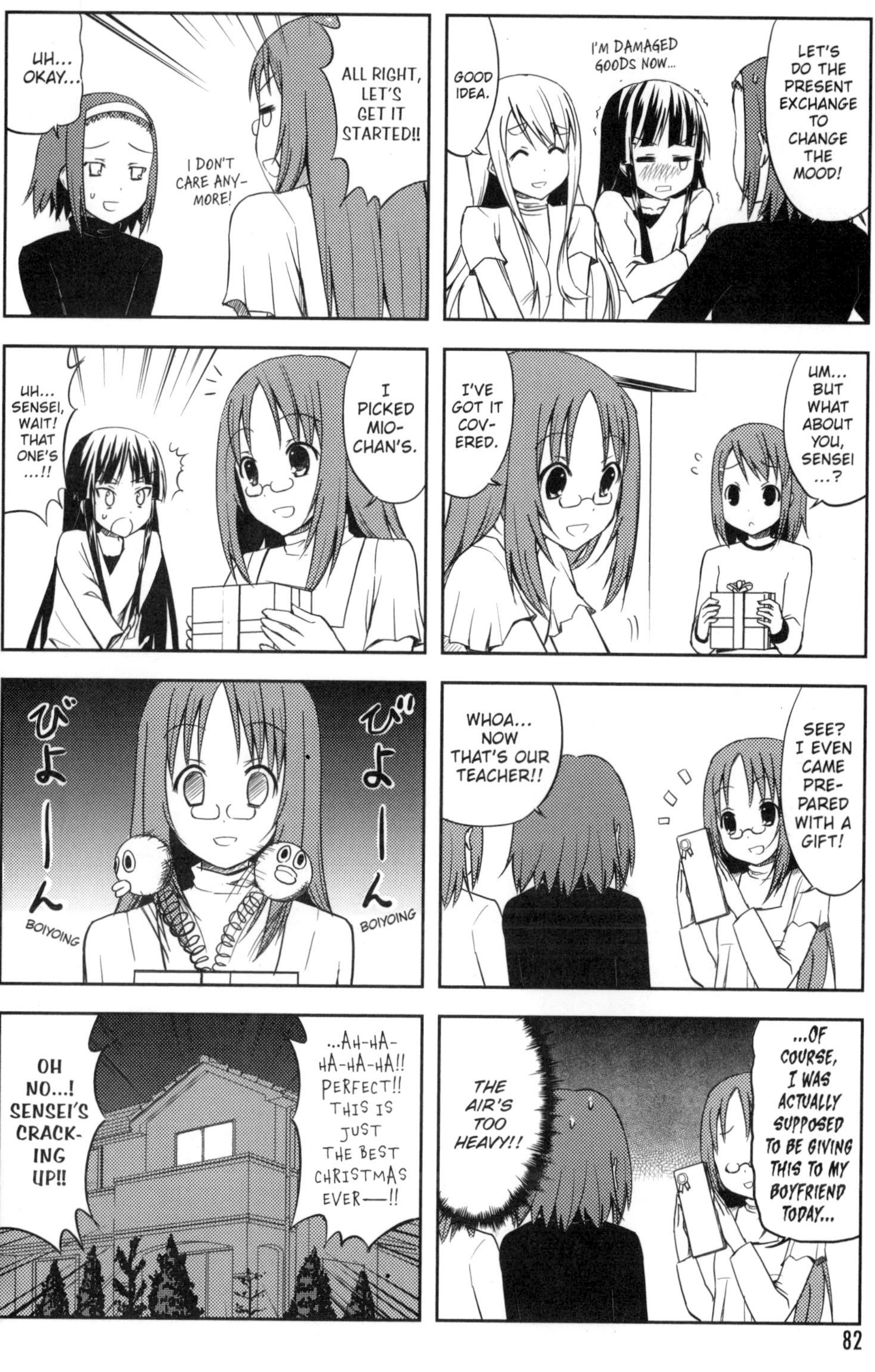
LET'S DO THE PRESENT EXCHANGE TO CHANGE THE MOOD!
I'M DAMAGED GOODS NOW...
GOOD IDEA.
UM... BUT WHAT ABOUT YOU, SENSEI...?
I'VE GOT IT COV-ERED.
SEE? I EVEN CAME PRE-PARED WITH A GIFT!
WHOA... NOW THAT'S OUR TEACHER!!
...OF COURSE, I WAS ACTUALLY SUPPOSED TO BE GIVING THIS TO MY BOYFRIEND TODAY...
THE AIR'S TOO HEAVY!!
ALL RIGHT, LET'S GET IT STARTED!!
I DON'T CARE ANY-MORE!
UH... OKAY...
I PICKED MIO-CHAN'S.
UH... SENSEI, WAIT! THAT ONE'S ...!!
びよーーん
BOIYOING
びよーーん
BOIYOING
...AH-HA-HA-HA-HA!! PERFECT!! THIS IS JUST THE BEST CHRISTMAS EVER—!!
OH NO...! SENSEI'S CRACK-ING UP!!

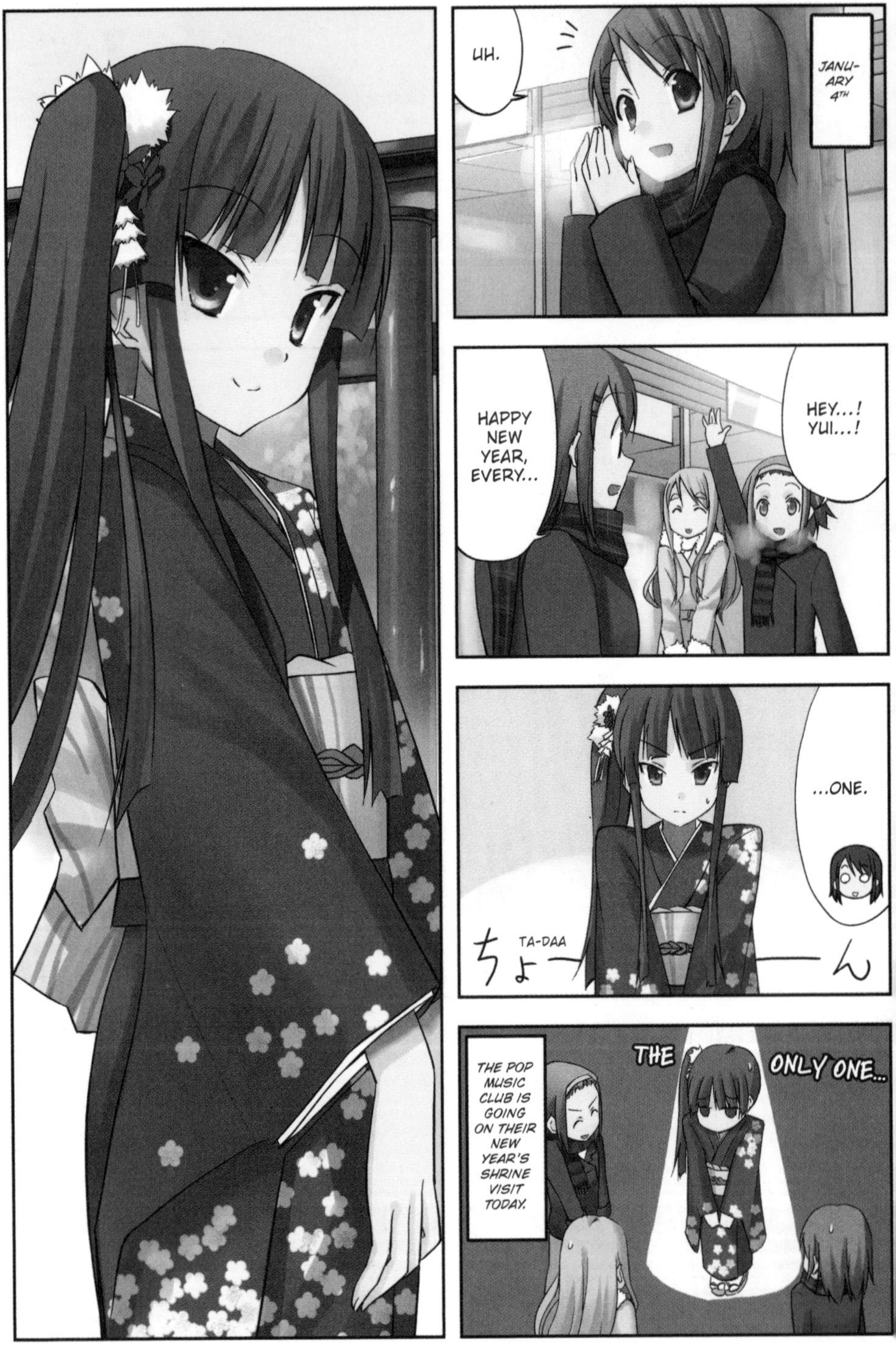
JANUARY 4TH
UH.
HEY...! YUI...!
HAPPY NEW YEAR, EVERY...
...ONE.
TA-DAA
ちょーーん
THE ONLY ONE...
THE POP MUSIC CLUB IS GOING ON THEIR NEW YEAR'S SHRINE VISIT TODAY.

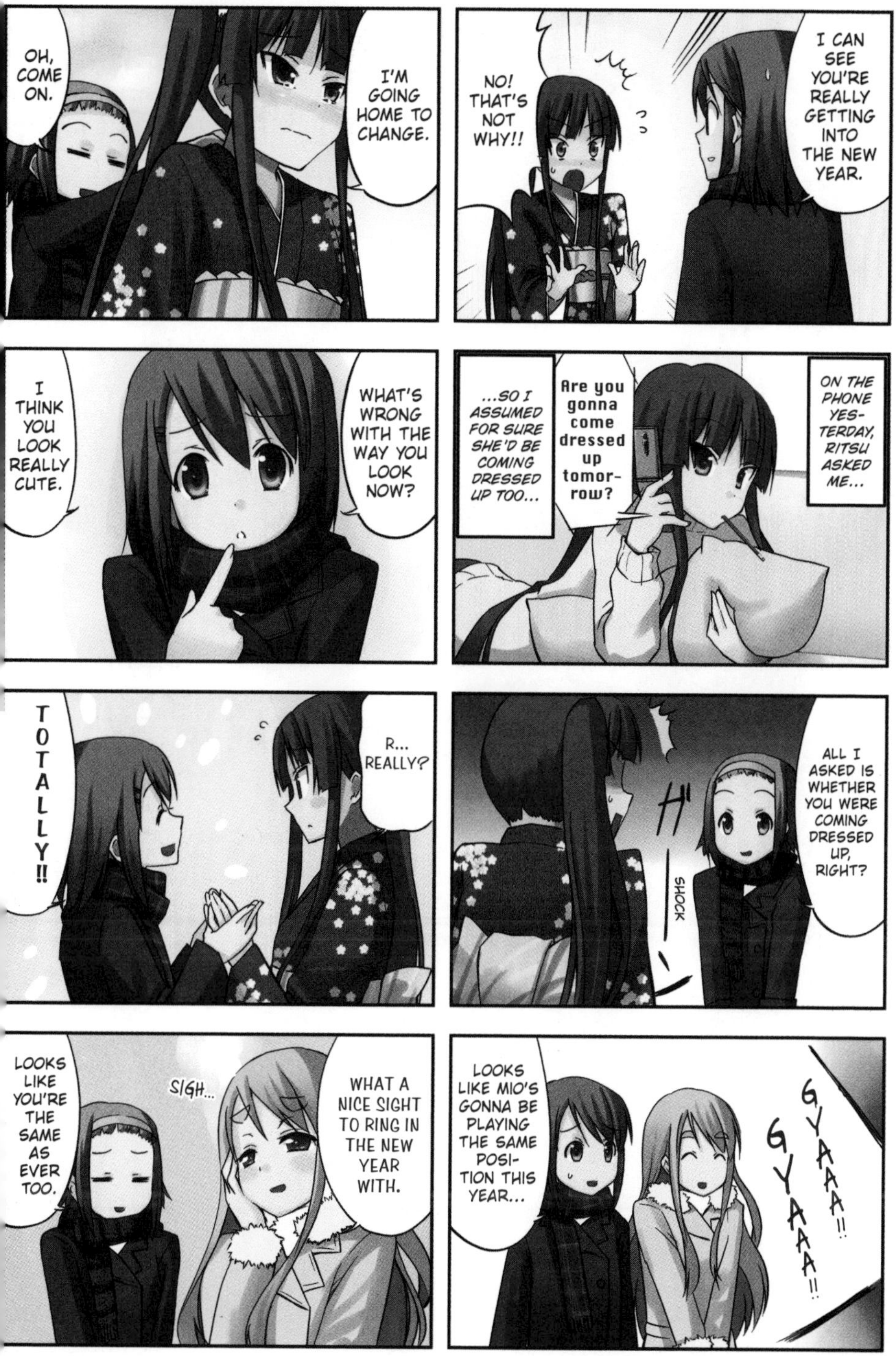
I CAN SEE YOU'RE REALLY GETTING INTO THE NEW YEAR.
NO! THAT'S NOT WHY!!
ON THE PHONE YESTERDAY, RITSU ASKED ME...
Are you gonna come dressed up tomorrow?
...SO I ASSUMED FOR SURE SHE'D BE COMING DRESSED UP TOO...
ALL I ASKED IS WHETHER YOU WERE COMING DRESSED UP, RIGHT?
SHOCK
LOOKS LIKE MIO'S GONNA BE PLAYING THE SAME POSITION THIS YEAR...
GYAAA!!
GYAAA!!
I'M GOING HOME TO CHANGE.
OH, COME ON.
WHAT'S WRONG WITH THE WAY YOU LOOK NOW?
I THINK YOU LOOK REALLY CUTE.
R... REALLY?
TOTALLY!!
WHAT A NICE SIGHT TO RING IN THE NEW YEAR WITH.
SIGH...
LOOKS LIKE YOU'RE THE SAME AS EVER TOO.

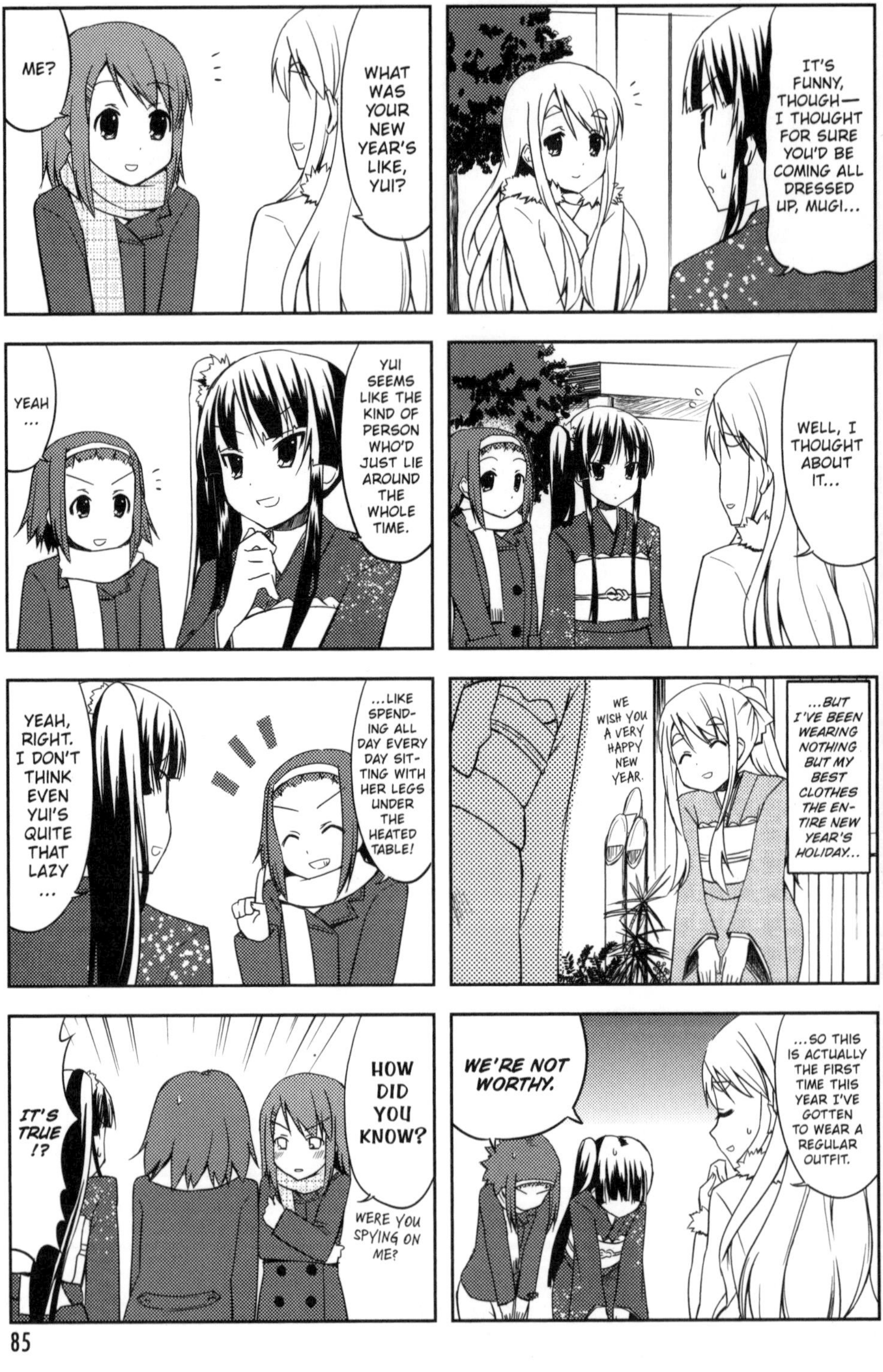
IT'S FUNNY, THOUGH— I THOUGHT FOR SURE YOU'D BE COMING ALL DRESSED UP, MUGI...
WELL, I THOUGHT ABOUT IT...
...BUT I'VE BEEN WEARING NOTHING BUT MY BEST CLOTHES THE ENTIRE NEW YEAR'S HOLIDAY...
WE WISH YOU A VERY HAPPY NEW YEAR.
...SO THIS IS ACTUALLY THE FIRST TIME THIS YEAR I'VE GOTTEN TO WEAR A REGULAR OUTFIT.
WE'RE NOT WORTHY.
WHAT WAS YOUR NEW YEAR'S LIKE, YUI?
ME?
YUI SEEMS LIKE THE KIND OF PERSON WHO'D JUST LIE AROUND THE WHOLE TIME.
YEAH ...
...LIKE SPENDING ALL DAY EVERY DAY SITTING WITH HER LEGS UNDER THE HEATED TABLE!
YEAH, RIGHT. I DON'T THINK EVEN YUI'S QUITE THAT LAZY ...
HOW DID YOU KNOW?
WERE YOU SPYING ON ME?
IT'S TRUE !?

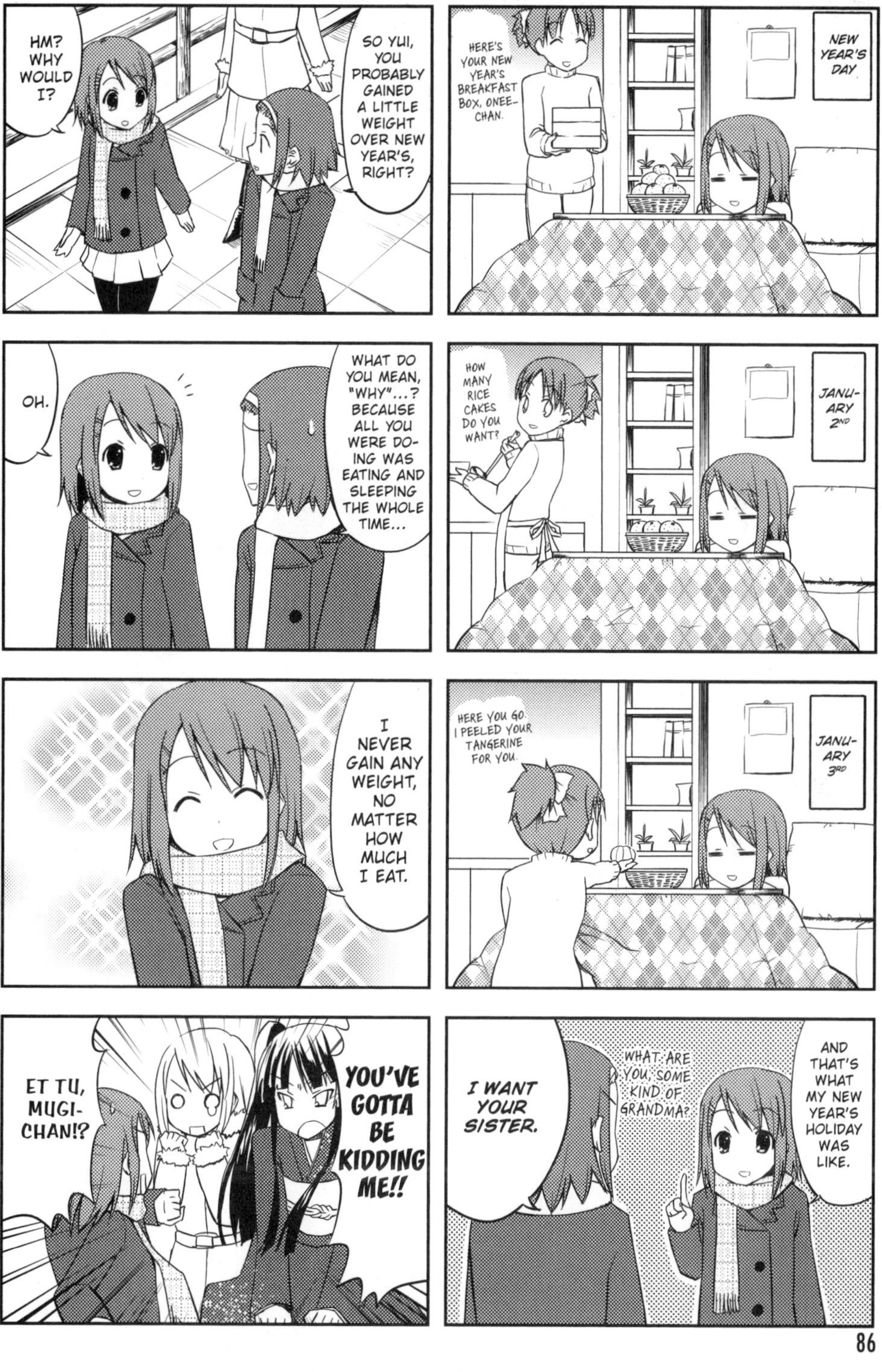
NEW YEAR'S DAY
HERE'S YOUR NEW YEAR'S BREAKFAST BOX, ONEE-CHAN.
JANUARY 2ND
HOW MANY RICE CAKES DO YOU WANT?
JANUARY 3RD
HERE YOU GO. I PEELED YOUR TANGERINE FOR YOU.
AND THAT'S WHAT MY NEW YEAR'S HOLIDAY WAS LIKE.
WHAT ARE YOU, SOME KIND OF GRANDMA?
I WANT YOUR SISTER.
SO YUI, YOU PROBABLY GAINED A LITTLE WEIGHT OVER NEW YEAR'S, RIGHT?
HM? WHY WOULD I?
WHAT DO YOU MEAN, "WHY"...? BECAUSE ALL YOU WERE DOING WAS EATING AND SLEEPING THE WHOLE TIME...
OH.
I NEVER GAIN ANY WEIGHT, NO MATTER HOW MUCH I EAT.
YOU'VE GOTTA BE KIDDING ME!!
ET TU, MUGI-CHAN!?

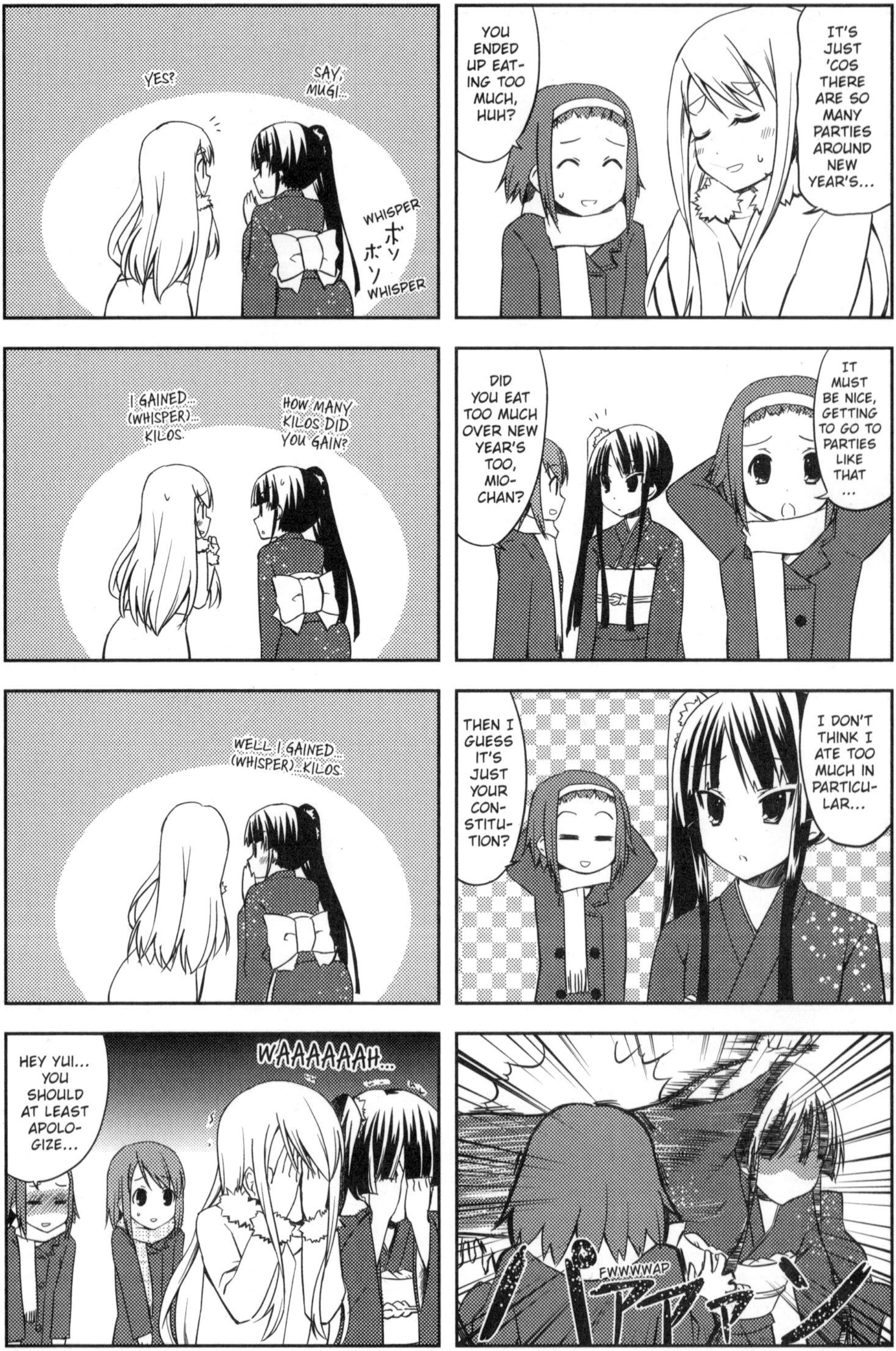
IT'S JUST 'COS THERE ARE SO MANY PARTIES AROUND NEW YEAR'S...
YOU ENDED UP EATING TOO MUCH, HUH?
IT MUST BE NICE, GETTING TO GO TO PARTIES LIKE THAT...
DID YOU EAT TOO MUCH OVER NEW YEAR'S TOO, MIO-CHAN?
I DON'T THINK I ATE TOO MUCH IN PARTICULAR...
THEN I GUESS IT'S JUST YOUR CONSTITUTION?
パァァン
FWWWWAP
SAY, MUGI...
WHISPER
ボソ
ボソ
WHISPER
YES?
HOW MANY KILOS DID YOU GAIN?
I GAINED... (WHISPER)... KILOS.
WELL I GAINED... (WHISPER)... KILOS.
WAAAAAAH...
HEY YUI... YOU SHOULD AT LEAST APOLOGIZE...

THE SLEEVE SLAP

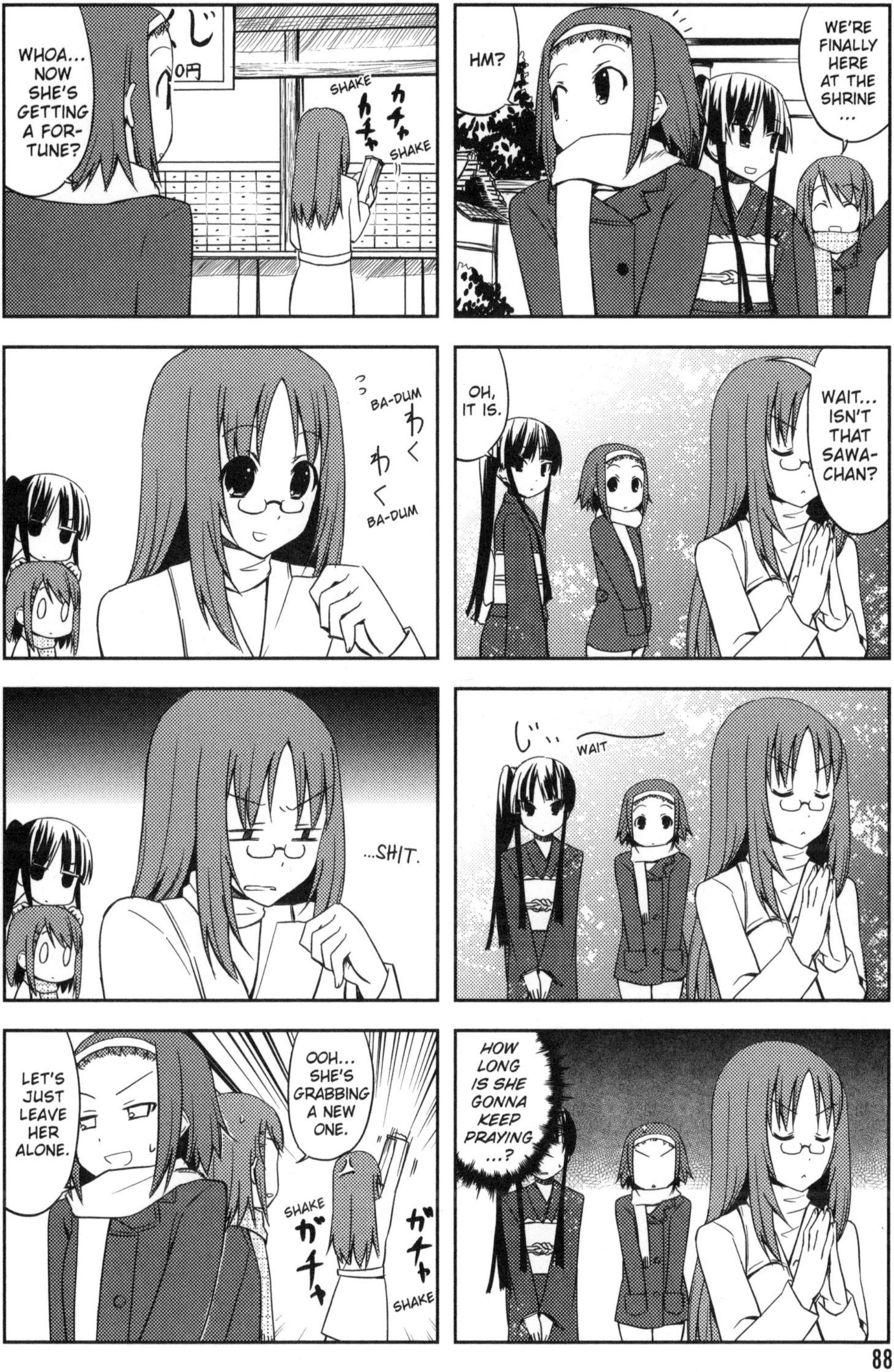
WE'RE FINALLY HERE AT THE SHRINE...
HM?
WAIT... ISN'T THAT SAWA-CHAN?
OH, IT IS.
じぃ WAIT
HOW LONG IS SHE GONNA KEEP PRAYING...?
WHOA... NOW SHE'S GETTING A FOR-TUNE?
カチャ SHAKE
カチャ SHAKE
わく BA-DUM
わく BA-DUM
...SHIT.
OOH... SHE'S GRABBING A NEW ONE.
LET'S JUST LEAVE HER ALONE.
ガチャ SHAKE
ガチャ SHAKE

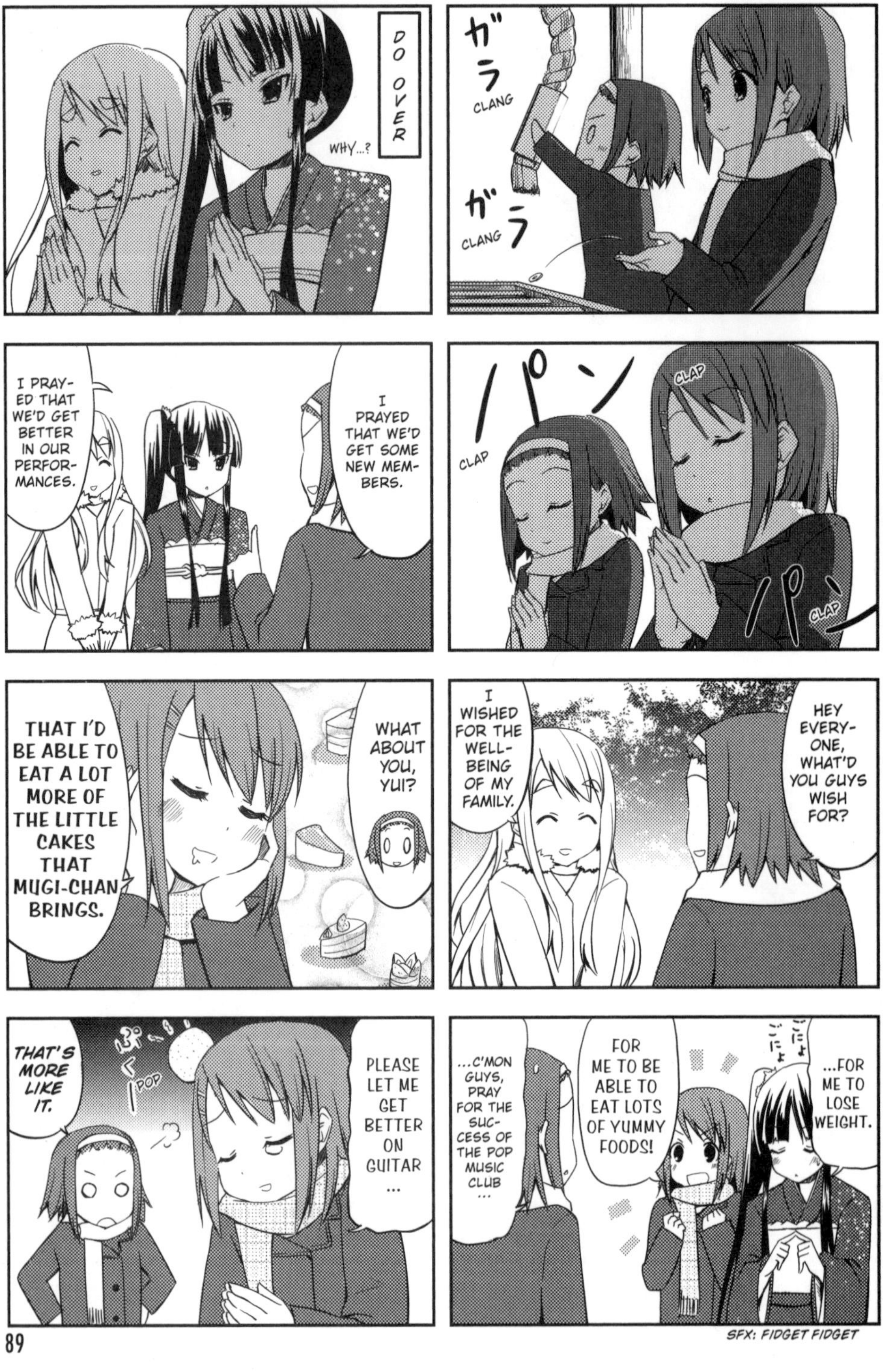
ガラ
CLANG
ガラ
CLANG
パン
CLAP
パン
CLAP
HEY EVERYONE, WHAT'D YOU GUYS WISH FOR?
I WISHED FOR THE WELL-BEING OF MY FAMILY.
...FOR ME TO LOSE WEIGHT.
ごにょごにょ
FOR ME TO BE ABLE TO EAT LOTS OF YUMMY FOODS!
...C'MON GUYS, PRAY FOR THE SUCCESS OF THE POP MUSIC CLUB ...
DO OVER
WHY...?
I PRAYED THAT WE'D GET SOME NEW MEMBERS.
I PRAYED THAT WE'D GET BETTER IN OUR PERFORMANCES.
WHAT ABOUT YOU, YUI?
THAT I'D BE ABLE TO EAT A LOT MORE OF THE LITTLE CAKES THAT MUGI-CHAN BRINGS.
PLEASE LET ME GET BETTER ON GUITAR ...
ぷくー
POP
THAT'S MORE LIKE IT.

SFX: FIDGET FIDGET

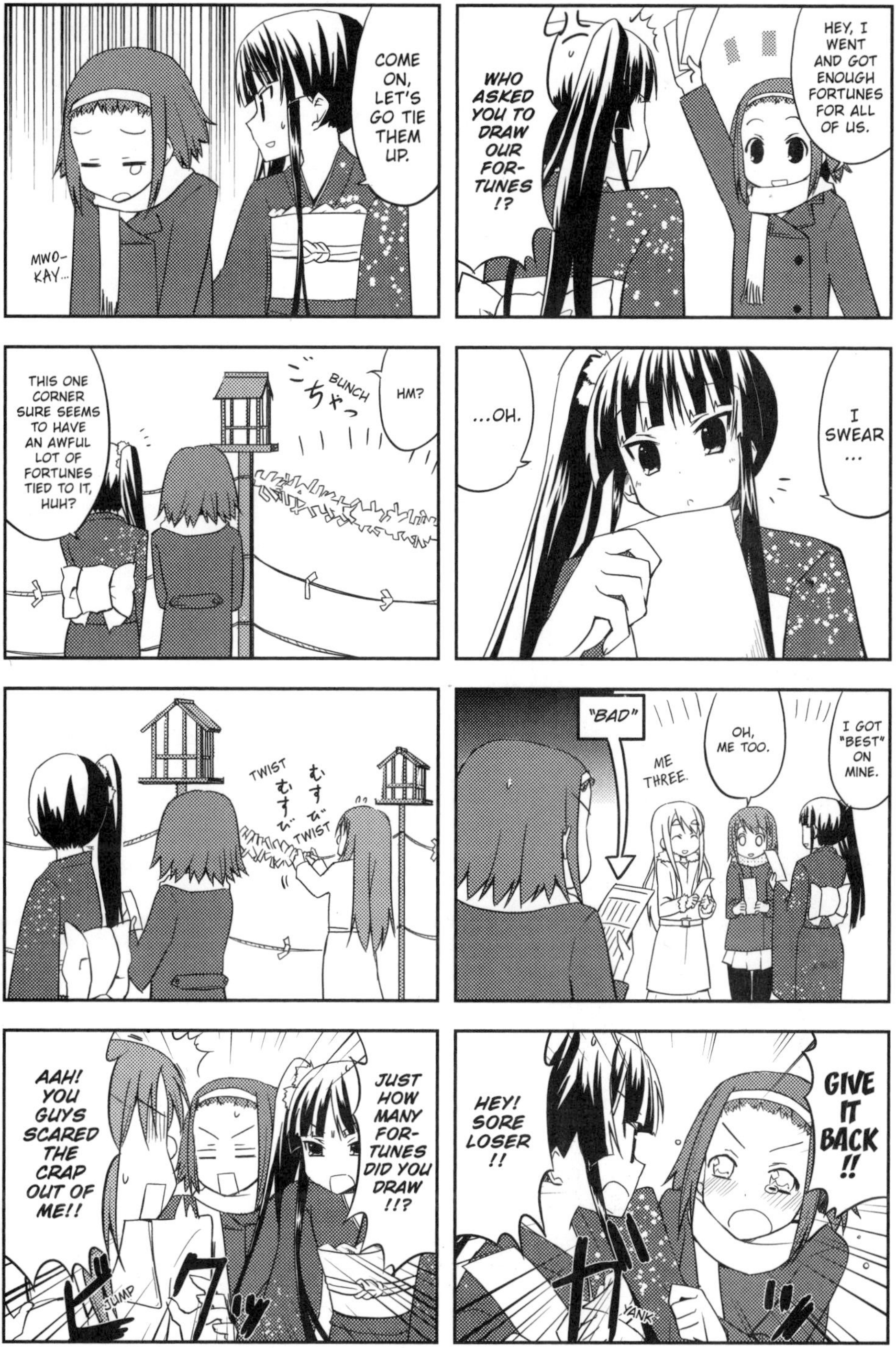
HEY, I WENT AND GOT ENOUGH FORTUNES FOR ALL OF US.
WHO ASKED YOU TO DRAW OUR FOR-TUNES !?
COME ON, LET'S GO TIE THEM UP.
MWO-KAY...
I SWEAR ...
...OH.
HM?
ごちゃっ
BUNCH
THIS ONE CORNER SURE SEEMS TO HAVE AN AWFUL LOT OF FORTUNES TIED TO IT, HUH?
I GOT "BEST" ON MINE.
OH, ME TOO.
ME THREE.
"BAD"
むすび
TWIST
むすび
TWIST
GIVE IT BACK !!
HEY! SORE LOSER !!
YANK
JUST HOW MANY FOR-TUNES DID YOU DRAW !!?
AAH! YOU GUYS SCARED THE CRAP OUT OF ME!!
JUMP

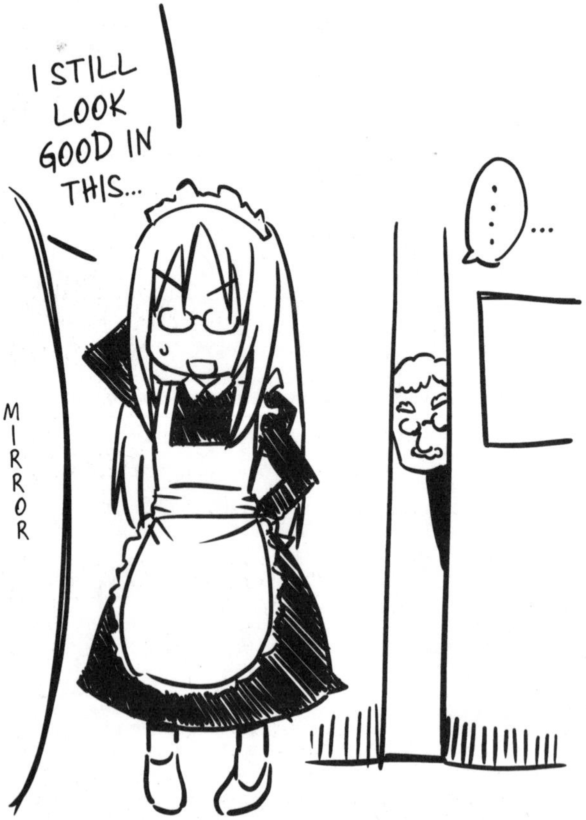
I STILL LOOK GOOD IN THIS...
MIRROR
...
...

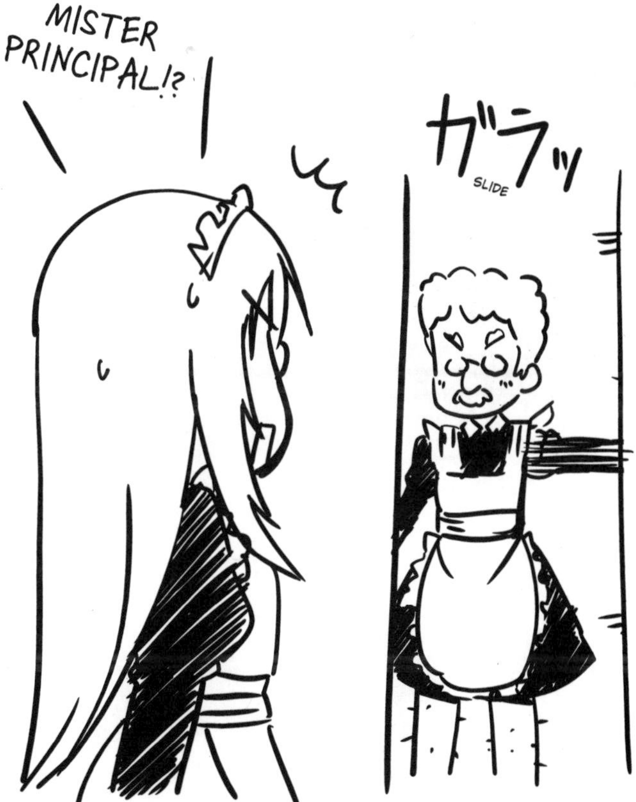
ガラッ
SLIDE
MISTER PRINCIPAL!?

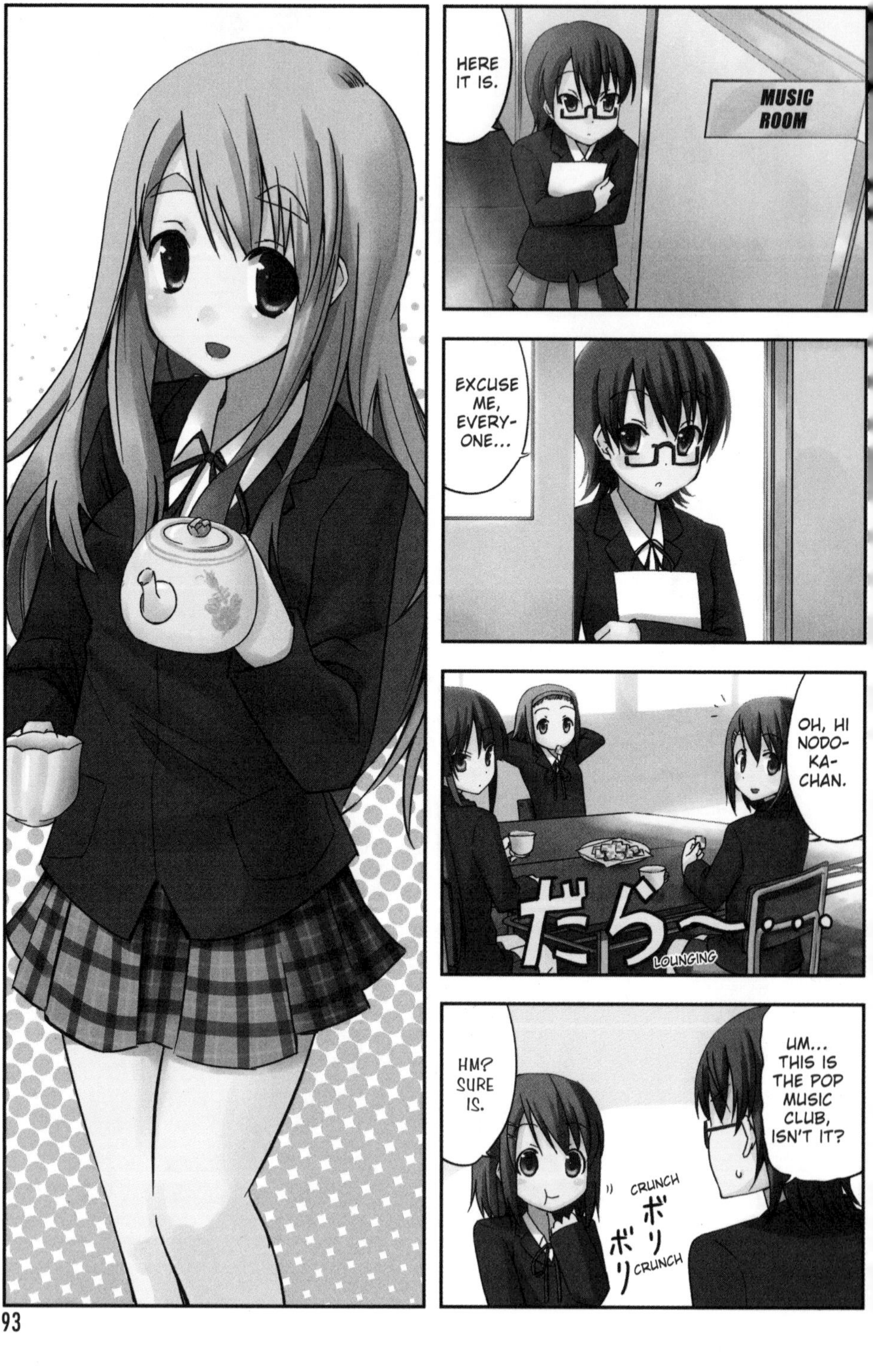
HERE IT IS.
MUSIC ROOM
EXCUSE ME, EVERYONE...
OH, HI NODOKA-CHAN.
だら〜…
LOUNGING
UM... THIS IS THE POP MUSIC CLUB, ISN'T IT?
HM? SURE IS.
ボリボリ
CRUNCH CRUNCH

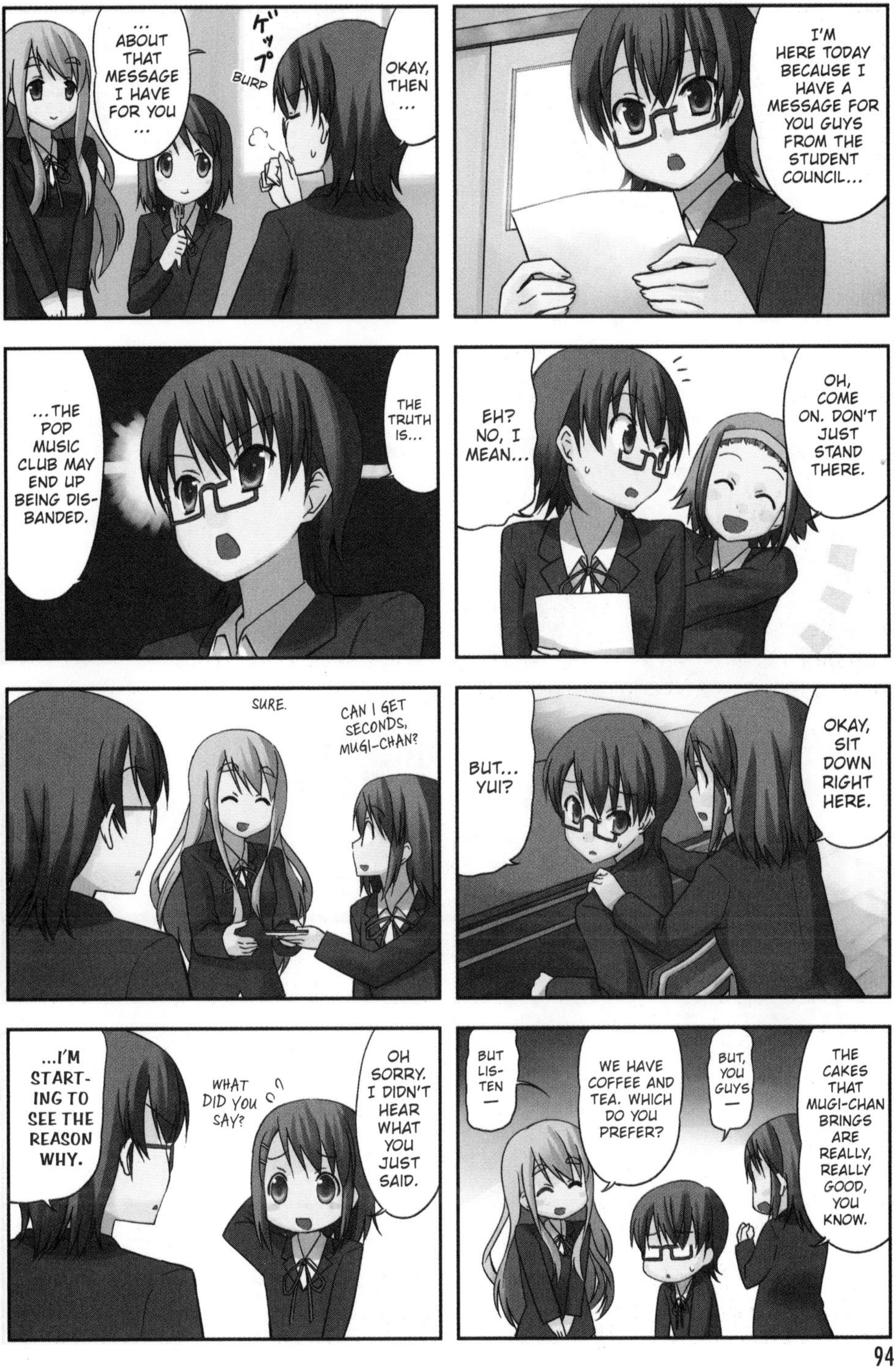
I'M HERE TODAY BECAUSE I HAVE A MESSAGE FOR YOU GUYS FROM THE STUDENT COUNCIL...
OH, COME ON. DON'T JUST STAND THERE.
EH? NO, I MEAN...
OKAY, SIT DOWN RIGHT HERE.
BUT... YUI?
THE CAKES THAT MUGI-CHAN BRINGS ARE REALLY, REALLY GOOD, YOU KNOW.
BUT, YOU GUYS —
WE HAVE COFFEE AND TEA. WHICH DO YOU PREFER?
BUT LIS-TEN —
OKAY, THEN...
ゲップ
BURP
...ABOUT THAT MESSAGE I HAVE FOR YOU...
THE TRUTH IS...
...THE POP MUSIC CLUB MAY END UP BEING DIS-BANDED.
CAN I GET SECONDS, MUGI-CHAN?
SURE.
OH SORRY. I DIDN'T HEAR WHAT YOU JUST SAID.
WHAT DID YOU SAY?
...I'M START-ING TO SEE THE REASON WHY.

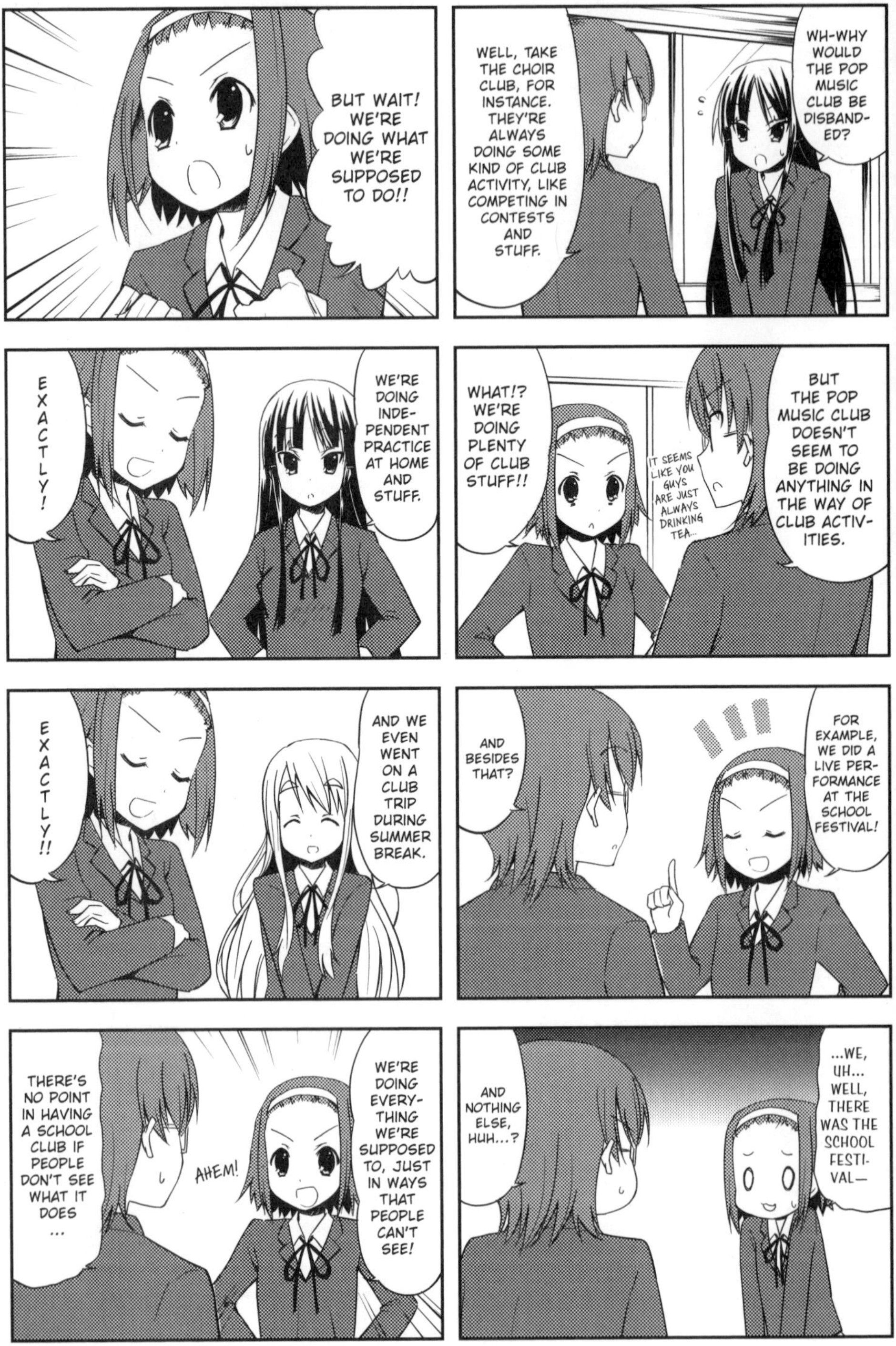
WH-WHY WOULD THE POP MUSIC CLUB BE DISBANDED?
WELL, TAKE THE CHOIR CLUB, FOR INSTANCE. THEY'RE ALWAYS DOING SOME KIND OF CLUB ACTIVITY, LIKE COMPETING IN CONTESTS AND STUFF.
BUT THE POP MUSIC CLUB DOESN'T SEEM TO BE DOING ANYTHING IN THE WAY OF CLUB ACTIVITIES.
IT SEEMS LIKE YOU GUYS ARE JUST ALWAYS DRINKING TEA...
WHAT!? WE'RE DOING PLENTY OF CLUB STUFF!!
FOR EXAMPLE, WE DID A LIVE PERFORMANCE AT THE SCHOOL FESTIVAL!
AND BESIDES THAT?
...WE, UH... WELL, THERE WAS THE SCHOOL FESTIVAL—
AND NOTHING ELSE, HUH...?
BUT WAIT! WE'RE DOING WHAT WE'RE SUPPOSED TO DO!!
WE'RE DOING INDEPENDENT PRACTICE AT HOME AND STUFF.
EXACTLY!
AND WE EVEN WENT ON A CLUB TRIP DURING SUMMER BREAK.
EXACTLY!!
WE'RE DOING EVERYTHING WE'RE SUPPOSED TO, JUST IN WAYS THAT PEOPLE CAN'T SEE!
AHEM!
THERE'S NO POINT IN HAVING A SCHOOL CLUB IF PEOPLE DON'T SEE WHAT IT DOES ...

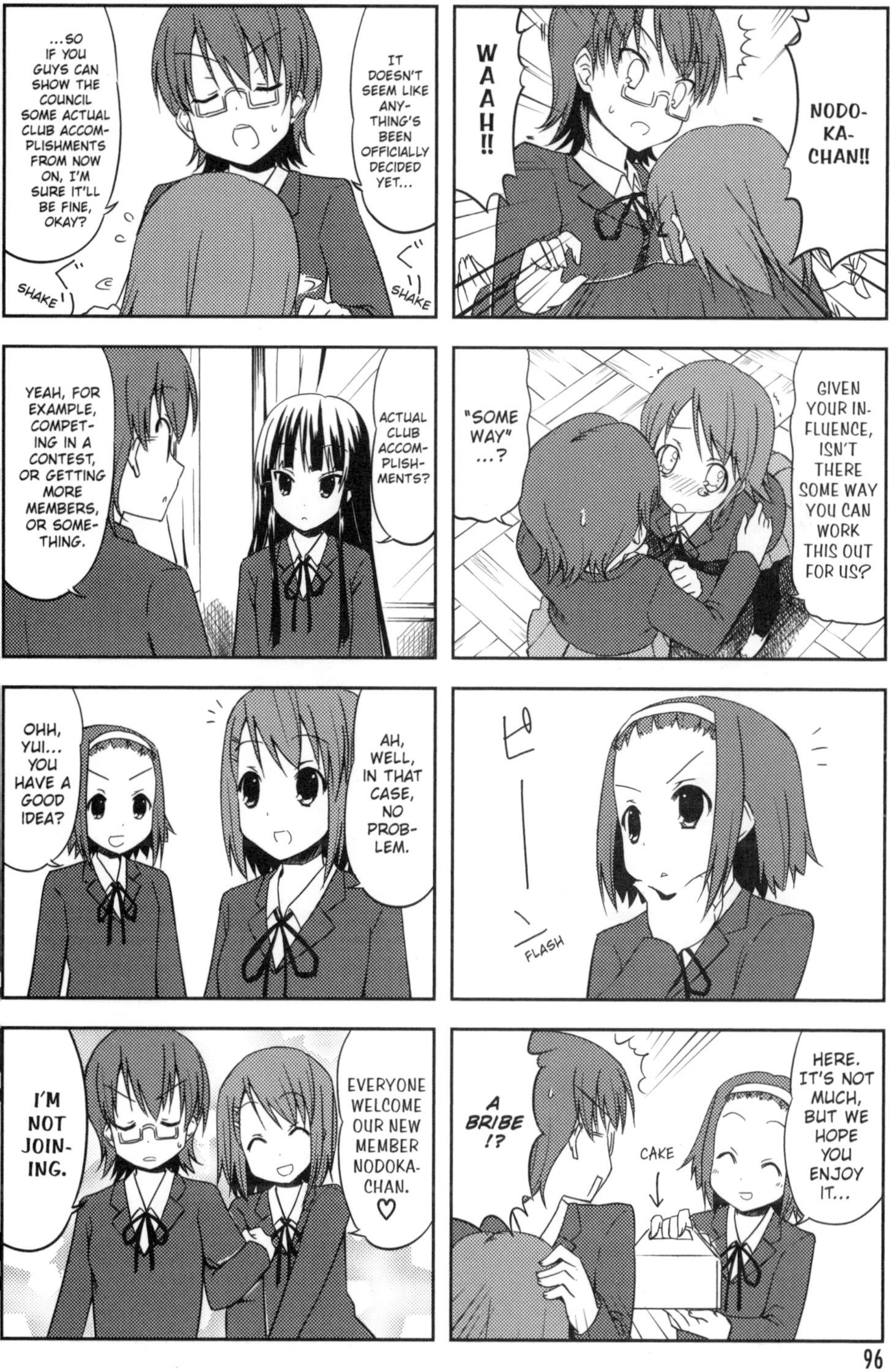
NODOKA-CHAN!!
WAAH!!
GIVEN YOUR INFLUENCE, ISN'T THERE SOME WAY YOU CAN WORK THIS OUT FOR US?
"SOME WAY" ...?
FLASH
HERE. IT'S NOT MUCH, BUT WE HOPE YOU ENJOY IT...
CAKE
A BRIBE !?
IT DOESN'T SEEM LIKE ANYTHING'S BEEN OFFICIALLY DECIDED YET...
...SO IF YOU GUYS CAN SHOW THE COUNCIL SOME ACTUAL CLUB ACCOMPLISHMENTS FROM NOW ON, I'M SURE IT'LL BE FINE, OKAY?
SHAKE
SHAKE
ACTUAL CLUB ACCOMPLISHMENTS?
YEAH, FOR EXAMPLE, COMPETING IN A CONTEST, OR GETTING MORE MEMBERS, OR SOMETHING.
AH, WELL, IN THAT CASE, NO PROBLEM.
OHH, YUI... YOU HAVE A GOOD IDEA?
EVERYONE WELCOME OUR NEW MEMBER NODOKA-CHAN. ♡
I'M NOT JOINING.

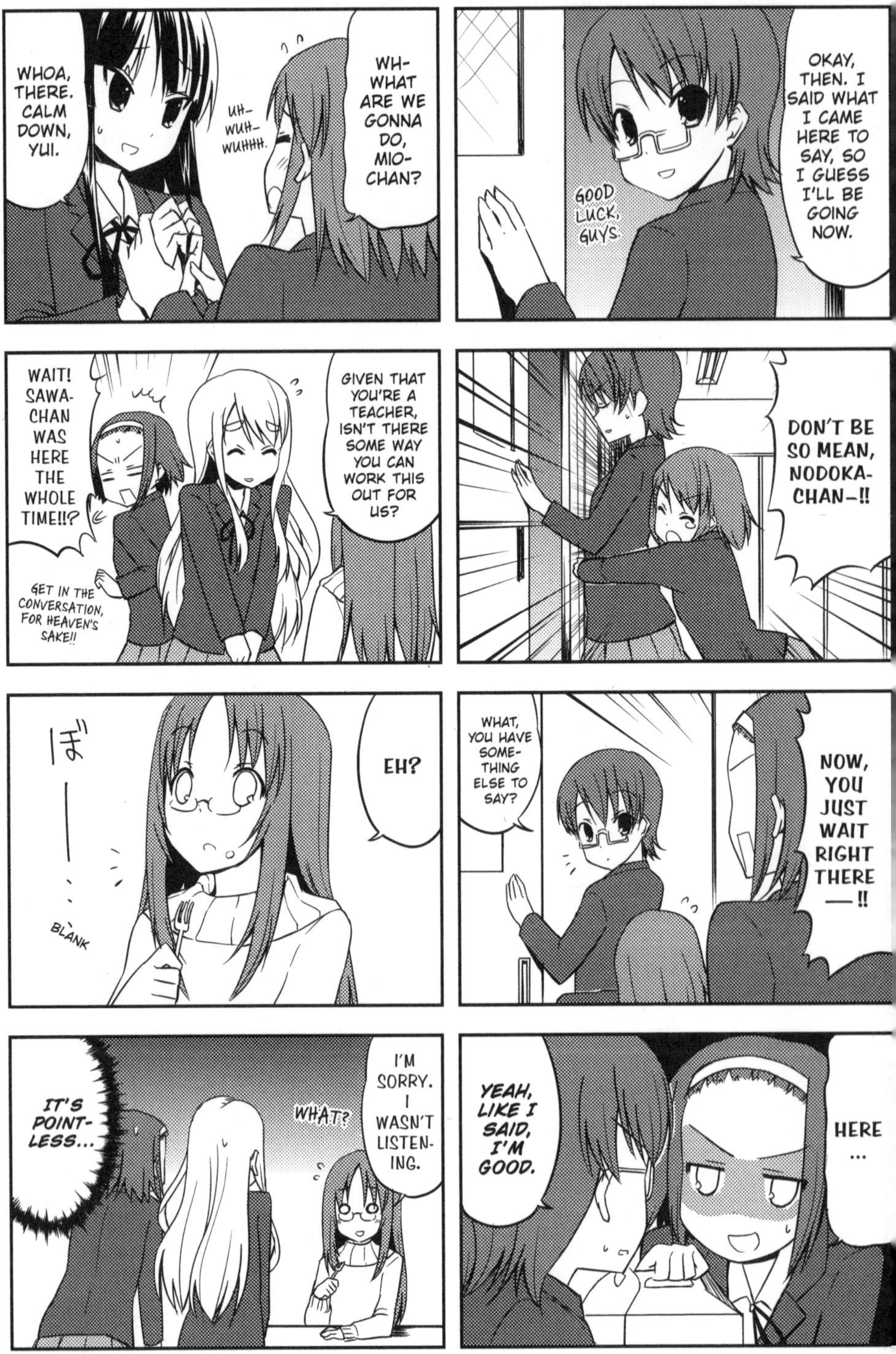
OKAY, THEN. I SAID WHAT I CAME HERE TO SAY, SO I GUESS I'LL BE GOING NOW.
GOOD LUCK, GUYS.
DON'T BE SO MEAN, NODOKA-CHAN—!!
NOW, YOU JUST WAIT RIGHT THERE—!!
WHAT, YOU HAVE SOMETHING ELSE TO SAY?
HERE...
YEAH, LIKE I SAID, I'M GOOD.
WH-WHAT ARE WE GONNA DO, MIO-CHAN?
UH-WUH-WUHHH.
WHOA, THERE. CALM DOWN, YUI.
GIVEN THAT YOU'RE A TEACHER, ISN'T THERE SOME WAY YOU CAN WORK THIS OUT FOR US?
WAIT! SAWA-CHAN WAS HERE THE WHOLE TIME!!?
GET IN THE CONVERSATION, FOR HEAVEN'S SAKE!!
EH?
ぼー
BLANK
I'M SORRY. I WASN'T LISTENING.
WHAT?
IT'S POINTLESS...

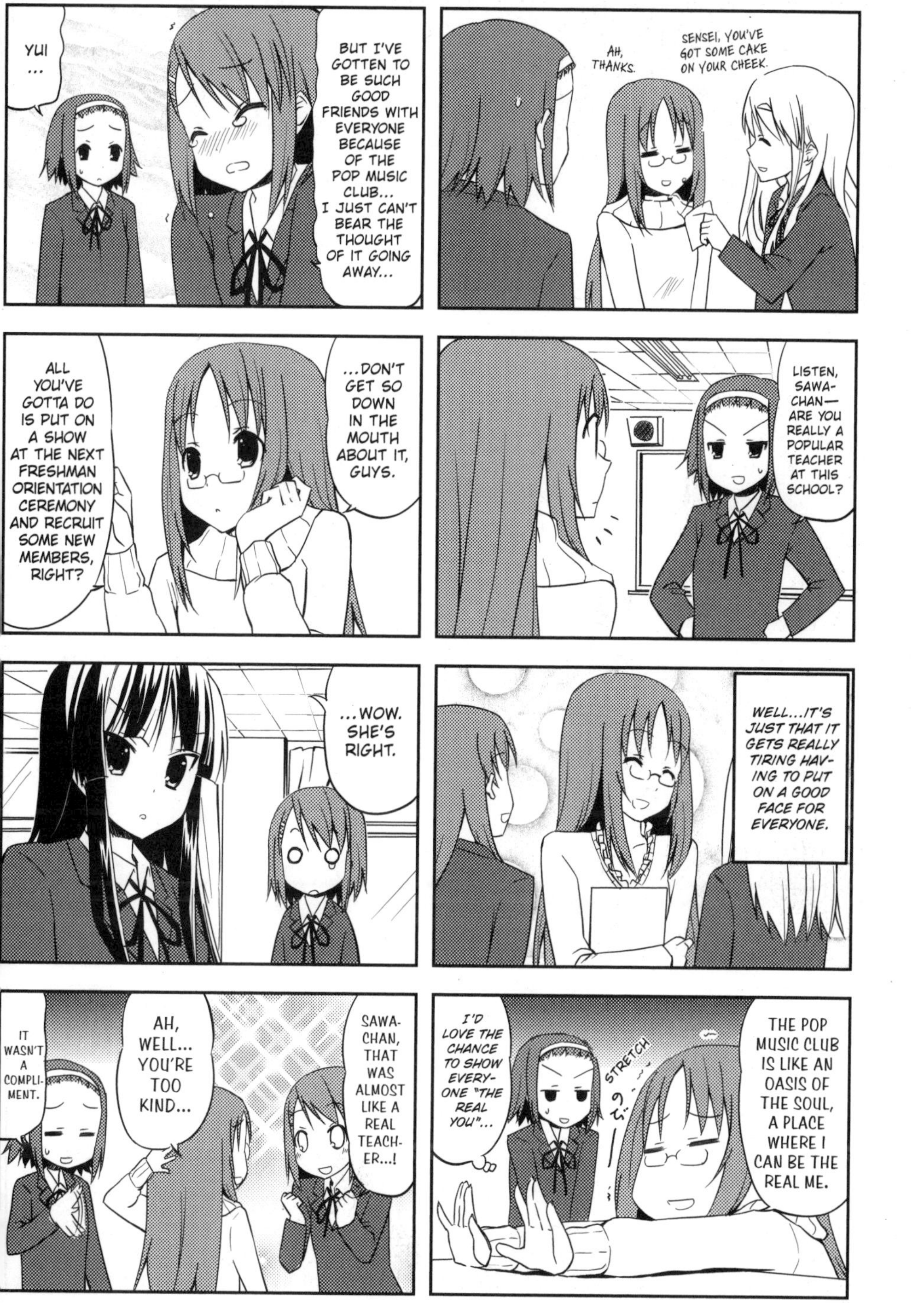
SENSEI, YOU'VE GOT SOME CAKE ON YOUR CHEEK.
AH, THANKS.
LISTEN, SAWA-CHAN— ARE YOU REALLY A POPULAR TEACHER AT THIS SCHOOL?
WELL...IT'S JUST THAT IT GETS REALLY TIRING HAV-ING TO PUT ON A GOOD FACE FOR EVERYONE.
THE POP MUSIC CLUB IS LIKE AN OASIS OF THE SOUL, A PLACE WHERE I CAN BE THE REAL ME.
STRETCH
I'D LOVE THE CHANCE TO SHOW EVERY-ONE "THE REAL YOU"...
BUT I'VE GOTTEN TO BE SUCH GOOD FRIENDS WITH EVERYONE BECAUSE OF THE POP MUSIC CLUB... I JUST CAN'T BEAR THE THOUGHT OF IT GOING AWAY...
YUI ...
...DON'T GET SO DOWN IN THE MOUTH ABOUT IT, GUYS.
ALL YOU'VE GOTTA DO IS PUT ON A SHOW AT THE NEXT FRESHMAN ORIENTATION CEREMONY AND RECRUIT SOME NEW MEMBERS, RIGHT?
...WOW. SHE'S RIGHT.
SAWA-CHAN, THAT WAS ALMOST LIKE A REAL TEACH-ER...!
AH, WELL... YOU'RE TOO KIND...
IT WASN'T A COMPLI-MENT.

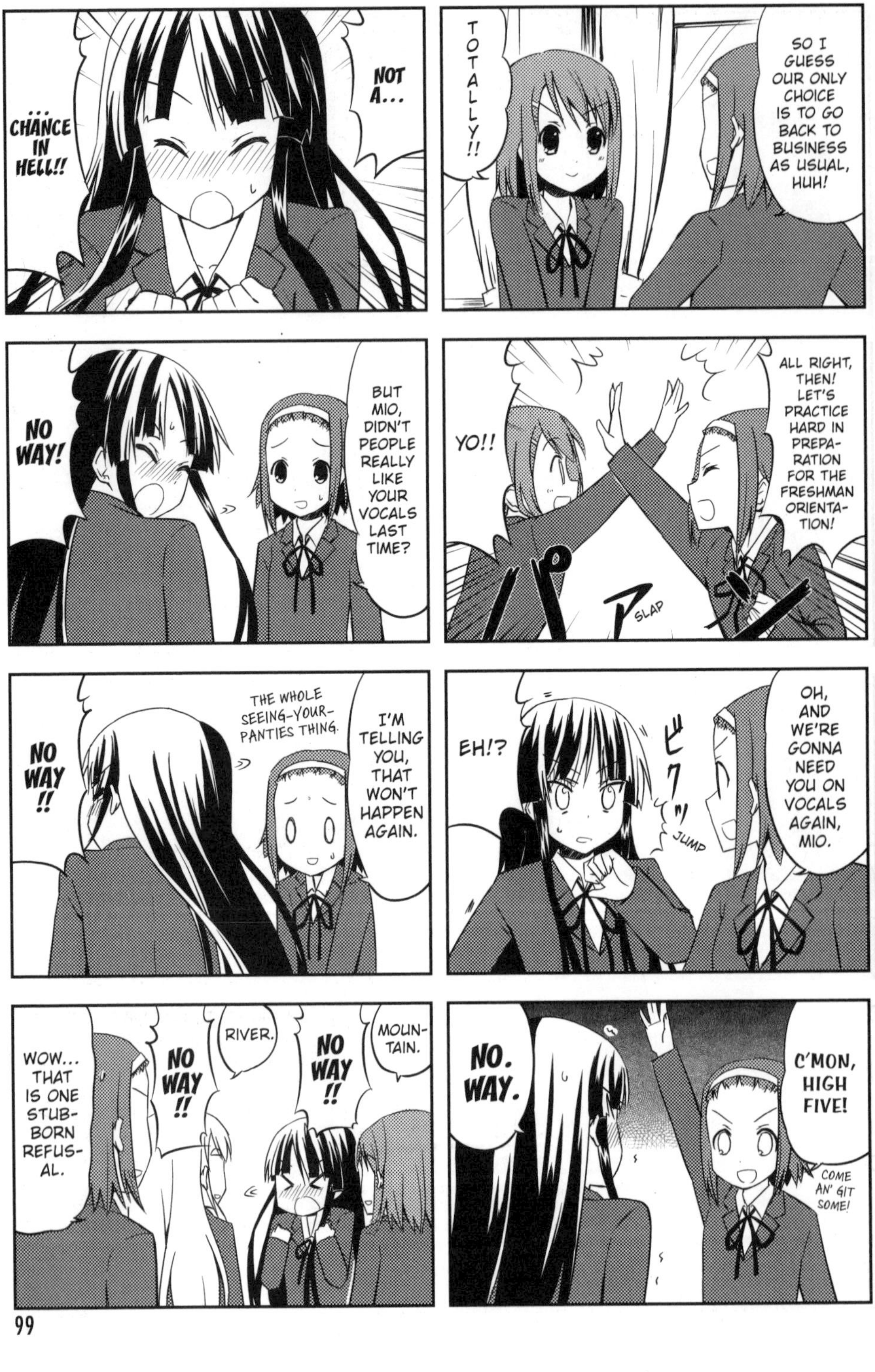
SO I GUESS OUR ONLY CHOICE IS TO GO BACK TO BUSINESS AS USUAL, HUH!
TOTALLY!!
ALL RIGHT, THEN! LET'S PRACTICE HARD IN PREPARATION FOR THE FRESHMAN ORIENTATION!
YO!!
パア
SLAP
OH, AND WE'RE GONNA NEED YOU ON VOCALS AGAIN, MIO.
ビクッ
JUMP
EH!?
C'MON, HIGH FIVE!
COME AN' GIT SOME!
NO. WAY.
NOT A...
...CHANCE IN HELL!!
BUT MIO, DIDN'T PEOPLE REALLY LIKE YOUR VOCALS LAST TIME?
NO WAY!
I'M TELLING YOU, THAT WON'T HAPPEN AGAIN.
THE WHOLE SEEING-YOUR-PANTIES THING.
NO WAY!!
MOUNTAIN.
NO WAY!!
RIVER.
NO WAY!!
WOW... THAT IS ONE STUBBORN REFUSAL.

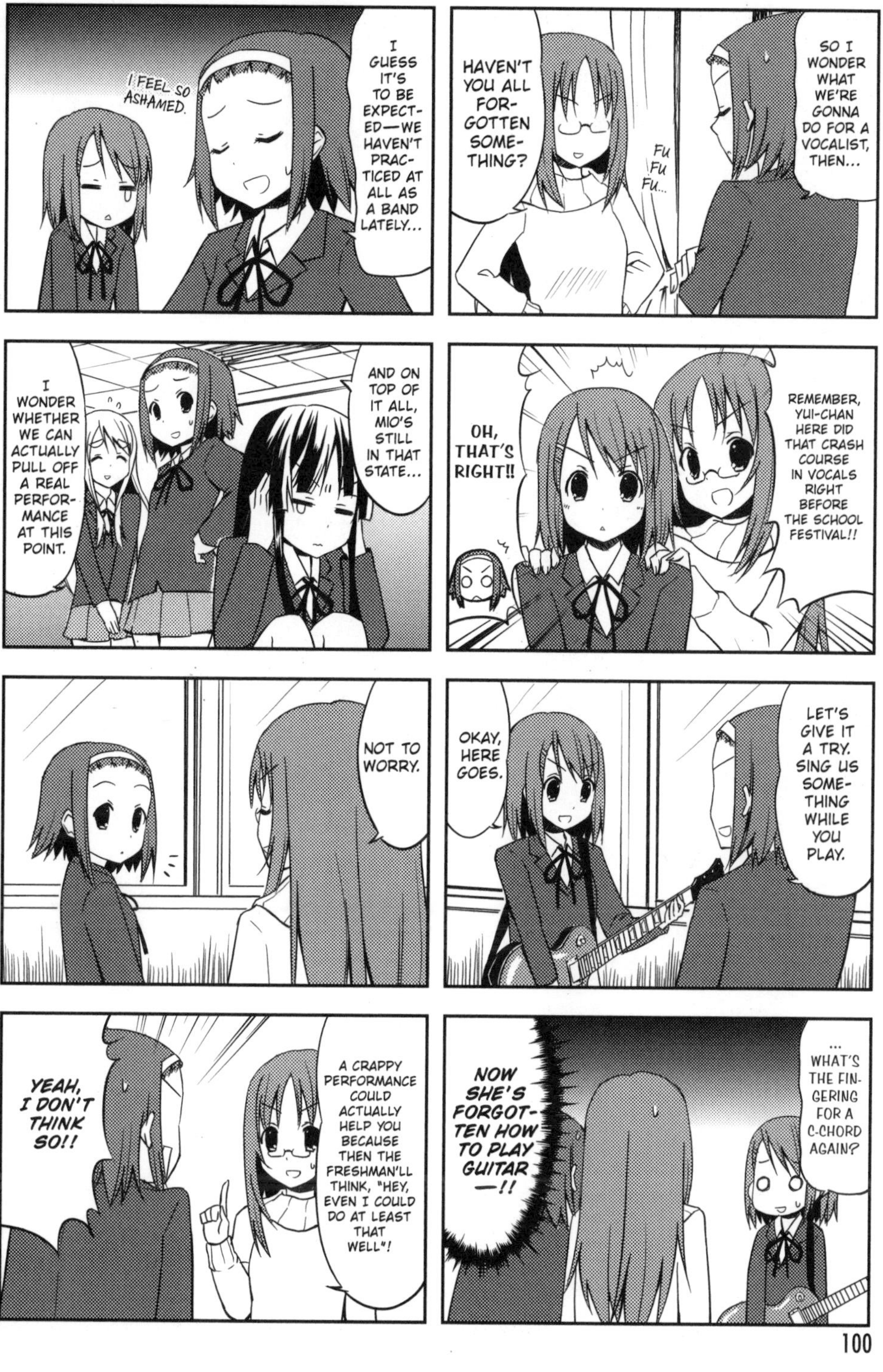
SO I WONDER WHAT WE'RE GONNA DO FOR A VOCALIST, THEN...
FU FU FU...
HAVEN'T YOU ALL FOR-GOTTEN SOME-THING?
REMEMBER, YUI-CHAN HERE DID THAT CRASH COURSE IN VOCALS RIGHT BEFORE THE SCHOOL FESTIVAL!!
OH, THAT'S RIGHT!!
LET'S GIVE IT A TRY. SING US SOME-THING WHILE YOU PLAY.
OKAY, HERE GOES.
... WHAT'S THE FIN-GERING FOR A C-CHORD AGAIN?
NOW SHE'S FORGOT-TEN HOW TO PLAY GUITAR—!!
I GUESS IT'S TO BE EXPECT-ED—WE HAVEN'T PRAC-TICED AT ALL AS A BAND LATELY...
I FEEL SO ASHAMED.
AND ON TOP OF IT ALL, MIO'S STILL IN THAT STATE...
I WONDER WHETHER WE CAN ACTUALLY PULL OFF A REAL PERFOR-MANCE AT THIS POINT.
NOT TO WORRY.
A CRAPPY PERFORMANCE COULD ACTUALLY HELP YOU BECAUSE THEN THE FRESHMAN'LL THINK, "HEY, EVEN I COULD DO AT LEAST THAT WELL"!
YEAH, I DON'T THINK SO!!

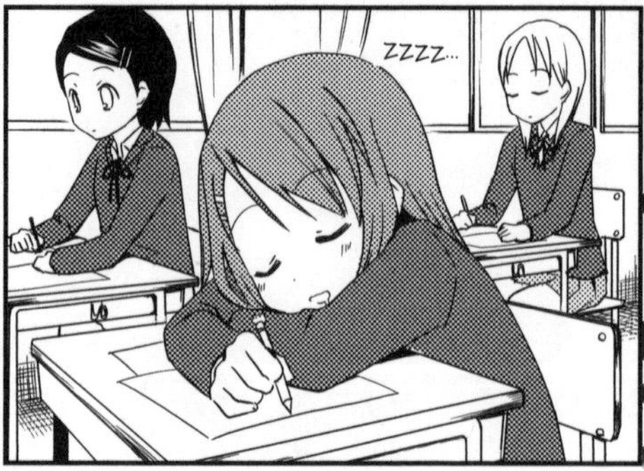
ZZZZ...

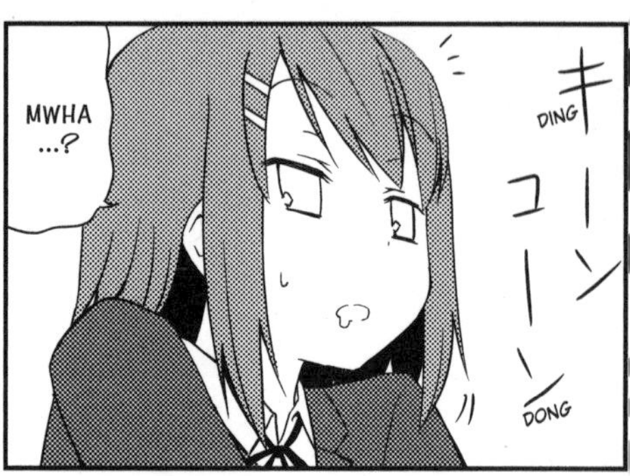
キーンコーン
DING
DONG
MWHA ...?

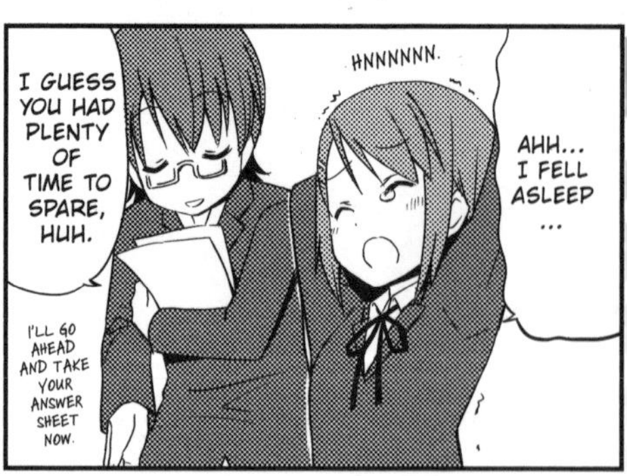
HNNNNNN.
AHH... I FELL ASLEEP ...
I GUESS YOU HAD PLENTY OF TIME TO SPARE, HUH.
I'LL GO AHEAD AND TAKE YOUR ANSWER SHEET NOW.

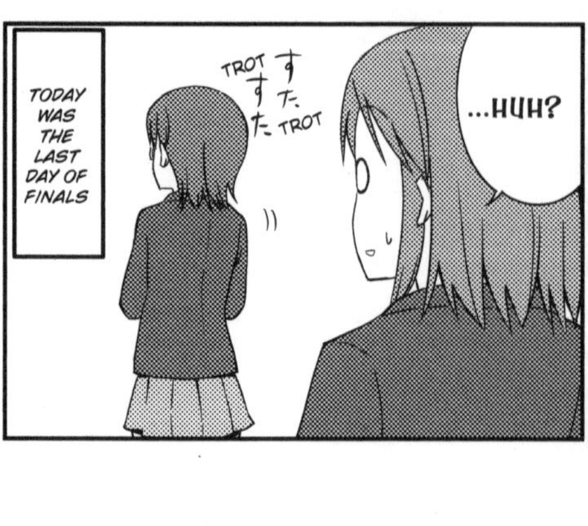
...HUH?
すたすた
TROT TROT
TODAY WAS THE LAST DAY OF FINALS

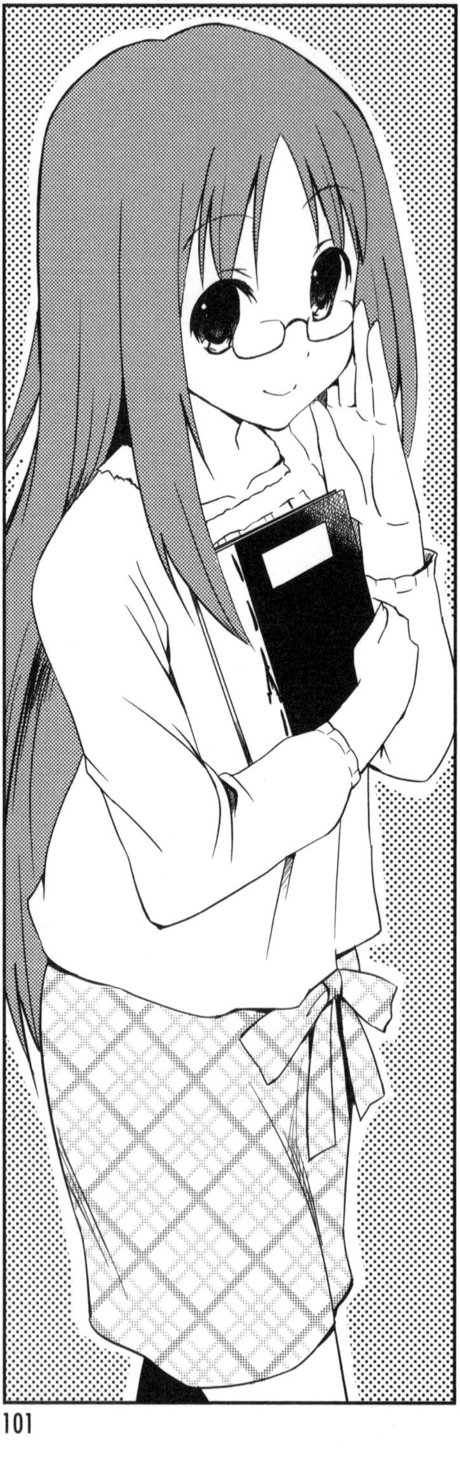

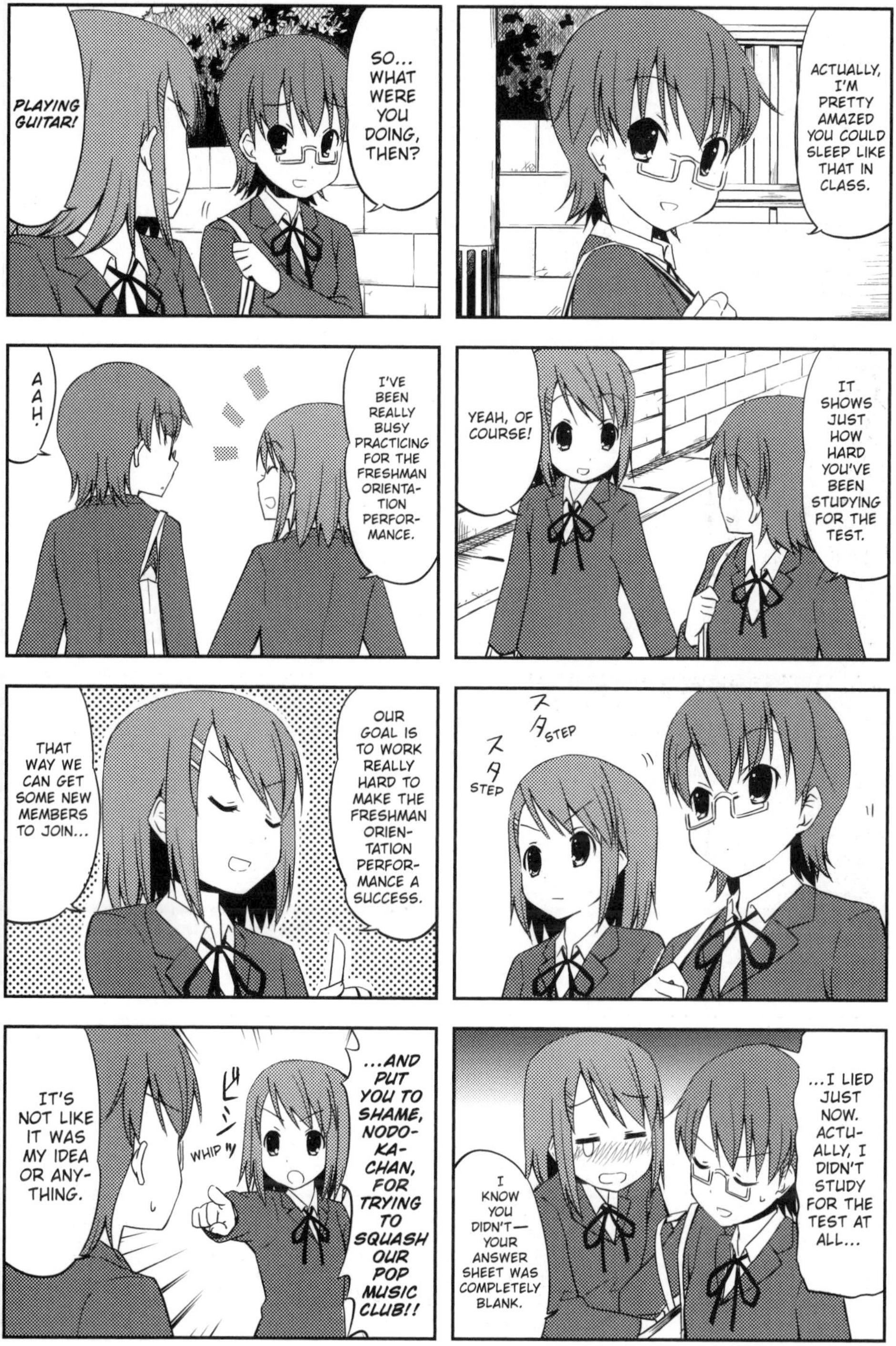
ACTUALLY, I'M PRETTY AMAZED YOU COULD SLEEP LIKE THAT IN CLASS.
IT SHOWS JUST HOW HARD YOU'VE BEEN STUDYING FOR THE TEST.
YEAH, OF COURSE!
スタ STEP
スタ STEP
...I LIED JUST NOW. ACTU-ALLY, I DIDN'T STUDY FOR THE TEST AT ALL...
I KNOW YOU DIDN'T— YOUR ANSWER SHEET WAS COMPLETELY BLANK.
SO... WHAT WERE YOU DOING, THEN?
PLAYING GUITAR!
I'VE BEEN REALLY BUSY PRACTICING FOR THE FRESHMAN ORIENTA-TION PERFOR-MANCE.
AAH!
OUR GOAL IS TO WORK REALLY HARD TO MAKE THE FRESHMAN ORIEN-TATION PERFOR-MANCE A SUCCESS.
THAT WAY WE CAN GET SOME NEW MEMBERS TO JOIN...
...AND PUT YOU TO SHAME, NODO-KA-CHAN, FOR TRYING TO SQUASH OUR POP MUSIC CLUB!!
ビシッ WHIP
IT'S NOT LIKE IT WAS MY IDEA OR ANY-THING.

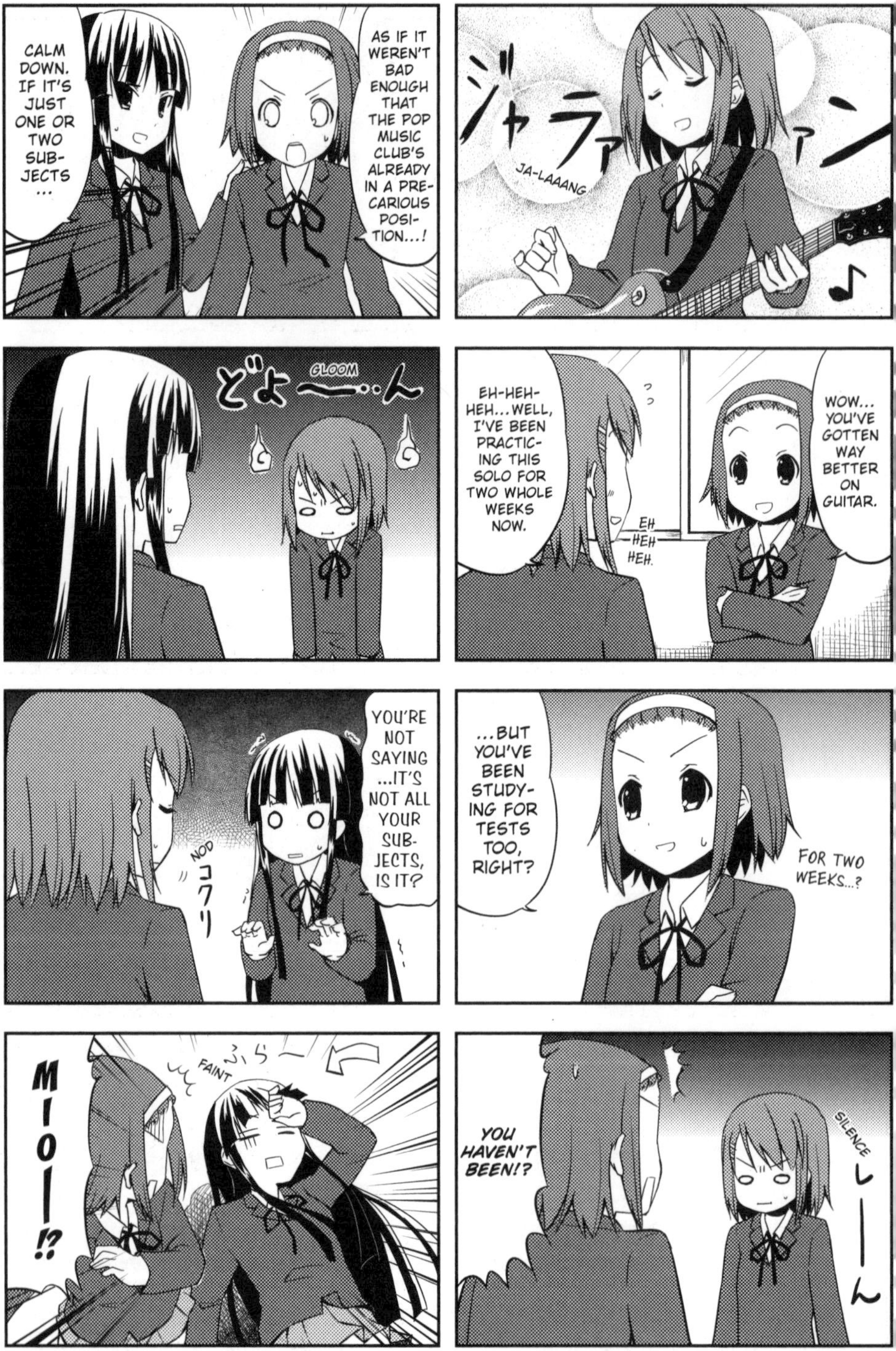
ジャラァアン
JA-LAAANG
WOW... YOU'VE GOTTEN WAY BETTER ON GUITAR.
EH-HEH-HEH... WELL, I'VE BEEN PRACTICING THIS SOLO FOR TWO WHOLE WEEKS NOW.
EH HEH HEH.
...BUT YOU'VE BEEN STUDYING FOR TESTS TOO, RIGHT?
FOR TWO WEEKS...?
SILENCE
しーん
YOU HAVEN'T BEEN!?
AS IF IT WEREN'T BAD ENOUGH THAT THE POP MUSIC CLUB'S ALREADY IN A PRECARIOUS POSITION...!
CALM DOWN. IF IT'S JUST ONE OR TWO SUBJECTS...
どよ〜〜ん
GLOOM
YOU'RE NOT SAYING ...IT'S NOT ALL YOUR SUBJECTS, IS IT?
NOD
コクリ
ふらー
FAINT
MIO!?

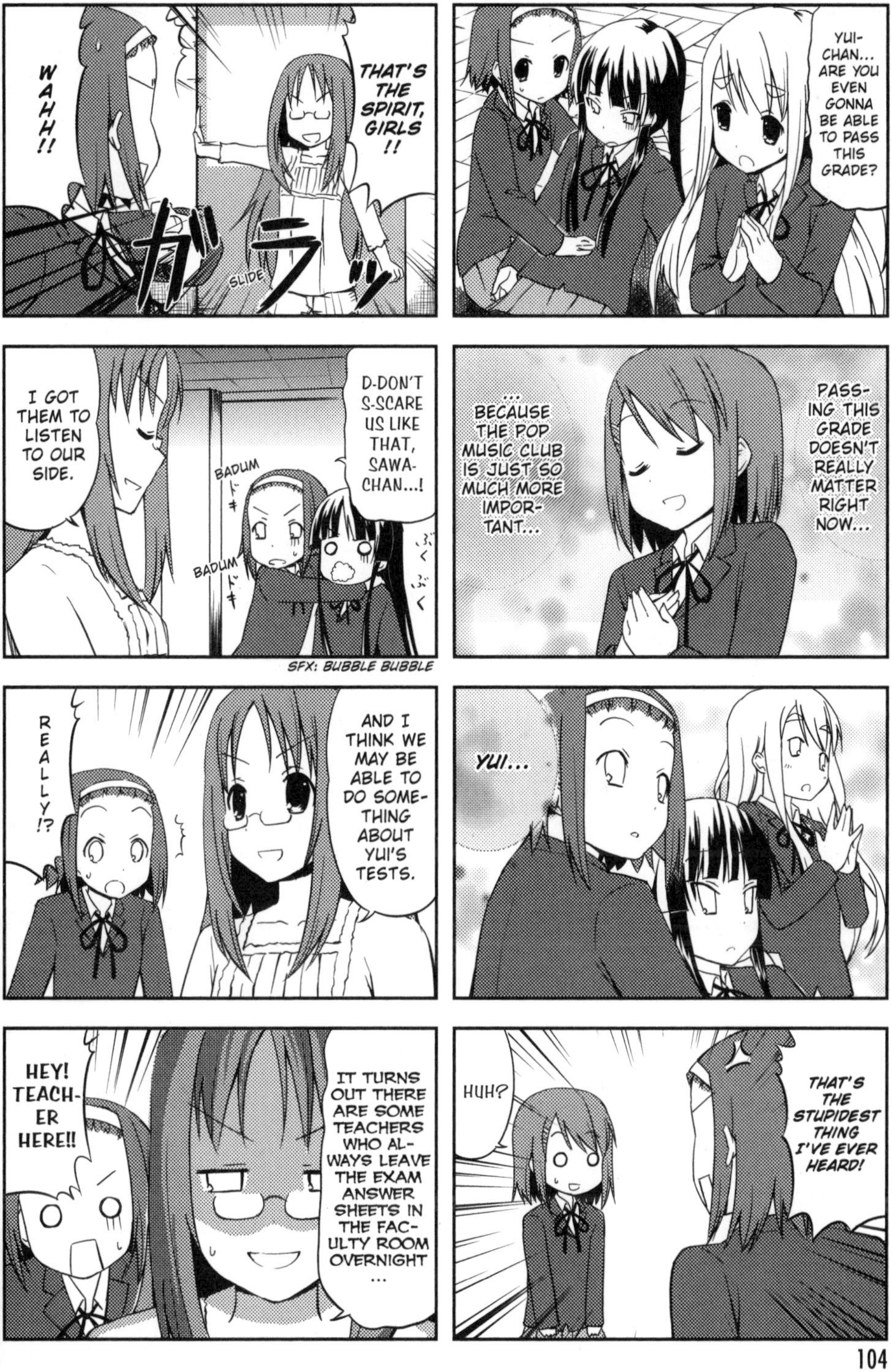
YUI-CHAN... ARE YOU EVEN GONNA BE ABLE TO PASS THIS GRADE?
PASSING THIS GRADE DOESN'T REALLY MATTER RIGHT NOW...
...BECAUSE THE POP MUSIC CLUB IS JUST SO MUCH MORE IMPORTANT...
YUI...
THAT'S THE STUPIDEST THING I'VE EVER HEARD!
HUH?
THAT'S THE SPIRIT, GIRLS!!
WAHH!!
ガラッ
SLIDE
D-DON'T S-SCARE US LIKE THAT, SAWA-CHAN...!
I GOT THEM TO LISTEN TO OUR SIDE.
BADUM ドキ
BADUM ドキ
ぶくぶく
SFX: BUBBLE BUBBLE
AND I THINK WE MAY BE ABLE TO DO SOMETHING ABOUT YUI'S TESTS.
REALLY!?
IT TURNS OUT THERE ARE SOME TEACHERS WHO ALWAYS LEAVE THE EXAM ANSWER SHEETS IN THE FACULTY ROOM OVERNIGHT...
HEY! TEACHER HERE!!

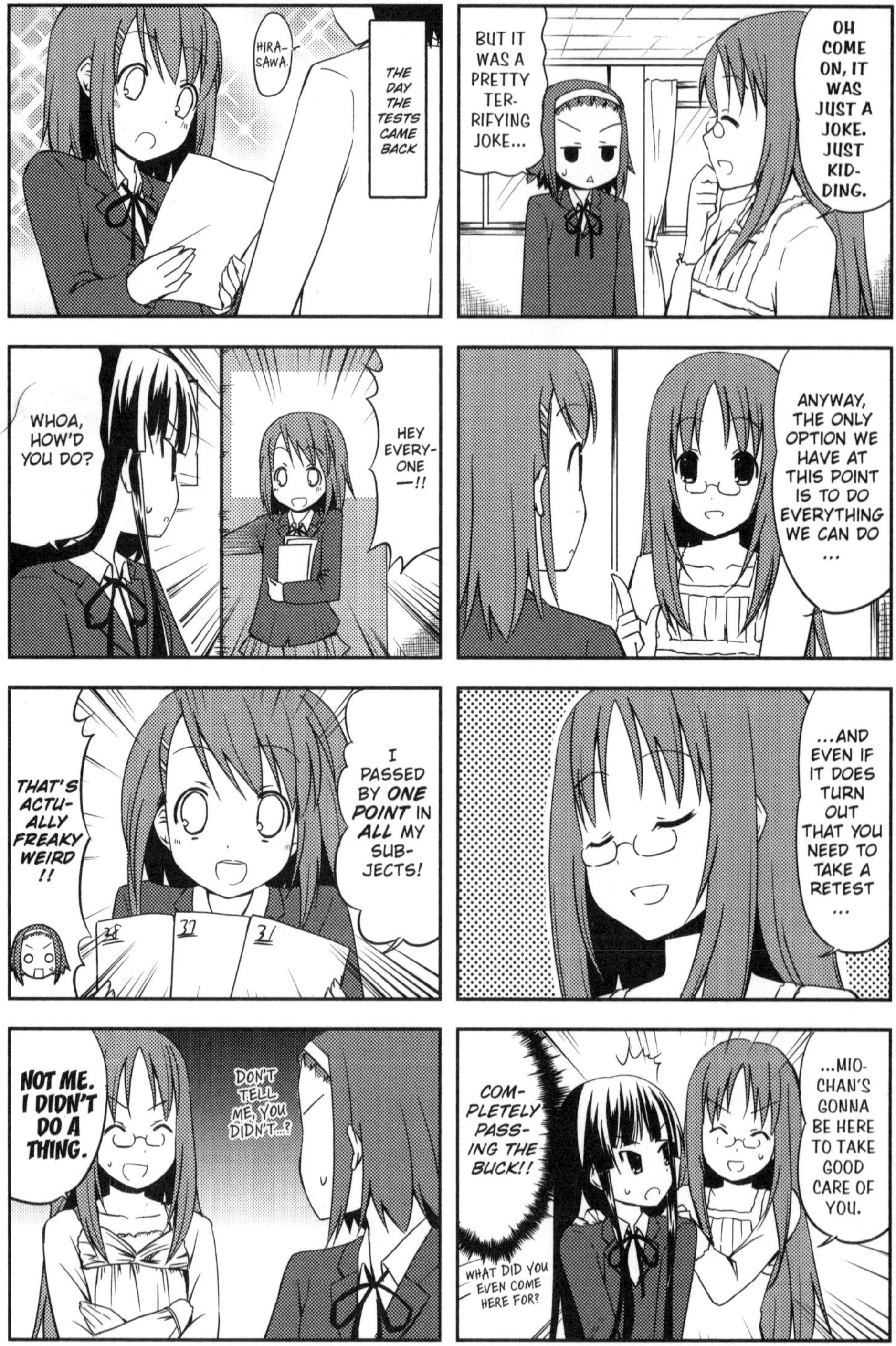
OH COME ON, IT WAS JUST A JOKE. JUST KIDDING.
BUT IT WAS A PRETTY TERRIFYING JOKE...
ANYWAY, THE ONLY OPTION WE HAVE AT THIS POINT IS TO DO EVERYTHING WE CAN DO ...
...AND EVEN IF IT DOES TURN OUT THAT YOU NEED TO TAKE A RETEST ...
...MIO-CHAN'S GONNA BE HERE TO TAKE GOOD CARE OF YOU.
COMPLETELY PASSING THE BUCK!!
WHAT DID YOU EVEN COME HERE FOR?
THE DAY THE TESTS CAME BACK
HIRA-SAWA.
HEY EVERYONE—!!
WHOA, HOW'D YOU DO?
I PASSED BY ONE POINT IN ALL MY SUBJECTS!
THAT'S ACTUALLY FREAKY WEIRD!!
DON'T TELL ME, YOU DIDN'T...?
NOT ME. I DIDN'T DO A THING.

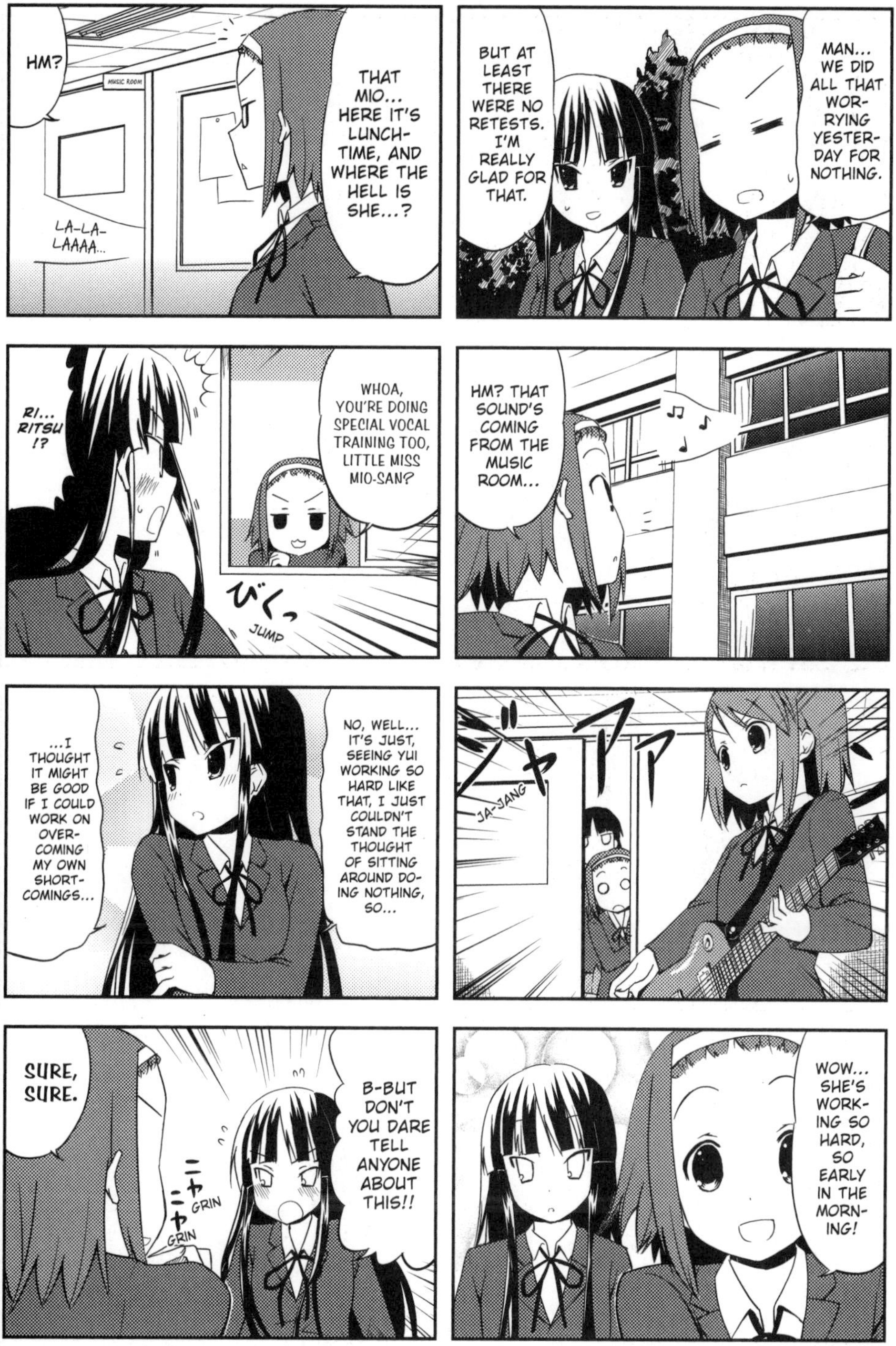
MAN... WE DID ALL THAT WORRYING YESTERDAY FOR NOTHING.
BUT AT LEAST THERE WERE NO RETESTS. I'M REALLY GLAD FOR THAT.
THAT MIO... HERE IT'S LUNCHTIME, AND WHERE THE HELL IS SHE...?
HM?
MUSIC ROOM
LA-LA-LAAAA...
HM? THAT SOUND'S COMING FROM THE MUSIC ROOM...
WHOA, YOU'RE DOING SPECIAL VOCAL TRAINING TOO, LITTLE MISS MIO-SAN?
RI... RITSU!?
びくっ
JUMP
ジャアア
JA-JANG
NO, WELL... IT'S JUST, SEEING YUI WORKING SO HARD LIKE THAT, I JUST COULDN'T STAND THE THOUGHT OF SITTING AROUND DOING NOTHING, SO...
...I THOUGHT IT MIGHT BE GOOD IF I COULD WORK ON OVERCOMING MY OWN SHORTCOMINGS...
WOW... SHE'S WORKING SO HARD, SO EARLY IN THE MORNING!
B-BUT DON'T YOU DARE TELL ANYONE ABOUT THIS!!
SURE, SURE.
ニヤニヤ
GRIN
GRIN

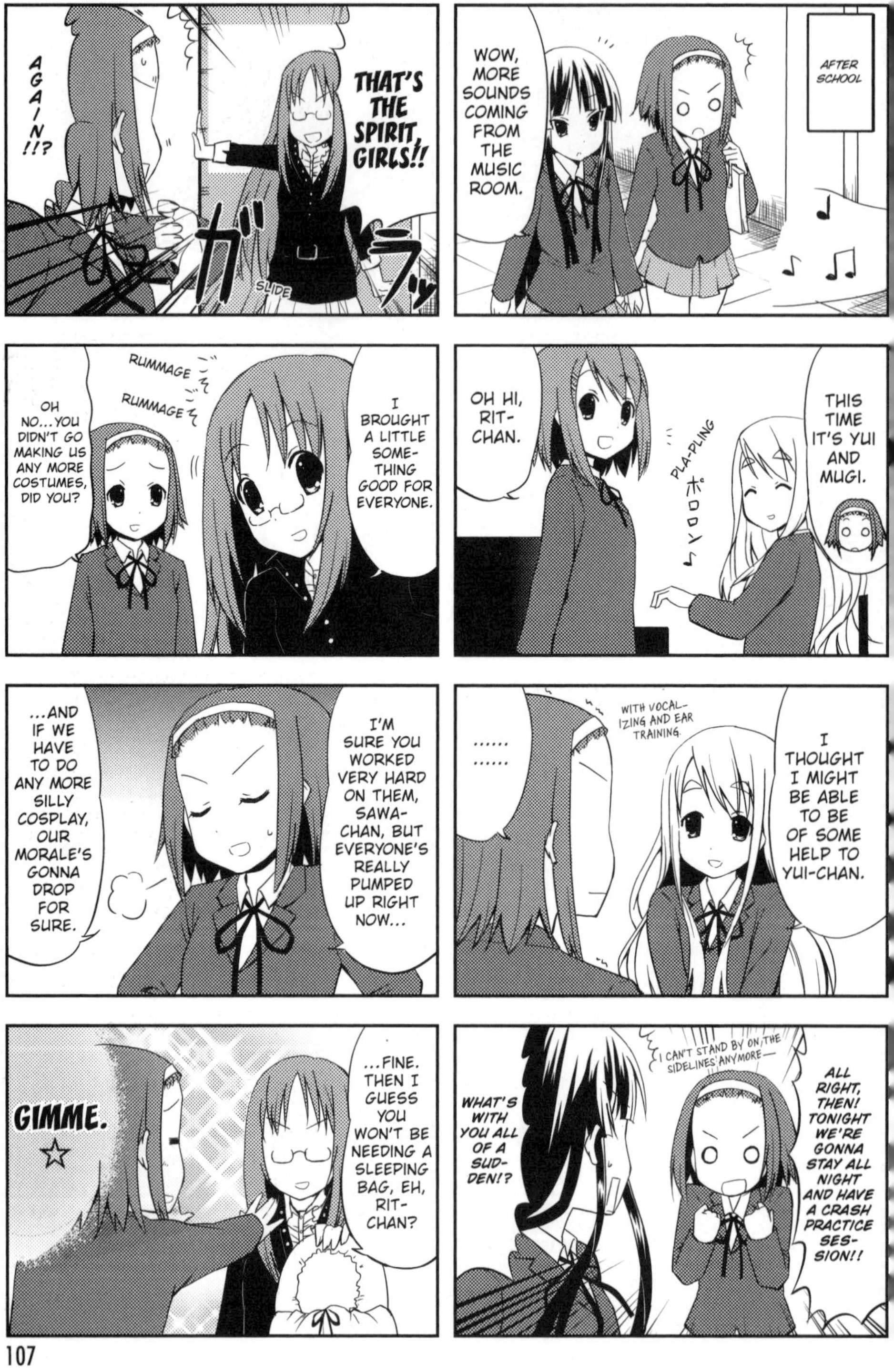
AFTER SCHOOL
WOW, MORE SOUNDS COMING FROM THE MUSIC ROOM.
THIS TIME IT'S YUI AND MUGI.
PLA-PLING
ポロロン♪
OH HI, RIT-CHAN.
I THOUGHT I MIGHT BE ABLE TO BE OF SOME HELP TO YUI-CHAN.
WITH VOCAL-IZING AND EAR TRAINING.
....
ALL RIGHT, THEN! TONIGHT WE'RE GONNA STAY ALL NIGHT AND HAVE A CRASH PRACTICE SES-SION!!
I CAN'T STAND BY ON THE SIDELINES ANYMORE—
WHAT'S WITH YOU ALL OF A SUD-DEN!?
THAT'S THE SPIRIT, GIRLS!!
ガラッ
SLIDE
AGAIN!!?
I BROUGHT A LITTLE SOME-THING GOOD FOR EVERYONE.
RUMMAGE
RUMMAGE
OH NO...YOU DIDN'T GO MAKING US ANY MORE COSTUMES, DID YOU?
I'M SURE YOU WORKED VERY HARD ON THEM, SAWA-CHAN, BUT EVERYONE'S REALLY PUMPED UP RIGHT NOW...
...AND IF WE HAVE TO DO ANY MORE SILLY COSPLAY, OUR MORALE'S GONNA DROP FOR SURE.
...FINE. THEN I GUESS YOU WON'T BE NEEDING A SLEEPING BAG, EH, RIT-CHAN?
GIMME. ☆

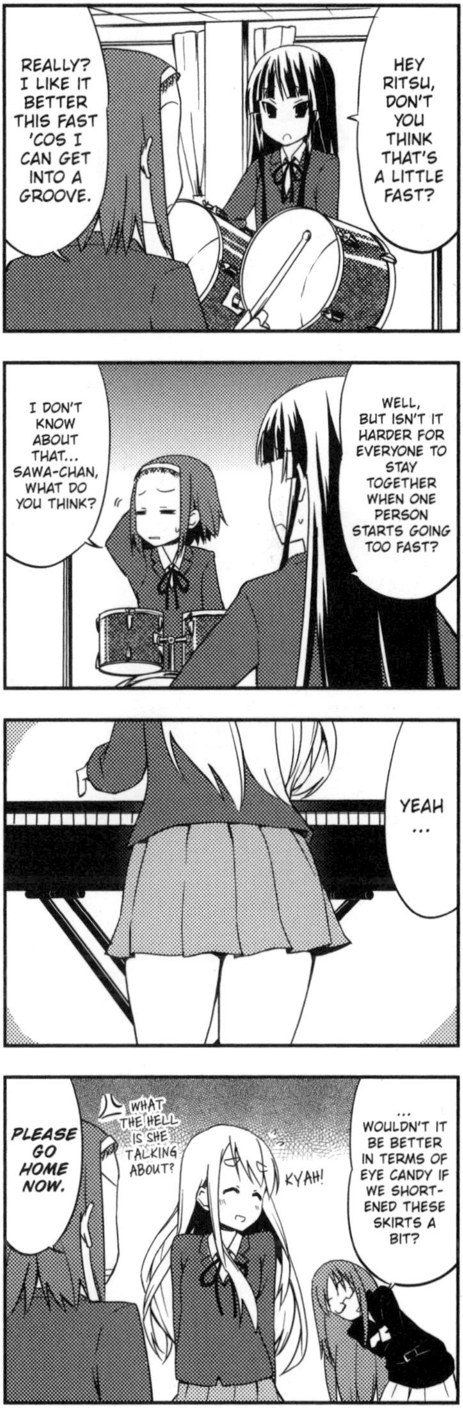
HEY RITSU, DON'T YOU THINK THAT'S A LITTLE FAST?
REALLY? I LIKE IT BETTER THIS FAST 'COS I CAN GET INTO A GROOVE.
WELL, BUT ISN'T IT HARDER FOR EVERYONE TO STAY TOGETHER WHEN ONE PERSON STARTS GOING TOO FAST?
I DON'T KNOW ABOUT THAT... SAWA-CHAN, WHAT DO YOU THINK?
YEAH ...
... WOULDN'T IT BE BETTER IN TERMS OF EYE CANDY IF WE SHORTENED THESE SKIRTS A BIT?
KYAH!
WHAT THE HELL IS SHE TALKING ABOUT?
PLEASE GO HOME NOW.
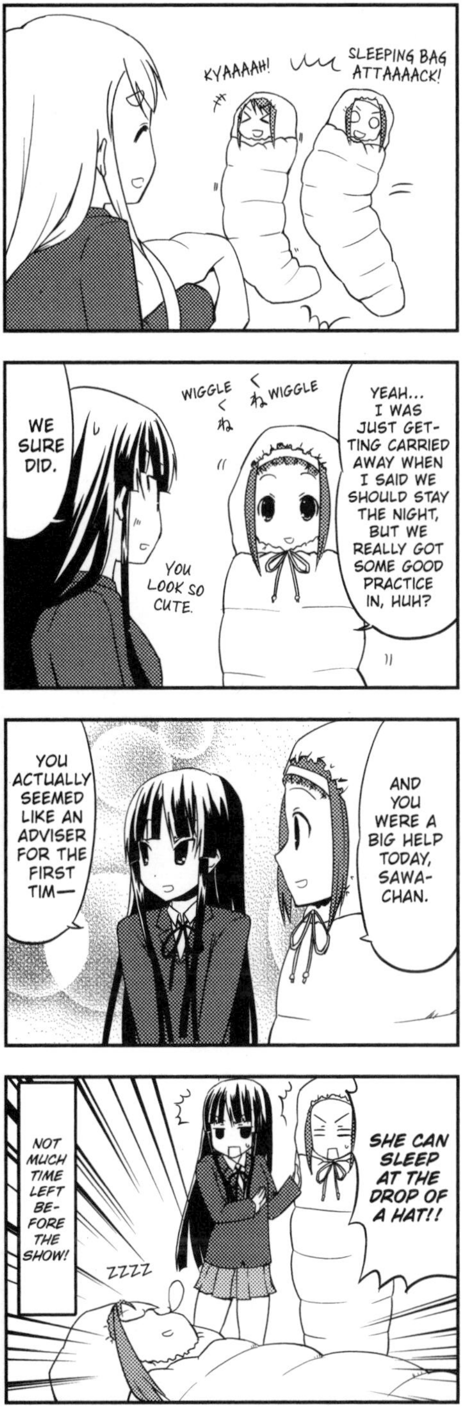
SLEEPING BAG ATTAAAACK!
KYAAAAH!
YEAH... I WAS JUST GETTING CARRIED AWAY WHEN I SAID WE SHOULD STAY THE NIGHT, BUT WE REALLY GOT SOME GOOD PRACTICE IN, HUH?
WIGGLE WIGGLE
YOU LOOK SO CUTE.
WE SURE DID.
AND YOU WERE A BIG HELP TODAY, SAWA-CHAN.
YOU ACTUALLY SEEMED LIKE AN ADVISER FOR THE FIRST TIM—
SHE CAN SLEEP AT THE DROP OF A HAT!!
ZZZZ
NOT MUCH TIME LEFT BEFORE THE SHOW!

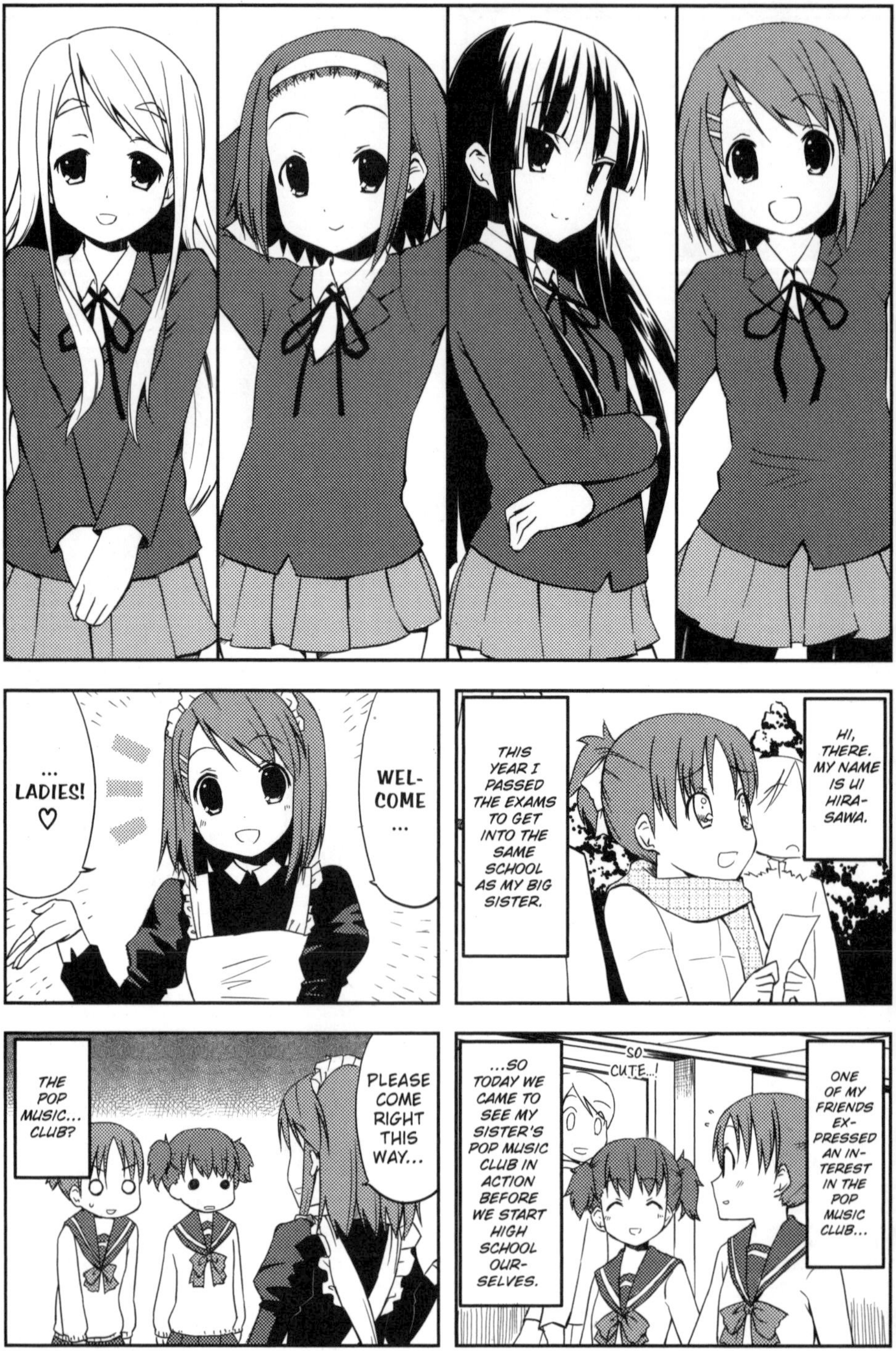
HI, THERE. MY NAME IS UI HIRA-SAWA.
THIS YEAR I PASSED THE EXAMS TO GET INTO THE SAME SCHOOL AS MY BIG SISTER.
WEL-COME ...
... LADIES! ♡
ONE OF MY FRIENDS EX-PRESSED AN IN-TEREST IN THE POP MUSIC CLUB...
SO CUTE...!
...SO TODAY WE CAME TO SEE MY SISTER'S POP MUSIC CLUB IN ACTION BEFORE WE START HIGH SCHOOL OUR-SELVES.
PLEASE COME RIGHT THIS WAY...
THE POP MUSIC... CLUB?

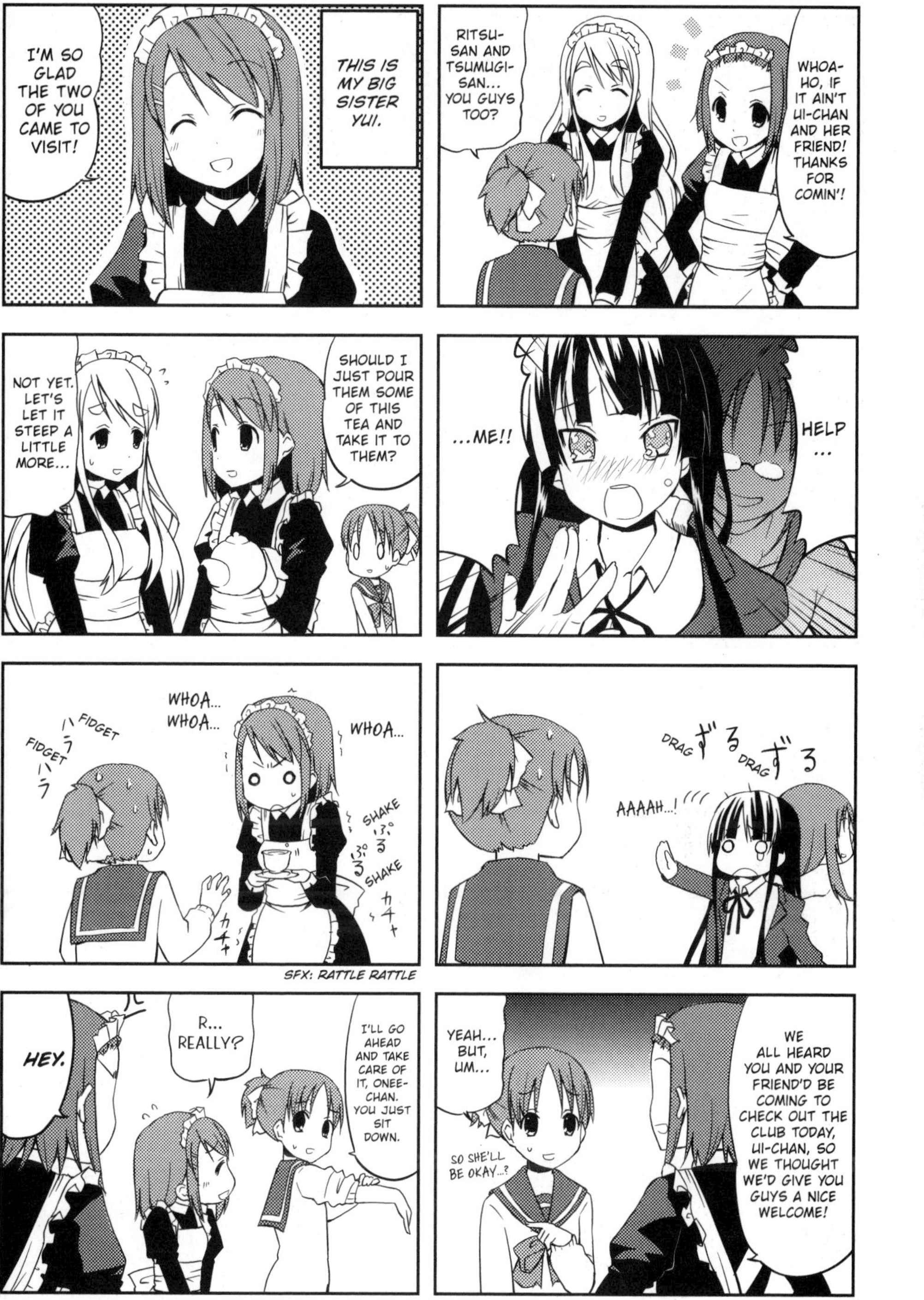
WHOA-HO, IF IT AIN'T UI-CHAN AND HER FRIEND! THANKS FOR COMIN'!
RITSU-SAN AND TSUMUGI-SAN... YOU GUYS TOO?
HELP...
...ME!!
DRAG ずる DRAG ずる
AAAAH...!
WE ALL HEARD YOU AND YOUR FRIEND'D BE COMING TO CHECK OUT THE CLUB TODAY, UI-CHAN, SO WE THOUGHT WE'D GIVE YOU GUYS A NICE WELCOME!
YEAH... BUT, UM...
SO SHE'LL BE OKAY...?
THIS IS MY BIG SISTER YUI.
I'M SO GLAD THE TWO OF YOU CAME TO VISIT!
SHOULD I JUST POUR THEM SOME OF THIS TEA AND TAKE IT TO THEM?
NOT YET. LET'S LET IT STEEP A LITTLE MORE...
WHOA...
SHAKE ぷる ぷる SHAKE
カチャ カチャ
WHOA... WHOA...
FIDGET ハラ FIDGET ハラ
SFX: RATTLE RATTLE
I'LL GO AHEAD AND TAKE CARE OF IT, ONEE-CHAN. YOU JUST SIT DOWN.
R... REALLY?
HEY.

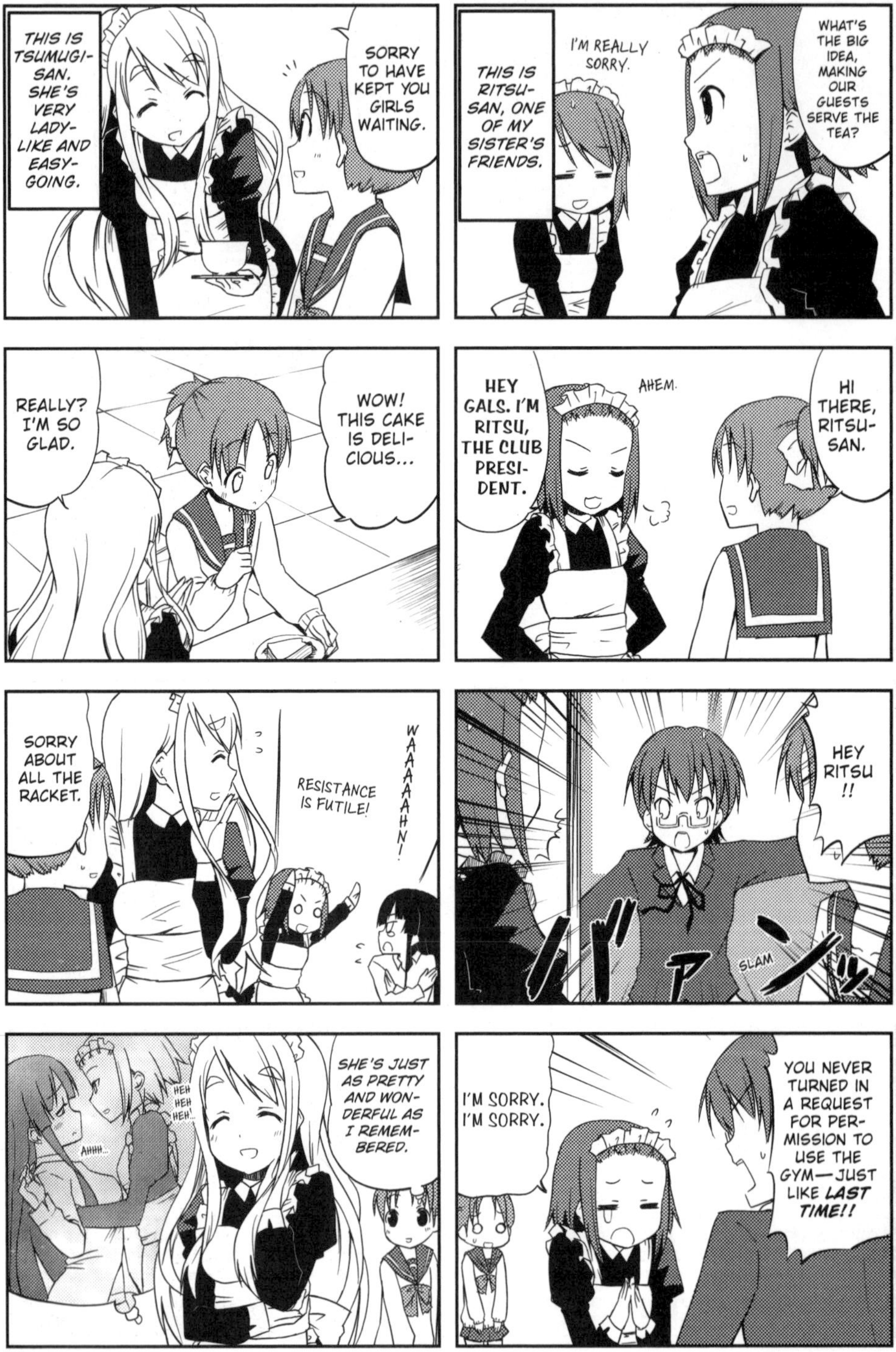

WHAT'S THE BIG IDEA, MAKING OUR GUESTS SERVE THE TEA?
I'M REALLY SORRY.
THIS IS RITSU-SAN, ONE OF MY SISTER'S FRIENDS.
HI THERE, RITSU-SAN.
AHEM.
HEY GALS. I'M RITSU, THE CLUB PRESIDENT.
HEY RITSU!!
SLAM
YOU NEVER TURNED IN A REQUEST FOR PERMISSION TO USE THE GYM—JUST LIKE LAST TIME!!
I'M SORRY. I'M SORRY.
SORRY TO HAVE KEPT YOU GIRLS WAITING.
THIS IS TSUMUGI-SAN. SHE'S VERY LADYLIKE AND EASYGOING.
WOW! THIS CAKE IS DELICIOUS...
REALLY? I'M SO GLAD.
WAAAAAAHN!
RESISTANCE IS FUTILE!
SORRY ABOUT ALL THE RACKET.
SHE'S JUST AS PRETTY AND WONDERFUL AS I REMEMBERED.
HEH HEH HEH...
AHHH...

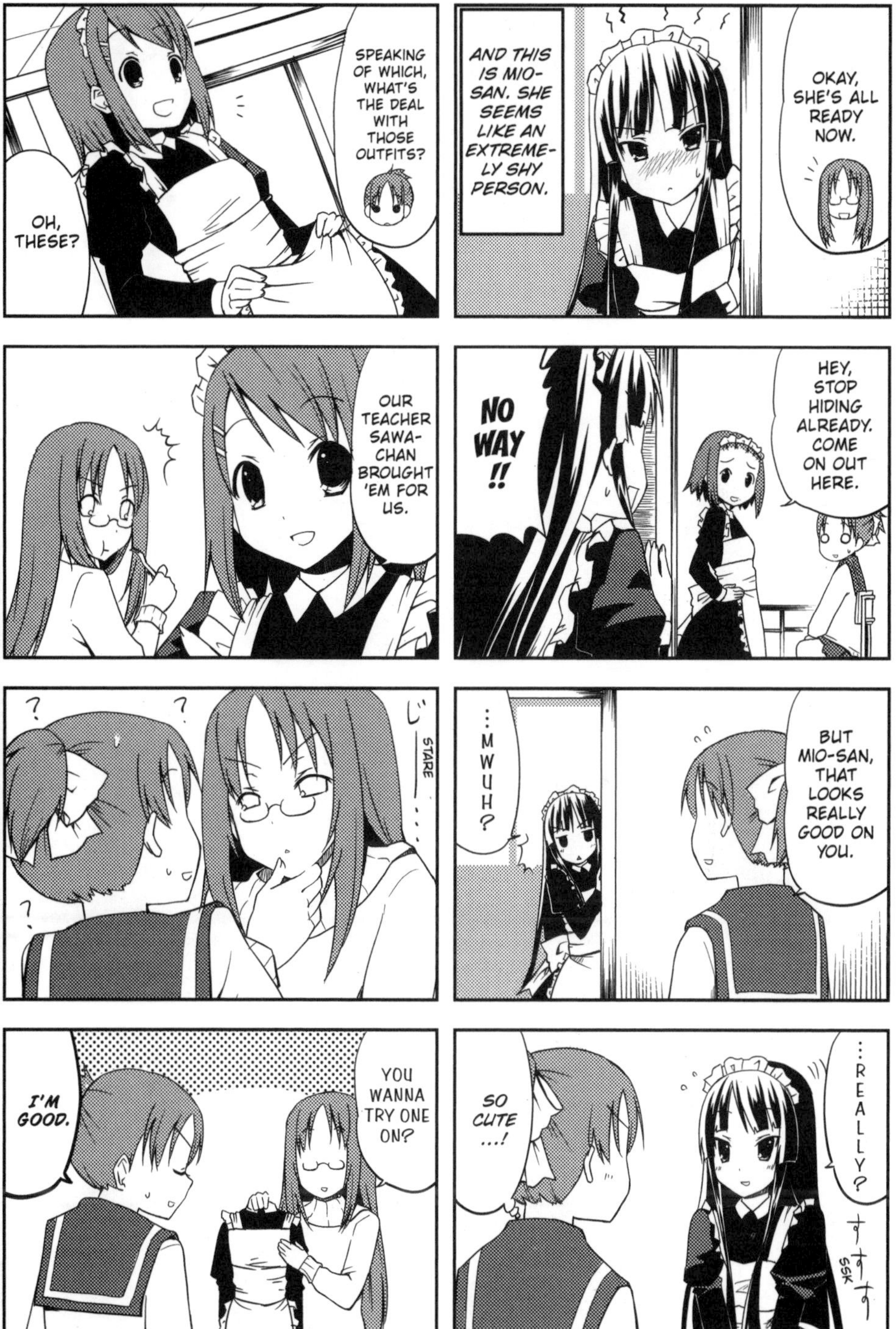
OKAY, SHE'S ALL READY NOW.
AND THIS IS MIO-SAN. SHE SEEMS LIKE AN EXTREMELY SHY PERSON.
HEY, STOP HIDING ALREADY. COME ON OUT HERE.
NO WAY!!
BUT MIO-SAN, THAT LOOKS REALLY GOOD ON YOU.
...MWUH?
...REALLY?
SO CUTE ...!
すすす SSK
SPEAKING OF WHICH, WHAT'S THE DEAL WITH THOSE OUTFITS?
OH, THESE?
OUR TEACHER SAWA-CHAN BROUGHT 'EM FOR US.
じー STARE...
YOU WANNA TRY ONE ON?
I'M GOOD.

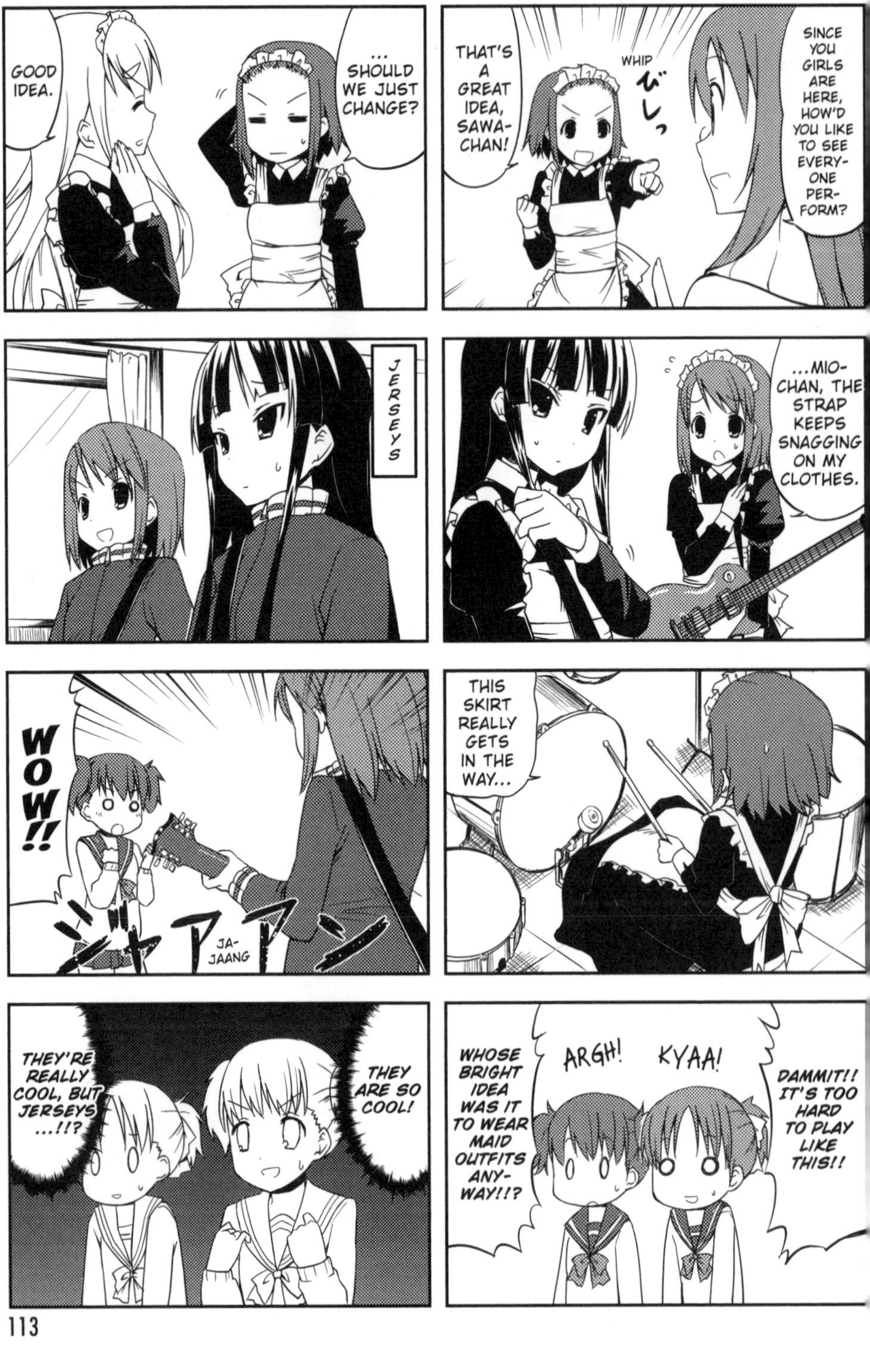

SINCE YOU GIRLS ARE HERE, HOW'D YOU LIKE TO SEE EVERYONE PERFORM?
WHIP びしっ
THAT'S A GREAT IDEA, SAWA-CHAN!
...MIO-CHAN, THE STRAP KEEPS SNAGGING ON MY CLOTHES.
THIS SKIRT REALLY GETS IN THE WAY...
DAMMIT!! IT'S TOO HARD TO PLAY LIKE THIS!!
KYAA!
ARGH!
WHOSE BRIGHT IDEA WAS IT TO WEAR MAID OUTFITS ANYWAY!!?
... SHOULD WE JUST CHANGE?
GOOD IDEA.
JERSEYS
WOW!!
JA-JAANG
THEY ARE SO COOL!
THEY'RE REALLY COOL, BUT JERSEYS ...!!?

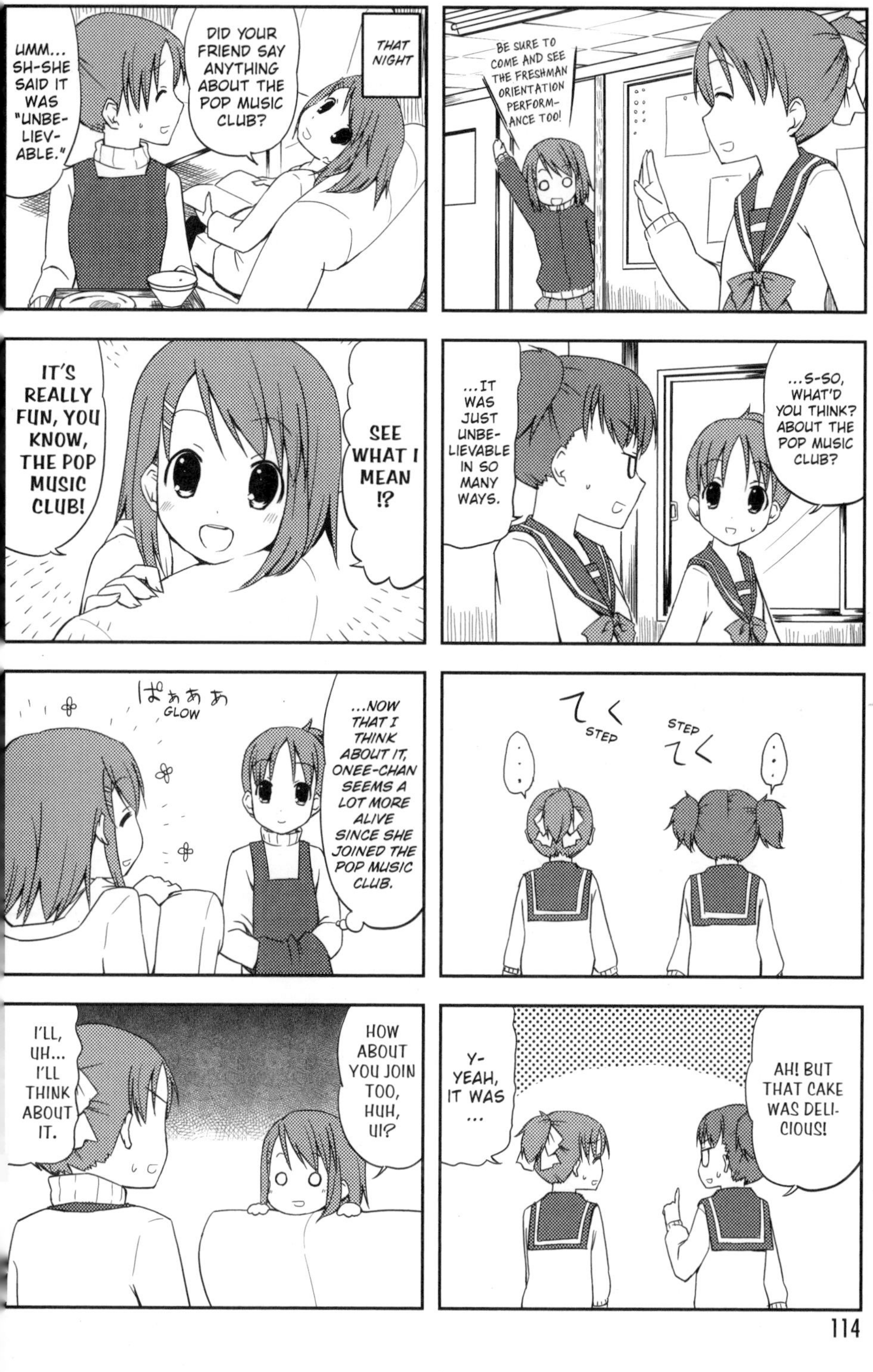
BE SURE TO COME AND SEE THE FRESHMAN ORIENTATION PERFORMANCE TOO!
...S-SO, WHAT'D YOU THINK? ABOUT THE POP MUSIC CLUB?
...IT WAS JUST UNBELIEVABLE IN SO MANY WAYS.
STEP てく
...
てく STEP
...
AH! BUT THAT CAKE WAS DELICIOUS!
Y-YEAH, IT WAS ...
THAT NIGHT
DID YOUR FRIEND SAY ANYTHING ABOUT THE POP MUSIC CLUB?
UMM... SH-SHE SAID IT WAS "UNBELIEVABLE."
SEE WHAT I MEAN!?
IT'S REALLY FUN, YOU KNOW, THE POP MUSIC CLUB!
...NOW THAT I THINK ABOUT IT, ONEE-CHAN SEEMS A LOT MORE ALIVE SINCE SHE JOINED THE POP MUSIC CLUB.
ぱぁあぁあ GLOW
HOW ABOUT YOU JOIN TOO, HUH, UI?
I'LL, UH... I'LL THINK ABOUT IT.

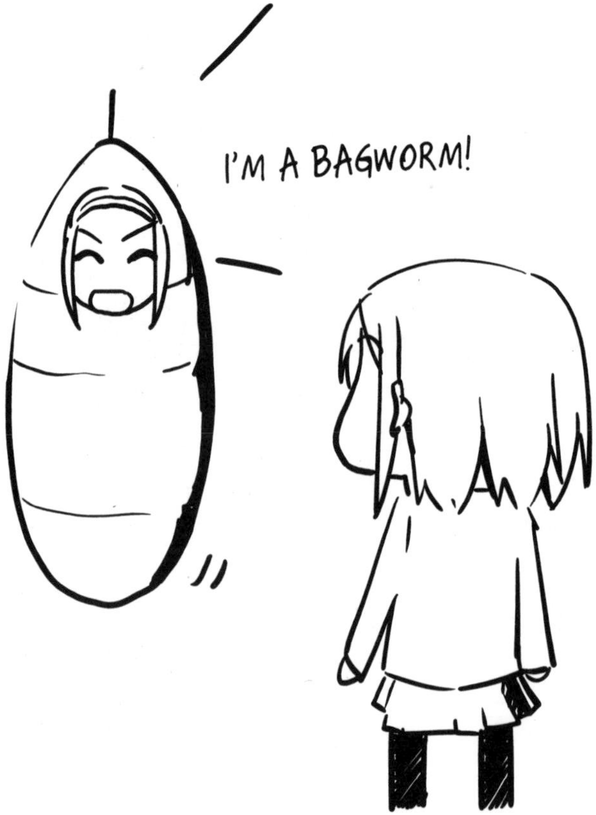
I'M A BAGWORM!

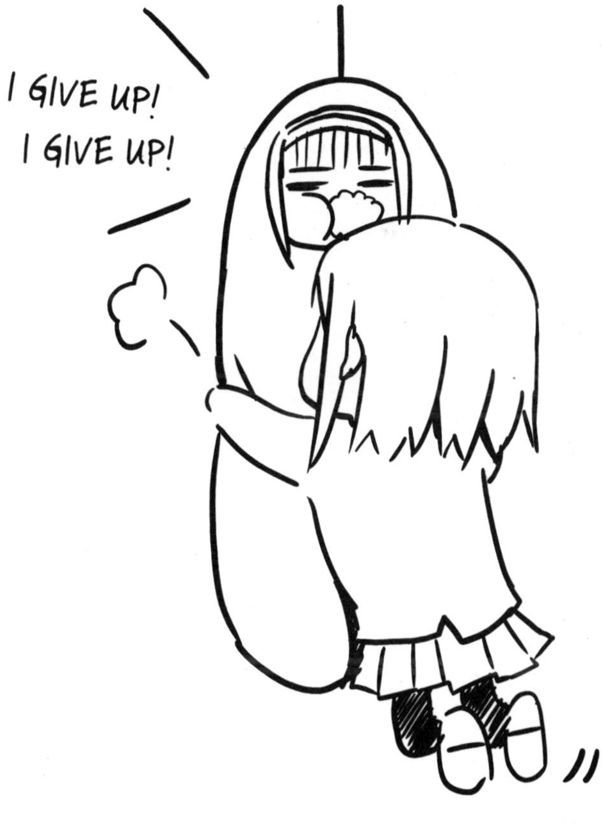
I GIVE UP!
I GIVE UP!

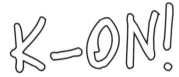

K-ON!

CONGRATULATIONS ON YOUR BOOK COMING OUT. KEEP ON WORKING HARD WHILE EATING NOTHING BUT CURRY!

–DAIOKI

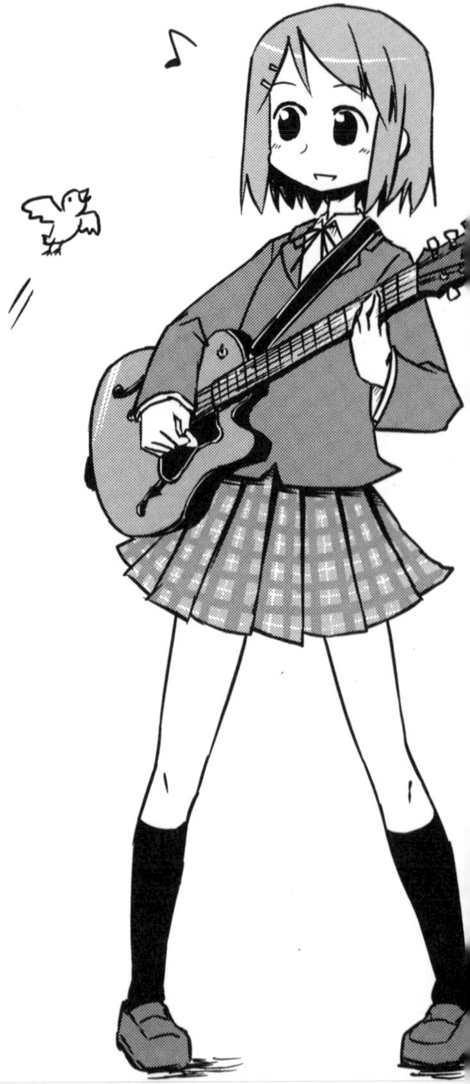

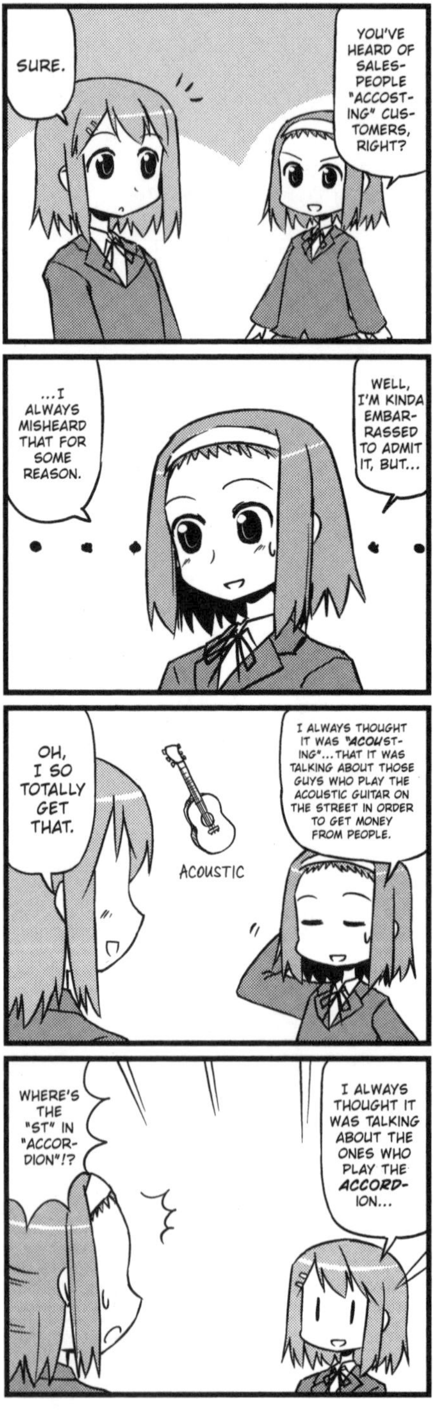
YOU'VE HEARD OF SALES-PEOPLE "ACCOSTING" CUSTOMERS, RIGHT?
SURE.
WELL, I'M KINDA EMBARRASSED TO ADMIT IT, BUT...
...I ALWAYS MISHEARD THAT FOR SOME REASON.
I ALWAYS THOUGHT IT WAS "ACOUSTING"...THAT IT WAS TALKING ABOUT THOSE GUYS WHO PLAY THE ACOUSTIC GUITAR ON THE STREET IN ORDER TO GET MONEY FROM PEOPLE.
ACOUSTIC
OH, I SO TOTALLY GET THAT.
I ALWAYS THOUGHT IT WAS TALKING ABOUT THE ONES WHO PLAY THE ACCORDION...
WHERE'S THE "ST" IN "ACCORDION"!?

AFTERWORD

HELLO, MY NAME IS KAKIFLY. I WANT TO THANK YOU FROM THE BOTTOM OF MY HEART FOR BUYING THE FIRST VOLUME OF *K-ON!* THIS BOOK IS MY VERY FIRST MANGA COMPILATION! SOMEHOW IT STILL DOESN'T SEEM QUITE REAL...BUT IF YOU ENJOY IT EVEN JUST A LITTLE BIT, THEN NOTHING WOULD MAKE ME HAPPIER!

BY THE WAY, THE GUITARS YOU SEE IN THE PHOTO ON THE OPPOSITE PAGE ARE FROM MY OWN PERSONAL GUITAR COLLECTION. AND DID YOU HAPPEN TO NOTICE ANYTHING JUST A BIT UNUSUAL IN THE PHOTO? THAT'S RIGHT——THE GUITARS ARE ALL LEFT-HANDED..AND NO, IT'S NOT A REVERSE-IMAGE PHOTO. THE WHOLE REASON WHY I MADE MIO LEFT-HANDED IN THIS SERIES IS BECAUSE I MYSELF AM LEFT-HANDED. I THINK IT'D BE REALLY GREAT IF ONE OF THESE DAYS I COULD MAKE A MANGA STORY AROUND THE IDEA OF GRUMBLING ABOUT WHAT A PAIN IT SOMETIMES IS TO BE LEFT-HANDED (LOL).

BEFORE I CLOSE, I'D LIKE TO THANK A FEW PEOPLE: MY EDITOR "S-HARA," WHO I'M CONSTANTLY MAKING TROUBLE FOR; MY FRIEND DAIOKI, WHO WAS KIND ENOUGH TO DRAW A FANTASTIC BONUS MANGA PAGE FOR THIS VOLUME AS A GUEST ARTIST; AND LAST BUT NOT LEAST, YOU, THE READER, WHO DID ME THE HONOR OF BUYING THIS BOOK. THANKS VERY MUCH TO ALL OF YOU!

UNTIL WE MEET AGAIN IN VOLUME 2!

KAKIFLY

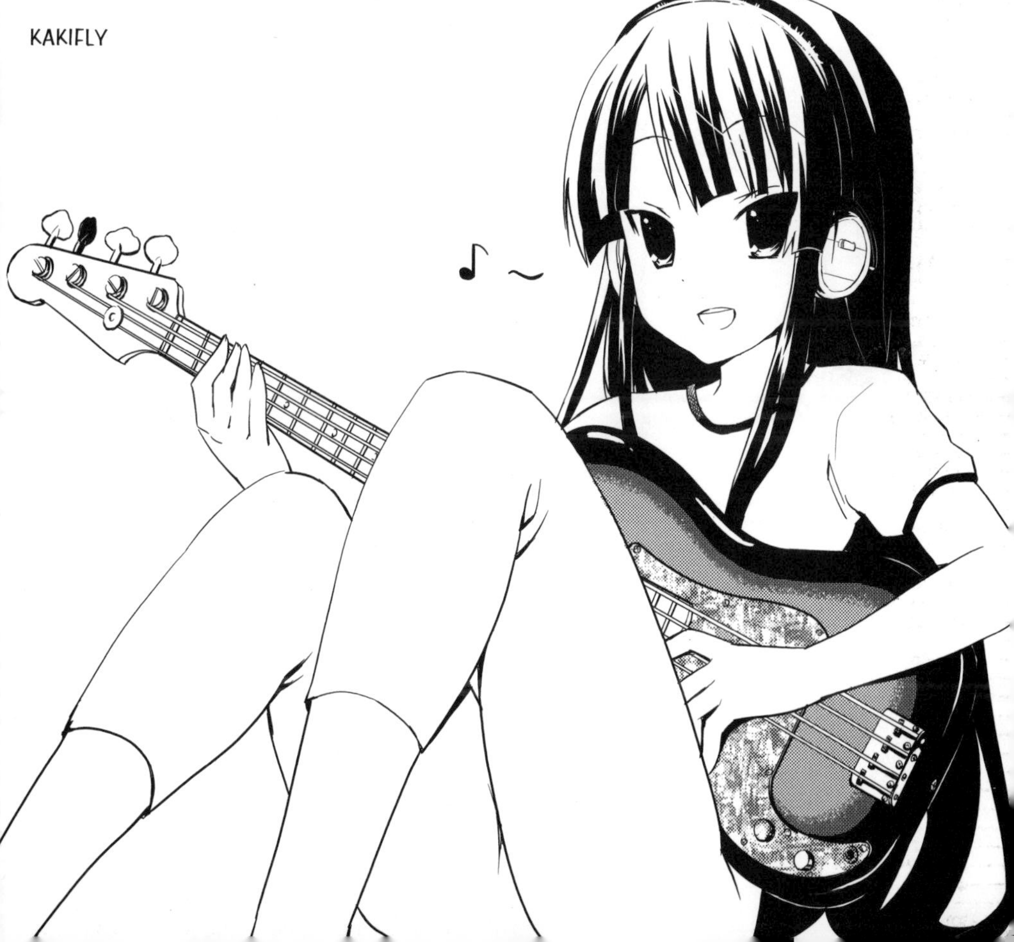

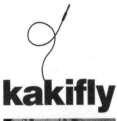

kakifly

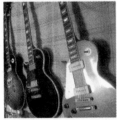

C O M M E N T S

Hi, my name is kakifly.
One food I don't like is
oysters. Thank you so
much for buying my book.

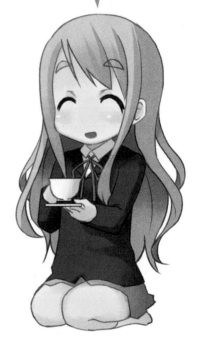

THANKS FOR
READING!

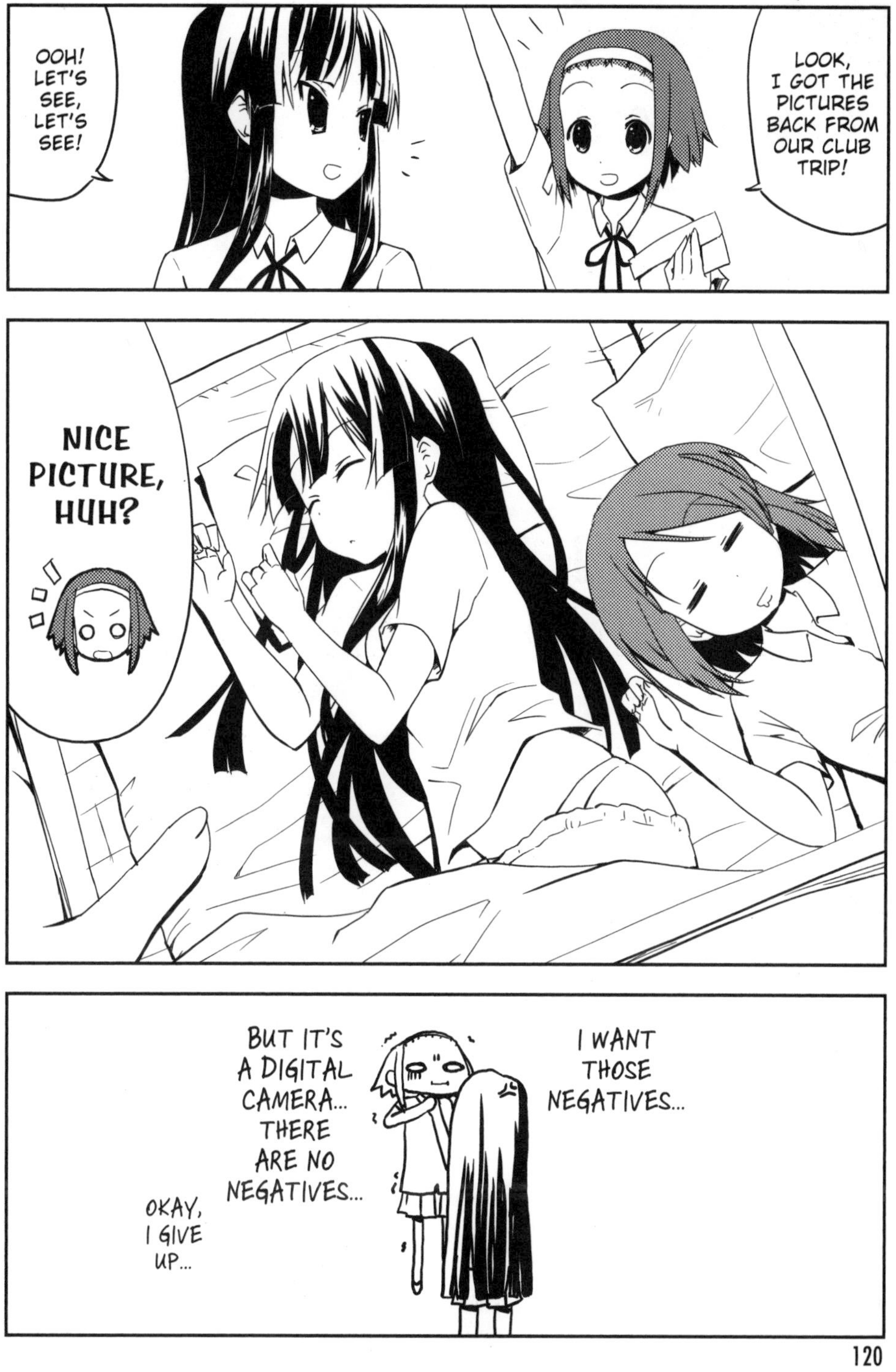
LOOK, I GOT THE PICTURES BACK FROM OUR CLUB TRIP!
OOH! LET'S SEE, LET'S SEE!
NICE PICTURE, HUH?
I WANT THOSE NEGATIVES...
BUT IT'S A DIGITAL CAMERA... THERE ARE NO NEGATIVES...
OKAY, I GIVE UP...

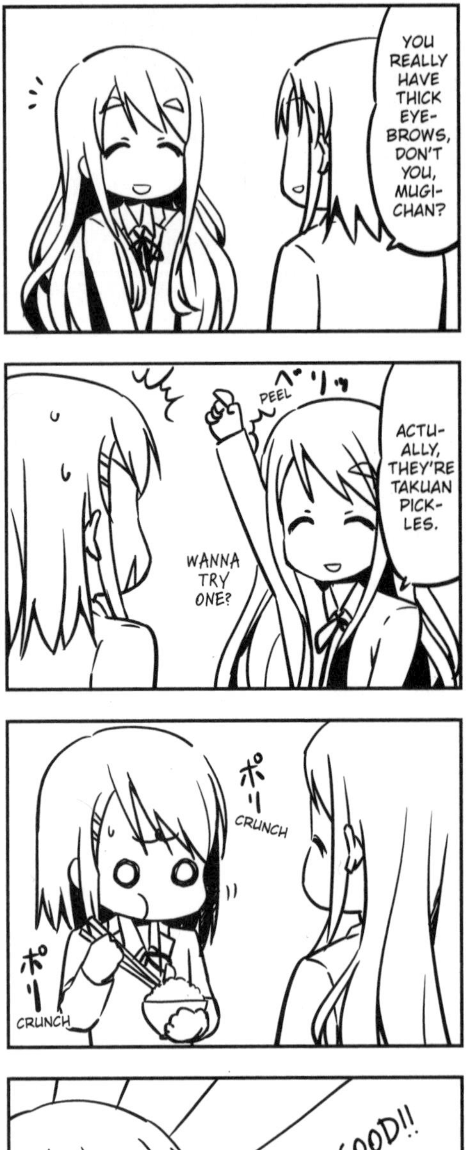
YOU REALLY HAVE THICK EYE-BROWS, DON'T YOU, MUGI-CHAN?
ペリッ
PEEL
ACTU-ALLY, THEY'RE TAKUAN PICK-LES.
WANNA TRY ONE?
ポリ
CRUNCH
ポリ
CRUNCH
THEY'RE GOOD!!

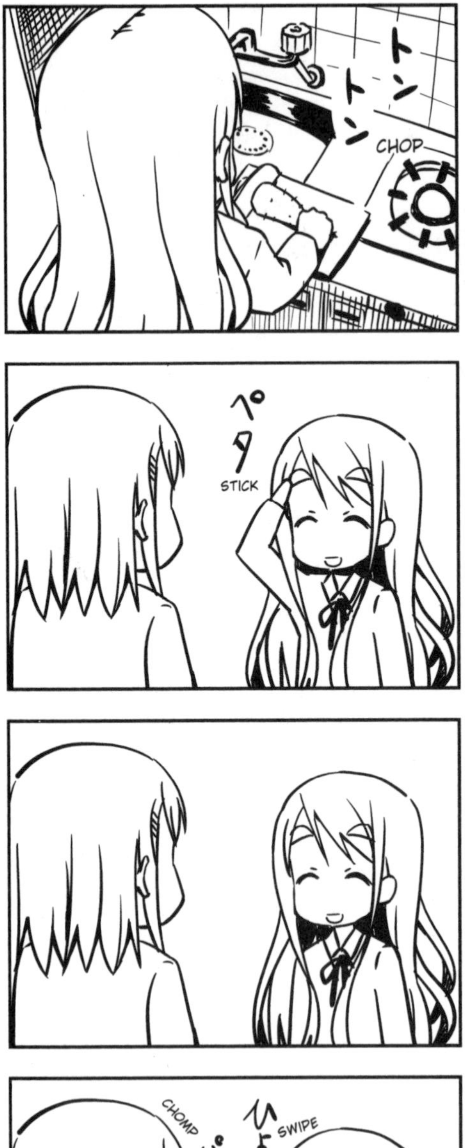
トン
トン
CHOP
ペタ
STICK
ひょい
SWIPE
パク
CHOMP

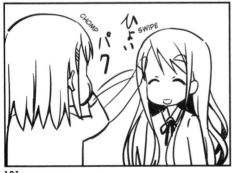

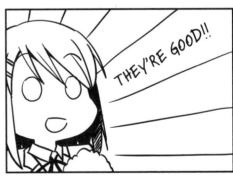

work nor engaging in any productive but unpaid economic activity (such as housework).

PAGE 11

Johannes Krauser II

The scary-looking character Yui pictures is a parody of Johannes Krauser II, alter ego of Souichi Negishi, the main character of the manga *Detroit Metal City*. When in character, Souichi paints his face with white makeup and draws the word "殺" (KILL) as a fake tattoo on his forehead.

PAGE 16

Yen Conversion

A general rule of thumb to use for converting Japanese yen to American dollars is ¥100 to 1 USD. Thus, ¥5,000 is about $50. You can't even get a dirt-cheap guitar for that price. Most low-end guitars in the US start around $100, though high-end guitars can cost upward of $1,000.

PAGE 23

Yui's guitar

The guitar that Yui buys in this volume is a Gibson Les Paul Standard model with Honey Burst finish. This guitar retails for around $3,500 new in the US, so even the roughly $1,500 price tag Yui sees is a pretty good deal. Getting one for around $500 would be an incredible steal.

PAGE 25

Charumera Song

This is the tune played by mobile ramen vendors (similar in concept to ice cream trucks) to alert potential customers to their presence. It's usually a canned recording of a specific melody played on a shrill-toned double-reed woodwind instrument called a *"charumera"* in Japanese (from Portuguese *charamela* because the instrument was first brought to Japan by Portuguese missionaries), or "shawm" in English. Thus, the musical phrase "chalalii~lala~" is strongly associated with ramen trucks in Japan.

PAGE 28

Gifts

Gift-giving is a very important component of business etiquette in Japan, and since such gifts tend to pass from the bottom to the top in terms of corporate hierarchy, the people in positions of most power receive the most (and most expensive) gifts.

PAGE 31

Chords Even A Monkey Could Learn

This is a parody of the *...For Dummies* books in the US There are various *Saru Demo Wakaru...* (Even A Monkey Could...) books of the same ilk in Japan.

Musical Notation

The notation Yui sees in the chord practice book is called tablature. It's a kind of musical shorthand showing how to finger chords on fretted instruments.

PAGE 35

Class 1-B

"Class 1-B" shows that Ritsu is in the 10th-grade, second cohort. Japanese high school students don't move around from room to room and participate in different class groupings like US students do. Instead, they belong to a fixed "cohort" (*kumi*) that stays grouped in the same room all year, and teachers for each subject visit the room during the appropriate times.

PAGE 37

Harumi

This is a "cameo" of the character Harumi Hosono from manga author Daioki's four-panel manga *Harumi Nation*. K-ON! author kakifly and Daioki are friends as well as colleagues, and Daioki even drew the bonus manga page for this volume of K-ON! on page 117.

PAGE 43

Salty/Brackish

Ritsu says the water is "salty" (*shoppai*), but the same word is wrestling slang (especially sumo wrestling) for "weak" (because the wrestlers toss salt into the ring before each bout, so a losing wrestler who spends a lot of time on the floor gets covered in salt). *"Shoppai"* is also more general slang for "sad" (because tears are salty). In this case, Yui misunderstands what Ritsu says and then "corrects" her.

TRANSLATION NOTES

COMMON HONORIFICS

no honorific: Indicates familiarity or closeness; if used without permission or reason, addressing someone in this manner would constitute an insult.

-san: The Japanese equivalent of Mr./Mrs./Miss. If a situation calls for politeness, this is the fail-safe honorific.

-sama: Conveys great respect; may also indicate that the social status of the speaker is lower than that of the addressee.

-kun: Used most often when referring to boys, this indicates affection or familiarity. Occasionally used by older men among their peers, but it may also be used by anyone referring to a person of lower standing.

-chan: An affectionate honorific indicating familiarity used mostly in reference to girls; also used in reference to cute persons or animals of either gender.

-senpai: Used to address upperclassmen or more experienced coworkers.

-sensei: A respectful term for teachers, artists, or high-level professionals.

K-ON!

The title *K-ON!* comes from the Japanese word *"kei-ongaku,"* meaning "light music" in the sense of casual or easy listening (i.e., not serious or innovative as in serious classical or jazz). In the context of school clubs in Japan, the term *"kei-ongaku-bu"* ("light music club") usually contrasts with *"ongaku-bu"* ("music club") in that it focuses on popular forms of music (pop, rock, folk, etc.) where the latter focuses on symphonic and choral forms.

kakifly

The author's name, "kakifly," comes from the Japanese word *"kaki-furai,"* meaning "fried oysters." It seems to be a running joke, as the author comments for this and future volumes reference his feelings toward oysters.

PAGE 2

Yui Hirasawa

Yui's last name is an allusion to Susumu Hirasawa, founder and former guitarist for the now-defunct Japanese techno band, P-Model. Her first name means "only."

Mio Akiyama

Mio's last name is an allusion to Katsuhiko Akiyama, former bassist for P-Model. Her first name means "wake (of waves)."

Ritsu Tainaka

Ritsu's last name is an allusion to Sadatoshi Tainaka, former drummer for P-Model. Her first name means "meter (of rhythm)."

Tsumugi Kotobuki

Tsumugi's last name is an allusion to Hikaru Kotobuki, former keyboardist for P-Model. Her first name means "woven (silk) cloth."

Sawako Yamanaka

Sawako's first and last names are an allusion to Sawao Yamanaka, vocalist and rhythm guitarist for the Japanese alternative rock band, The Pillows.

Nodoka Manabe

Nodoka's last name is an allusion to Yoshiaki Manabe, lead guitarist for The Pillows. Her first name means "serene."

Ui Hirasawa

Ui's first name means "gloomy/vexing."

PAGE 3

Pop Music Club

"Pop Music Club" is literally "Light Music Club" (*"kei-ongaku-bu,"* used in the sense discussed in the note above), but in this context the term stands in contrast to classical/traditional music and refers to typical pop music.

PAGE 9

School Clubs

Participating in after-school clubs is a very big deal in Japanese high schools, as it's one of the only chances for students to interact outside their fixed class groups.

NEET

"NEET" is an acronym for "Not in Education, Employment, or Training." It's a technical term in both the UK and Japan, referring to the class of relatively young (defined as between the ages of 15 and 34 in Japan) individuals who are unemployed, not in any school or job training, and neither actively seeking

winter foods is a stereotypical winter scene in Japan.

PAGE 86
New Year's Breakfast Box
It's traditional to eat special New Year's box meals (collectively referred to as *osechi* food) for the first meal after the turn of the new year. Each element of the meal has some symbolic significance, so that eating it is supposed to bring good luck. Typical examples of *osechi* components are: *zoni* (sweet rice cake soup); *toso* (spiced saké); the traditional "three appetizers" of *kuromame* (black soybeans), *kazunoko* (herring roe), and *tataki gobo* (burdock root salad) or *tazukuri* (dried sardines); and various boiled vegetables (including lotus root, seaweed, pickled plums, etc). Many homes also incorporate various seafood elements like lobster, shrimp, red snapper, and so forth. The food tends to be arranged in a stack of boxes, each with individual compartments.

PAGE 89
Clang and Clap
When offering prayers at a Shinto shrine, it's usual to ring the bell (to summon the attention of the spirits) and then clap your hands together twice (for the same reason), holding them together after the second clap as you make your prayer.

PAGE 90
Tying Up Fortunes
If you draw a bad fortune at a Shinto shrine, the rule is that you have to tie it to a special string at the shrine (and under no circumstances take the fortune home with you!) so that the bad luck will stay at the shrine and not follow you home.

PAGE 101
Classroom Duties
In Japan it's common for students to perform many of the duties (often on a rotating basis) that would normally be handled by teachers in the US, such as taking roll and collecting test papers.

PAGE 107
Vocalizing and Ear Training
Both are technical musical terms related to singing. "Vocalizing" involves breath control, projection, timbre, and volume—in general, aspects contributing to the quality of vocal production when singing. "Ear training" is practice in hearing and reproducing the precise pitch intervals and timing of notes in a melody, sometimes involving sight-reading as well.

PAGE 109
Maid Café
Yui is greeting Ui and her friend like a waitress at a maid café would, all dressed up in a French maid outfit and using polite/formal language. Hence Ui's joke: "...Club" instead of "...Café" or something, which is what she's thinking.

PAGE 119
Guitar Photo
The guitars shown here (kakifly's own) are three left-handed Gibson Les Paul models, the same brand that Yui plays in the story.

PAGE 121
Takuan
Takuan pickles are made from daikon radishes. They usually acquire bright yellow coloring from the pickling process and are served in thick half-round slices (roughly the shape of Tsumugi's eyebrows.)

PAGE 58
Shredding
"Shredding" is guitar-player slang for playing lightning fast.

PAGE 58
Tapping
"Tapping" is a guitar technique involving sounding notes by hammering onto the frets with the fingertips (instead of sounding the strings while holding down on the frets in the usual manner). It was first popularized by rock guitarist Eddie Van Halen.

PAGE 58
Playing with Teeth
Playing with your teeth is a guitar stunt where the musician plucks the strings with the upper teeth. It was first performed by legendary blues guitarist T-Bone Walker but was later made popular by (and is most associated with) Jimi Hendrix.

PAGE 61
Mio's Song Lyrics
The song lyrics that Mio wrote were actually made into a song for the anime version of *K-ON!* and performed by the anime voice cast. And in case you're wondering, the Japanese lyrics sound every bit as silly as the English translation. That's why Ritsu gets goose bumps when she hears them aloud.

PAGE 63
Sawa-chan
The diminutive suffix *–chan* is an inappropriate form of address for one's teacher. Ritsu should address Sawako by last name, using the title *–sensei* instead, but Sawako doesn't really seem to mind much because she wishes she were a student again anyway.

PAGE 64
Yui's False Modesty
False modesty is a culturally accepted Japanese response in a situation like this. It would seem arrogant of Yui to immediately agree to be the lead singer (thereby implying that she thought she was the right choice all along), so she pretends to hem and haw in order to appear modest and encourage the others to work on "convincing" her, after which she

will "reluctantly" accept the appointment. Of course it backfires here.

PAGE 69
"Friends since we were babies"
The word *osana-najimi* (literally "familiar at infancy") implies that they grew up in the same neighborhood and/or played together from the time of their earliest memories, before either was of school age.

PAGE 83
New Year's Shrine Visit
A New Year's shine visit (*hatsumode*) refers to the Japanese tradition of visiting one's local neighborhood Shinto shrine immediately after the change of the year. (Some people even wait in line so they can make their visit right after midnight.) This is done to offer prayers for health and prosperity in the new year and maybe also to pick a fortune (a piece of paper telling the visitor what their future prospects are) so they can either rest easy (if the fortune is "Good" or better) or take steps to avoid calamity (if the fortune is "Bad" or worse).

PAGE 84
Playing the Same Position
The phrase "same position" is a sports reference in Japanese (e.g., a position in baseball). In this case it means that Mio will have the same role vis-à-vis Ritsu—namely, being strung along by Ritsu's whims.

PAGE 85
New Year's Holiday
"New Year's holiday" ("*sanganichi,*" literally "the three days") refers to the first three days of the new year, which are a national holiday in Japan.

Heated Table
The "heated table" (*kotatsu*) is a typical piece of furniture in Japanese sitting rooms. It's a small coffee table with a space heater mounted to the underside and quilted material draped around the sides to trap the heat in the space underneath. When people sit at the table, they place their legs inside the heated space to keep warm. Sitting around the heated table eating tangerines and other

Music Theory 101

Reading the Musical Staff:

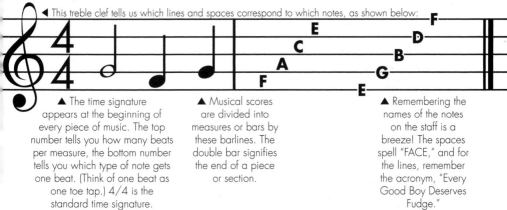

◄ This treble clef tells us which lines and spaces correspond to which notes, as shown below:

▲ The time signature appears at the beginning of every piece of music. The top number tells you how many beats per measure, the bottom number tells you which type of note gets one beat. (Think of one beat as one toe tap.) 4/4 is the standard time signature.

▲ Musical scores are divided into measures or bars by these barlines. The double bar signifies the end of a piece or section.

▲ Remembering the names of the notes on the staff is a breeze! The spaces spell "FACE," and for the lines, remember the acronym, "Every Good Boy Deserves Fudge."

Types of Musical Notes:

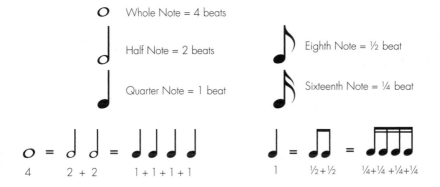

Whole Note = 4 beats

Half Note = 2 beats

Quarter Note = 1 beat

Eighth Note = ½ beat

Sixteenth Note = ¼ beat

$$O = 4 \quad \text{♩♩} = 2 + 2 \quad \text{♩♩♩♩} = 1 + 1 + 1 + 1$$

$$\text{♩} = 1 \quad \text{♫} = ½ + ½ \quad \text{♬♬} = ¼ + ¼ + ¼ + ¼$$

Get that foot tapping! Try clapping or humming the rhythm below:

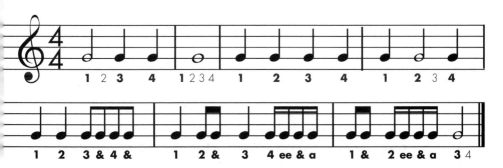

1 2 3 4   1 2 3 4   1   2   3   4   1   2 3 4

1   2   3 & 4 &   1   2 &   3   4 ee & a   1 &   2 ee & a   3 4

READING GUITAR CHORD NOTATION:

C
X O O
3 2 1
A
X O O
2 3 4
Am
X O O
2 3 1
D
X X O
1 3 2
Dm
X X O
2 3 1
E
O O O
2 3 1
Em
O O O O
2 3
F
X X
3 2 1 1
G
O O O
2 1 3

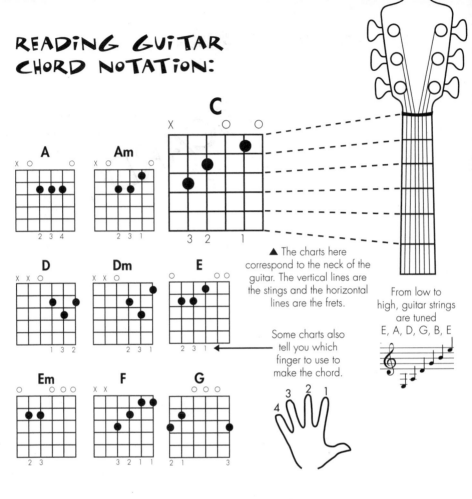

▲ The charts here correspond to the neck of the guitar. The vertical lines are the stings and the horizontal lines are the frets.

From low to high, guitar strings are tuned E, A, D, G, B, E

Some charts also tell you which finger to use to make the chord.

4
3
2
1

Grab your guitar and try strumming this familiar tune!

G C G C G D G
Twinkle, twinkle little star, how I wonder what you are.

G C G D G C G D
Up above the world so high, like a diamond in the sky.

G C G C G D G
Twinkle, twinkle little star, how I wonder what you are.

See how many of your favorite pop songs you can play using the chords G, C, D, and Em! You'll be jamming in no time!

Translation: Jack Wiedrick

Lettering: Hope Donovan

K-ON! vol. 1 © 2008 Kakifly. All rights reserved. First published in Japan in 2008 by HOUBUNSHA CO., LTD., Tokyo. English translation rights in United States, Canada, and United Kingdom arranged with HOUBUNSHA CO., LTD through Tuttle-Mori Agency, Inc., Tokyo.

English Translation © 2010 by Yen Press, LLC

Yen Press
1290 Avenue of the Americas
New York, NY 10104

www.YenPress.com

Yen Press is an imprint of Yen Press, LLC. The Yen Press name and logo are trademarks of Yen Press, LLC.

First Yen Press Edition: November 2010

ISBN: 978-0-316-11933-7

13

LSC-C

Printed in the United States of America

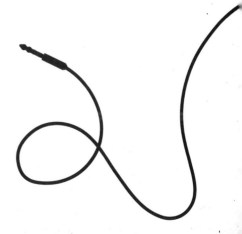